Praise for *Hatters, Railwaymen and Knitters*

'A delight. It's the kind of book, filled with astute observations of small details, that might just convince the most confirmed football sceptic why football has such a place in our culture....a book to savour and to make you think.'
New Statesman

'Superlative...The book is beautifully written; pessimistic and damning, yet joyful and full of love for the game...wonderful.'
When Saturday Comes

'Quality and heartfelt football writing.'
David Conn, *The Guardian*

'Highly recommended.'
Oliver Kay, *The Times*

'Gray brilliantly interweaves social history, modern day public and political life and, of course, football itself...Highly recommended.'
The Telegraph

'Like a footballing version of Bill Bryson's *Notes from a Small Island*.'
FourFourTwo

'A wryly-observed history lesson on lower league football and proper Englishness.'
Loaded

'More than just a tale of sport, Gray's quest becomes a voyage of discovery...His humour and passion may well win over even the most reluctant of football fans.'
Easyjet Traveller

'[Gray] writes like Lowry paints. Superb.'
BBC Lancashire

'A story of towns, their people, their histories, their clubs, and a ruddy bloody great read.'
Love Middlesbrough

'Among urban blight, his astute eye can pick out details that are funny, redeeming or both...Book of the Week.'
Bradford Telegraph and Argus

D0412833

'Daniel Gray does an excellent job of writing a football book that is about more than football.'
No Nay Never

'Superb…a shrewdly observed and at times caustic cocktail of social history and travelogue.'
Middlesbrough Evening Gazette

'300 pages of great prose… a beautiful book about England, one worth reading.'
Staten Island Advance

'A wonderful read and like some of the very best football books out there, the actual football is merely a footnote…Really enjoyable and beautifully paced, this is one to read and keep as in ten years' time it could feel even more relevant than it does right now.'
In Bed with Maradona

'It is perhaps obvious to compare Gray to Nick Hornby given the subject matter, yet the comparisons stretch beyond a passion for football… Beautifully written, nostalgic and reflective, this will also appeal to fans of Simon Armitage, Stuart Maconie and Tim Moore.'
Books with Bunny

'Recognising the interconnectedness of town and team, Gray offers social histories of the places he visits for the weekend, coupling them with droll travel writing…a celebration of the game and where its roots and its guts lie… I heartily recommend you pick up a copy as an antidote to the cold cynicism that pervades the peak of the football pyramid.'
Football 365

Hatters, Railwaymen and Knitters

Travels through England's football provinces

DANIEL GRAY

B L O O M S B U R Y
LONDON · NEW DELHI · NEW YORK · SYDNEY

First published in Great Britain 2013
This paperback edition published 2014

Copyright © 2013 by Daniel Gray

The moral right of the author has been asserted

Extracts from *The Road to Wigan Pier* ... George Orwell
(Cop_____ ... __8, 1937) reprinted with permission of
Bill Hamilton, Literary Executor of the Estate of the Late Sonia
Brownell Orwell

Exc____ ... by J.B. Priestley reprinted with
perm_____ ... of United Agents ... behalf of the Estate of J.B. Priestley

E_____ ... ___ooot
(Cop_____ © Esther Morgan, 2008) reprinted with permission ...

Bloomsbury Publishing Plc

50 Bedford Square
London
WC1B 3DP

www.bloomsbury.com

Bloomsbury is a trademark of Bloomsbury Publishing Plc

Bloomsbury Publishing, London, New Delhi, New York and Sydney

A CIP catalogue record for this book is available from the British Library

ISBN 978 1 4088 3099 4

10 9 8 7 6 5 4 3 2 1

Typeset by Saxon Graphics Ltd, Derby
Printed and bound in Great Britain by CPI Group (UK) Ltd, Croydon CR0 4YY

Contents

Introduction

I love the idea of England, perhaps because I don't live there. Distance has allowed romance to blossom and an imagined England to sprout. Geographically, I'm not far away – Scotland remains where it always was, sandwiched somewhere between Carlisle and Iceland. Politically and socially though, it splinters and shuffles away regardless of the independence referendum. I have become complacent, barely engaging with England because I presume it will always be there for me when I need it.

As I thought about writing this book, I realised I had grown jealous of Scotland. Here was a place, it seemed, with uniform identity and firm direction. What was England? A country divided in so many ways, filled with people who were Yorkshire or Cornish or Cockney before they were English. Having lived apart from England for nigh on a decade, in my thirtieth year I decided it was time to become reacquainted and see in what form, if any, she was holding together. How many Englands were there? I'd view her changes and measure whether she lived up to that red rose-coated England in my mind. My interest was not in the sociology of 'Englishness', which other books have fought manfully to define, but in how England's places and football teams combine to make the entirety. It was in the moods, looks, accents and smells of those places, in overheard conversations and one-liners. If that meant inadvertently defining types of Englishness along the way, then so be it.

Before I set out, I didn't half miss England. I missed the north-south divide, and I missed the flashes and dashes of Tudor and

Georgian that creep up in the most unlikely of English places. I missed red bricks, canals, fish and chips cooked to order, town markets, reasonably sized hills, 'dry spells', small breweries, pubs with coal fires and beer gardens, people calling you 'love', proper seaside resorts, my family.

I also missed English football, or the incarnation of it that it is possible to miss, literally and figuratively. I missed the early rounds of the FA Cup, Ceefax page 312 ('News in Brief'), teams I held childhood preconceptions and prejudices about, small-club sponsorship deals with local garages, goalkeepers throwing kitbags into the net and hanging a towel on it, diving headers and referees with other jobs you could read about on the back of the programme. In short, then, I missed an English game that existed only in my mind, much like England the country. Feeling so uncertain of England it seemed that football, no matter how inaccurate my vision of it, was a constant – the thing I could easily recognise and possibly reconnect with. Despite all its post-1992 disfigurements, England still does the game brilliantly. Its wider, more important social trimmings are ingrained as in no other land. It was therefore unrivalled as cause to visit myself upon the provinces, in search of England.

These misty-eyed thoughts were brought on too, by the fact I was about to turn thirty. Thirty doesn't seem significant from the vantage of, say, forty or sixty. Middle age has not been reached, you're still young enough to meet your life partner or divorce her, and you can choose just about any career. Any career, that is, apart from football: for a footballer, thirty is usually the last stopping point before retirement. When you define most things via football as I do, that makes thirty important. A thirty-year-old born in the early 1980s probably started going to football when it was distinctly old school, and so will soon be in a unique position.

For me that meant artful Victorian stadiums with ear-splitting atmosphere, but also appalling treatment by the authorities and hearing monkey chanting at black players. As such, another reason for visiting myself upon England would be to find out if clubs had managed to cling on to or recapture the former without the trappings of the latter.

Thirty is also important because it is a bridging age for all generations: our parents are often pensionable, and we start to have children of our own. For my fellow thirty-ites this feels heightened – we are the only generation to have grandparents who fought in a world war and kids with mobile phones.

Thirty was also on my mind because in 2011, England seemed to be repeating itself. My birth year, 1981, saw a Royal Wedding take place against the backdrop of a divisive, one-track-minded Tory government and strikes. Young people, often black, but always disillusioned, rioted and left streets in tatters. On those same streets, fascistic movements mobilised beneath boozy breath and sought to divide the nation. Rupert Murdoch acquired *The Times*, and his name dominated dinner-party discourse. Rumblings began over the future of the Falkland Islands, with a bullish government in Buenos Aires and one here holding an exaggerated view of Britain's world place. It seemed that 'Wills & Kate', public sector strikers, Tottenham looters, English Defence League members, tabloid hackers and David Cameron had joined a hugely destructive (not to mention ugly) tribute band which probably churned out synth pop, dominant in 2011 as in 1981. It seemed appropriate to look at our country then and now, and what better vehicle on which to ride than football?

In the 1981-82 season, Ron Atkinson's avuncular brand of racism had found temporary respite at Manchester United (some of his best centre-backs were black, you know). Bobby Robson busily enthused Ipswich to high places, Villa won the European Cup and Liverpool channelled black armbands positively, winning the Division One title in tribute to the recently deceased Bill Shankly. Spurs won the cup in front of an aggregate Wembley crowd of 192,000, and at Southampton Kevin Keegan defied heavy hair to score twenty-six times. On the day I was born, Swansea City of Wales were England's top team. It was the last time they would rise so far for, inevitably, thirty years. To unleash attacking football, teams would be awarded three points for a win for the first time in 1981-82. English sides had won six consecutive European Cups and the national team had a World Cup in Spain to prepare for (team song: 'This Time (We'll Get It Right)').

Thirty, 1981, 2011: the numbers and coincidences seemed too good to ignore. One afternoon in my local, I looked long and hard at the four league tables from that 1981-82 season, and at a map of England (someone else was dominating possession of the pub's communal newspaper). Searching for patterns or clever concepts – teams from seaside resorts and ports? One of each team name suffix, from Athletic to Wanderers? – the least imaginative stuck out. Visiting the teams who finished first, second and bottom of the four divisions (with one notable exchange deal) gave a diverse geographical spread of England, and a huge range of footballing levels from the Football League to the South West Peninsula Premier. Seasons make a fan aware that time is passing. I have long defined my life by them, memories of old ones and hopes for new, so taking a past season as a route map seemed appropriate. If I couldn't find England in Bradford, Ipswich or Crewe, or its football somewhere among six different divisions I was either a particularly bad writer or drunk. For good measure, I'd also spend time in the very centre of England watching our national team on telly – Hinckley in the summertime, anyone?

In thirteen towns I'd observe England and see if she was worth loving and missing. As well as looking at them now, I'd pick out the ways in which they'd contributed to the making (and mythologising) of England, from Middlesbrough's role in the Empire to Luton's in revolutionising the make-up of my homeland. While interesting social histories in their own right, these stories all help build a picture of who England is today. I approached them in a positive manner, keen to avoid the sneers of Crap Town and Chav Town culture and embrace their uniqueness and even their foibles. I wanted the book to celebrate the provinces and pinpoint why parochialism matters and is not always a bad thing. This is embodied in the way a band from outside London is often identified by their place of origin ('Woking's The Jam'; 'Sunderland band The Futureheads'); the implication is that the place has influenced the musicians – even in a negative way – who will now influence the country.

Past highlights of the clubs I visit would also feature. This was not only because football, or my version of it, is a sport based almost entirely on nostalgia, but because team histories paint and taint the character of a club and its host town. In addition, club histories are the narrative detail of football itself. Through an hour fine or dark, each gives a perspective of our game's evolution. There are its Victorian origins in Sheffield United, its glowing pre-war days in Bradford, its wartime in Orient, its 1930s heights in Middlesbrough and 1950s in Burnley. Shankly's Carlisle take us through the 1960s, Robson's Ipswich the 1970s and Elton's Watford the 1980s. Chronological pieces of micro-history to make the whole, but also themes that illustrate the game – Crewe as a team for the pleasure of industrial workers or Chester's confused twenty-first-century ownership structures.

I know I was born in the wrong era. I am nostalgic for a time of overlapping half-backs and family-run sweetshops on every corner, a time I never knew. Sepia days I do not remember will be part of the story, but it will very keenly offer a glimpse of England and its clubs today. It is a snapshot rather than mass observation, the view from the direction I happen to be looking in, but it will capture the England in which I travelled and the game I saw, and what it was like to be thirty almost a hundred years after the Great War. I would complete each leg of my tour by public transport for full communal experience. Think of it as a charabanc tour of places you had forgotten.

When I think of England I think of football, albeit in silhouette. It is time to re-familiarise myself and try to fall in love all over again.

Part One

In the Winter:
Scabs, Blades, Hatters and Tractor Boys

Chapter One

Middlesbrough

There was Chunky and there was Moustache and there was me. There were also four women in slippers. Always in slippers. From five o'clock every other Saturday we'd loiter on the bruised cobbles outside Ayresome Park, Middlesbrough Football Club's fading stately home. We all shared one aim: to obtain the scruffy autographs of footballers no one now remembers.

Moustache always brought a small radio, which he perched on his shoulder like a ghetto blaster. He'd broadcast the results from elsewhere for the benefit of Chunky and me and the Slipper Sisters. In his heyday, before years of watching Middlesbrough had turned him humourless, it was said that he'd record himself delivering shock results on a tape and then play them to the amazement of others. I never stopped to ponder quite how a man with a Teesside accent thicker than wet cement pulled off a convincing James Alexander Gordon.

Without ever knowing his real name, I liked him. Ditto Chunky, who wore a Middlesbrough sun hat covered in pin badges and peered out from behind lenses the width of ice cubes. Chunky kept his autograph books and pens in a boot-bag which, when we'd finished and the last steward was begging us to leave the premises, he'd cradle like a newborn as we walked away. The Slipper Sisters preferred to keep their distance from us – before moving in for the autograph kill at the last minute. Amazingly, they achieved signatures without once unfolding their arms, probably welded in position thanks to years of indifference to north-eastern winters.

The ritual was always the same. At around 5.15 p.m. the beeping reverse tones of the away team coach sounded – a bugle choking a note that the hunt was about to begin. Moustache, Chunky and I would file smoothly into the small gap between the vehicle's rear and the flaky red iron gates of old Ayresome. From there, we could doorstep players – both 'ours' and the opposition's – as they stepped out into the cool air. 'Can I 'ave yer autograph please?' we'd bark at young full-backs and surprised Plymouth Argyle physiotherapists. (This was Division Two in the early 1990s. We only knew what Boro players looked like, as well as the odd few who had made it to the hallowed and sarcastic pages of 90 Minutes magazine. Often we would turn to the Slipper Sisters as a player signed, and mouth 'Who's that?' I've no idea why we thought they'd know. Perhaps they looked erudite and worldly in that footgear.)

When it came to our players the ritual was similar, only with the odd matey extra ('Can I 'ave yer autograph please, John?'). Chunky would always ask for – and, to my annoyance, sometimes get – free tickets for away matches, while Moustache would let each player know their rating out of ten for that afternoon's performance.

Important things happened to me on those evenings. Some of them were individual firsts: a tottering Malcolm Macdonald emerging from the guests' lounge and becoming the first man to passively intoxicate me; mistakenly taking part in my first ever demonstration when five men in moccasins and chinos pushed their way in-between us to holler: 'Sack the board'.

Beyond those landmarks were the first stirrings of something greater: my sense of identity. I barely knew these people, nor did I live in the same town as them, yet I belonged here in a way I didn't elsewhere. The tired terrain seemed more familiar and welcoming than that of my school and village, the creaking bricks of Ayresome more homely than our dull new-build. With only a small immediate family to speak of, the players whose names I collected hundreds and thousands of times, filled the gaps that cousins or uncles might ordinarily have occupied. Christ, they even ruffled my hair. On the pitch, these were men who gave me a sense of forgetful happiness more than anything or anyone else could. They taught me crushing disappointment too.

This football club was the establishment to which my own fortunes and moods were tied. On those autograph dusks I learned to care deeply and feel deeply cared about.

So far, so very sentimental, but even today thinking of Ayresome and its ghosts is like looking through a dog-eared family photo album. I know my link was – and is – far from unique. Indeed, it comforts me to suppose that young people are still forging similar bonds now, still waiting for autographs and learning to define themselves through their team as I did. I just fear they're not. I fear that theirs is a football and an England very different to mine. One in which there is very little to relate and cling and belong to.

I hope I'm wrong, because hope is important and because in Middlesbrough it can seem that the team is all that the people have left. Where before they could belong to epic steelworks or the mighty structures moulded by their artisanship, now industry has died and often taken dignity with it. The club is both a beacon for belonging and a metaphor for the town's decline – since my darling Ayresome was put to sleep, our new Riverside abode sits grandly, yet sheepishly, by the docks, industry dearly departed, promised replacements resembling thin air.

I'm five days shy of thirty years old as we cross the border from Scotland into England. The clouds over the green and silky North

Sea resemble grey candyfloss from the vantage of my first class seat, whose purchase has been justified entirely on the grounds of an approaching birthday. It matters not that I have paid to be here: I still feel that my eviction is imminent and I'm sure the ticket inspector can smell my lowly yearly income when he checks my ticket. Amazingly, a woman with a trolley then starts handing out free food and drinks. I say yes to the tea, the coffee, the orange juice, the croissant and the biscuit, so that by the time she leaves East Coast trains are basically *paying me* to travel. When a man two rows from me declines the refreshment trolley, I am momentarily tempted to grab him by the lapels and slap his face while exclaiming 'are you mad? This is free. FREE. WHAT'S WRONG WITH YOU?' Instead, I read the label on my pastry that says 'Somerset Cheddar and Vine Ripened Tomato Croissant', then in smaller, explanatory letters, 'Somerset Cheddar and Vine Ripened Tomato in a Croissant'.

In Berwick-upon-Tweed, outside English pebbledash houses covered in English ice, St George flags will the morning to work up a bluster. The casual and widespread flying of such flags is something new to me about England, and I wonder whether it reflects a resurgent patriotism and the reclaiming of this symbol from the far right, or the fact that Asda flog them for a fiver. There are plenty here, perhaps reflecting Berwick's frontier land status.

From behind net curtains England awakes to bacon sandwiches and *Soccer Saturday*. The land flattens and fog cuddles Lindisfarne and then Alnmouth, the latter unfeasibly idyllic like a Constable drawing of a *Daily Express* 'Win a Dream Cottage' prize. I've twenty minutes to spare in Newcastle station so I cross a bridge to watch the hustle and bustle of Saturday morning England on the move. There are blokes in their sixties, rucksacked-up and ready to go. The eldest distributes train tickets among them, Dad playing Dad to the Dads. Pairs and trios of women eye up and put down stag-do arrivals, everyone on their way to what must now make up 20 per cent of the UK economy: the weekend away.

Then it happens. They start with 'Jingle Bells' and move neatly into 'We Three Kings'. A brass band. The sound, to me, of England, my England. It is a *Truman Show* moment: someone somewhere is directing this, turning up the emotion level to eleven to tell me something – that I am *home*. Of course, this is a homely feeling shaped by my upbringing as a treacly Yorkshireman, and thus my version of England. It reminds me that we all have our Englands to bear. That includes Duncan Bannatyne, I think as I while away another ten minutes in WHSmith where the front of *North-East Life* magazine bears the legend 'Bannatyne's Love of Stockton-on-Tees'.

The 10.30 to Nunthorpe will pass through Bannatyne's darling Stockton. It is a stinking beast of a train, a two-carriage smog-powered bus on wheels. Every time it splutters a little bit of George Monbiot dies. The heating is fixed high and constantly turned on, boiling us all in our winter coats. I expect to turn around and see nothing left of the man behind me save for a pair of glasses perched upon the oily remnants of his blue cagoule.

This is not the quickest way to Middlesbrough. It is the scenic route. In a pleasingly sardonic tone, the weary conductor reads from a list of destinations: Sunderland, Seaham, Hartlepool, Seaton Carew ... Outside, the theme colour is rust: rusty post-coal sea, rusty industrial shells, rusty allotments, rusty-red back-to-backs, rusty piles of old cars and bits of unrecognisable machine, rusty under-used track that Beeching forgot. Everywhere there is space – space between former mining villages, space between track and sea, space between streets of occupied houses and boarded-up houses. Industry, mainly coal, once filled the gaps in landscapes and lives.

This forgotten line takes in St James' Park, the Gateshead Stadium, the Stadium of Light, Victoria Park and the Riverside. By more backyards with St George flags we approach Hartlepool, an impressive wreck with patches of lonely beauty. The heritage marina and museum sit pristine, awaiting visitors like a dolled-up student house awaiting party guests. Ghosts are everywhere on this railway line and in this area. Ghosts and spaces. There are even ghosts of optimism: shiny office blocks skirt Seaham, Thornaby, Stockton, Middlesbrough and elsewhere, most awaiting tenants.

Beyond the silver turrets of chemical Teesside stand rigidly, flanked by postcard hills. Aldous Huxley called this view 'a magnificent kind of poem'. It is a giant sci-fi set that against today's blue winter sky makes my heart leap with joy.

At Seaton Carew, the Teesside Riviera home of 'Canoe Man' John Darwin, five teens board, a gangly mix of hormones and excitement. 'Warrizit ahmaskin for, an 'alf return?' asks one of the girls in a rhythmic machine gun accent. We pass by the home of Billingham Synthonia, the only club in England named after an agricultural fertiliser, then Duncan Bannatyne's idyll, Stockton, beyond whose scrapyards full of railway history I was born.

Our passenger wagon rolls on by acres of disused sidings and passes Newport Bridge, a giant's Meccano construction. As we queue to leave the train, I gesture for an old man carrying an animal box to alight in front of me. 'I should think so, son,' he says, looking down in the direction of his pet and back at me, as if he were holding the world's last baby panda.

The Saturday into which we emerge is the full stop on a week of sad sentences for this area. BBC *Newsnight* announced that

Redcar and Cleveland, Middlesbrough then Hartlepool were the three English council areas most vulnerable to the effects of government cuts. A Middlesbrough family was more likely to fall into poverty than a family from anywhere else. The *Daily Mail* threw pissy sleet on the blizzard in its own special way, screeching: 'That's a bit steep! Parking spaces in London cost £96,000 (£13,000 more than average HOUSE in Middlesbrough)'.

Leaving Middlesbrough station – once an attractive, oval-roofed hub, but since the Luftwaffe and Network Rail visited, an Anytown halt – my eyes fix on the row of buildings ahead. Looking upwards I see some fine Germanic flourishes that recall the town's tradition of cosmopolitan industry. Looking downwards I see a young woman in a corset puking up on the wall outside Spensley's Emporium, now the only bar in town offering pre-match strippers. The Premier League good times are emphatically over.

Surveying the scene is a sturdy statue of Henry Bolckow, the father of modern Middlesbrough. As rain bounces off vomit, he gives the impression of wishing he'd stayed celibate. That, though, would have robbed the world of a vital community, one christened 'an infant Hercules' by Gladstone. For a century Middlesbrough was as important to the British Empire as any place. What happened to it speaks for all of post-industrial England.

The air in Middlesbrough often hangs silently where once it roared to a white-hot chorus of clanks and hisses. Most of her iron and steel plants are flattened, crushed by market forces and other things no one here had a say in or asked for. Thankfully, the blood, sweat and toil that caked the walls have lasted long into the night. Never did the grafters of Teesside strain in vain. Their bridgework still straddles Sydney Harbour, the Nile, the Bosporus, the Yangtze and Victoria Falls. In separate pieces of one-upmanship on local rivals up the road, they made the Tyne Bridge and the Angel of the North ('Built by Teessiders for Geordies', one peace-making worker welded to the inside of the latter). Theirs too are the rails spanning the former countries of the Empire. Sometimes, they even let southerners have a piece of the action: Canary Wharf, the Thames Barrage and the new Wembley all bear the motif: 'Made in Middlesbrough'.

The town's evolution from farmhouses to foundries happened at a speed only possible during the industrial revolution. In his *English Journey* J. B. Priestley reflected negatively on the haste in which Middlesbrough was built, writing that it was:

> ... more like a vast dingy conjuring trick than a reasonable town ... [with] inhabitants whose chief passions, we were always told, were for beer and football. It is a dismal town, even with beer or football.

Prior to the mid-nineteenth century, 'Middlesbrough' had been one farm among many. It had no claims to fame, other than being next door to the village from which Captain Cook hailed. Between 1831 and 1891 the town's population grew from 150 to 75,000.

In 1829, 'six solid, broad-brimmed, broad-fronted, broad-bottomed' Quakers bought 'Middlesbrough' for £30,000. The group – described in this way by Newcastle MP Joseph Cowen – saw that if the world's first industrial railway line (the Stockton and Darlington) could be extended by a few miles to the east, the transportation of coal southwards via the North Sea became possible. With their railway completed, coal and money piled into Middlesbrough. By new docks north of the River Tees, a town was hastily planned and built for incoming workers. The land remained boggy to the extent that locals communicated between houses using speaking trumpets, to avoid stepping outdoors and sinking.

The coal market, however, was unsustainable and despite her youth Middlesbrough needed reinvention. Enter Henry Bolckow. A German, he moved to the area with fellow iron-founder John Vaughan. One afternoon in 1850, Vaughan tripped while walking in local hills. In doing so, he kicked up a tuft of earth and examined its strange colour. It turned out to be ironstone. Vaughan and Bolckow immediately bought the land and built a quarry. Luck had given birth to an iron industry quickly stoked by local slog. People flocked to the town to establish or staff foundries as the area became England's answer to America's gold rush settlements. Optimism abounded and was typified by the motto that Bolckow – first mayor, then MP – chose for Middlesbrough: *Erimus* ('We Shall Be').

By the 1870s, Middlesbrough was making a third of the UK's iron, and the visiting Gladstone saluted: 'This remarkable place, the youngest child of England's enterprise. It is an infant, gentlemen, but it is an infant Hercules.' This innocuous farm had grown into a living, belching behemoth, its tentacles spreading across the world. As Joseph Cowen (a Geordie, remember) wrote:

The iron it supplies furnishes railways to Europe; it runs by Neapolitan and Papal dungeons; it startles the bandit in his haunts in Cilicia; it streaks the prairies of America; it stretches over the plains of India; it surprises the Belochees; it pursues the peggunus of Gangotri. It has crept out of the Cleveland Hills, where it has slept since the Roman days, and now, like a strong and invincible serpent, coils itself around the world.

The industrialist organisers of Middlesbrough iron's world tour attempted to care for their workers by building housing and social institutions. Demand outstripped supply, a price of growth that reinforced the town's status as almost completely working-class. It was a man's world too: Middlesbrough had one of the highest men to women ratios in the land, a fact which harked back to its class make-up – there were simply no middle-class families for women to work for as happened in more established industrial towns.

Diversity instead came from immigration. Middlesbrough was a melting pot; by 1871, over half those living here had come from elsewhere. Most were Irish: outside of Liverpool, this was (and still is) the most Hibernian place in England. These days, there is a recognisably Irish tint to the local accent ('me mam') and approach to the past tense ('I could've went'). When Yorkshire wool-combers arrived in Middlesbrough in the 1850s, they sent a note back to Bradford warning against English reinforcements:

If you send men here in Large Numbers and the Masters begin to turn the Irish off it will very likely lead to a disturbance.

Though an infant, Middlesbrough was already a dirty old town. Yet in the same way that some of us from the area embrace the silver-chimneyed skyline of its chemical industry today, grime meant industry, ergo work. When the 1926 General Strike ended and the works fired up once more, local women took to the streets excitedly screaming, 'Look! The smoke, the smoke!'

At the end of the nineteenth century, Middlesbrough was changing again. Steel production had begun its slow march to outmuscling iron. In huge plants, the shells of the above-mentioned bridges and buildings were created and then shipped along the Tees. It is physically impossible for anyone born in these environs not to cry when local boy Chris Rea's paean to this lost world, 'Steel River', strikes up on the jukebox or radio. Rea's song, written in the 1980s, is a nostalgic trawl through what has gone and a bitter longing for its impossible return. His lost Steel River Tees was a colossus whose banks wheezed with industry and whose waters carried local inventions to the world. She survived the bombs of the Luftwaffe, but now ran so tranquilly that salmon had moved back in.

Rea's bustling Tees died when globalisation and Thatcher happened to Middlesbrough. For a while, a chemical sector spearheaded by ICI maintained jobs and upheld a sense of working worth. In recent decades, that has withered. A few plants remain, along with one steelwork, mothballed and then given the kiss of life early in 2011. There, men, and now women, will make things like they always have, this time rivets for the new World Trade Centre in New York. Regeneration schemes have come and gone with little to show, new names and new millions amounting to nothing permanent apart from poverty (the local unemployment rate usually tops the division or at least qualifies for the Champions League). The public sector jobs that papered cracks in the 1990s are now disappearing: Round Two for a Tory government in London; 'here we go again' for the locals. As always here, the football club's fortunes have mirrored the town's.

As I stand beneath Henry Bolckow's statue, I wish they'd let Middlesbrough build things, let us show that round here, our brains are in our hands. I think of all the words I've read about the rise of this town and look around me at all the signs of its fall.

Erimus, we shall be. *Erimas*, we were.

I'm off round for Cloughie. He'll cheer me up.

On a Saturday match morning in December 2011, 11 Valley Road is neat and tidy. It is the only brown and beige house in a row of red and faded whites, a cosmetic uniqueness that invites the onlooker to take notice. A small green plaque boasts that 'International Footballer and Football Manager Brian Clough was born here'. Number 11 is a well-kept house on a well-kept working-class council estate, the type that seldom makes the news and is never the centrepiece of gritty, grotty television drama. There's green everywhere: gardens to the front and back, trees and patches of grass crammed into all spare space – tiny pitches and trunks for goalposts. A middle-aged neighbour crosses the road arms folded. She is wearing slippers. (Could it be …?) Birds sing, crows caw like belching tramps and the sun shines gloriously for a glorious son.

Just beyond little Brian's house are the playing fields of the Acklam Iron and Steelworks Athletic Club. Here, the young man who later liked to call everyone 'young man' first smashed leather through proper goal frames. Working as a clerk at ICI through the week, the teenage Clough spent his Saturdays breaking nets among the fertilisers of Billingham Synthonia. Soon Ayresome Park called and signed Clough to Middlesbrough.

Clough's time with his hometown club was explosive. Between 1955 and 1961, he scored 204 goals in 222 matches. When he left for Sunderland, the town wept. Clough's teammates may not have felt the same – in 1959, nine of them had signed a 'round robin' letter demanding that their arrogant leader be stripped of his captaincy. Clough responded with a transfer request – refused – and a surfeit of goals.

I continue to the top of Valley Road and cross into Albert Park. 'Alcohol Free Zone' shout scolding signs on every bench. By the pretty boating lake the wooden hut cafe belts out Christmas hits. A lad of fifteen wearing a grey tracksuit yaps at me from his BMX: 'How mate. You look like Harry Potter mate.' 'You look like a scruffy twat who fiddles with himself too much' I reply, an hour or so later.

Just after the bandstand there is a statue to Clough, unveiled in 2007. Rather than the manager recalled in bronze elsewhere, here he is twenty-four and in training gear, his boots slung over a shoulder, purposeful, on his way to training or a match. Today a couple of teenagers take turns to slap his legs and backside. Oh to think what punishment he would have meted out. Probably a kiss.

All of this – his Valley Road family home, Albert Park, the walks to Ayresome – was vital to who Clough became. 'I was the kid who came from a little part of paradise,' he later said:

> ... to me it was heaven. Everything I have done, everything I've achieved, everything that I can think of that has directed and affected my life – apart from the drink – stemmed from my childhood.

Middlesbrough first played here in Albert Park, on the site of its archery strips. The club was formed, goes the local legend, in 1876 at a tripe supper by cricketers looking for a winter hobby. Four years later, Middlesbrough Football Club was evicted from the park for making a mess of the grass, and moved in with the cricket club next door. In 1895 and 1898, Boro won the FA Amateur Cup, firstly against Old Carthusians (who didn't bring the trophy, so certain were they of retaining it), and latterly against Uxbridge.

Between war memorials, flowerbeds and a lady in a Leona Lewis T-shirt feeding pigeons, I leave Albert Park in search of a short-lived, long-forgotten football rivalry. On Linthorpe Road, Abyss Tanning promises endless bronzing of the type often popular in the north-east. I take a right on to the cobbles of Clive Road, one of many parallel strands of terraced housing that the local Victorian writer Florence Bell called 'little brown streets'. At the street's corner with Ayresome Park Road, I pause where once stood Paradise Ground, home to Middlesbrough Ironopolis FC.

Ironopolis of Paradise were formed by local romantics in 1889 and played in maroon and green stripes. Their dreamy-eyed naming policy veiled a steely financial rationale: Ironopolis were formed to make money. Where Middlesbrough FC refused to go professional and pay their players, Ironopolis would. The formation of a second team split the footballing public. Both played at home on the same Saturdays, and for a couple of seasons in the same Northern League.

The rivalry was bitter, and acidity intensified when Boro reneged on a merger deal aimed at Football League membership in 1892. From then on, their nickname among half the town became 'The Scabs'. Ironopolis stole a march in 1893, gaining admission to Division Two at the same time as Arsenal, Liverpool and Newcastle United. Despite avoiding relegation, a year later Ironopolis were bankrupt. The town was simply not big enough for the both of them. The Scabs won. To enforce their point, Boro moved in over the road, so that the north-west corner of Paradise became the south-east of Ayresome Park.

Once we had graduated from the terraces, it was Clive Road that I'd walk down with my dad to take our seats in the South Stand. Preferring to keep in my mind an image of the area as it was, this is the first time I've been back. Everything seems small like junior school furniture, memory having inflated the appearance of the past. Red bollards mark the ground's boundaries and the two-up two-downs across from our turnstile remain, but the turnstile is now a hedge in someone's garden. In recognition of times gone by, they have erected a 'South Terrace' plaque above their double-glazed door. Around the corner, silver dots mark the

Holgate End, our Kop. When it was rafter-full and bouncing, we sang and danced till we were woozy. When it was sparse and dripping with urine, we dreamt of moving to the seats. It was Old Football and I feel lucky to have been there. Thank God I am turning thirty and not twenty. Mine is the last generation to have lived in that world.

The homes now here are part of a roomy estate built after Boro left Ayresome in 1995. The development company did try to reflect that which had gone before: a bronze football marking the former centre-spot sits on a lawn and a sculpture of Alf Tupper-ish boots adorns the doorstep location of Pak Doo-Ik's winner for North Korea against Italy at the 1966 World Cup. Streets are named 'The Turnstile', 'The Midfield' and 'The Holgate'.

Walking among these houses I scarcely see their classic Barratt designs or think about who lives in them. What I see is the Portakabin ticket office beneath the away corner and what I think of is the time my dad pretended to be going in to enquire about an away match and came out with two season tickets. I see the ghosts of Ayresome, strolling to the ground early and chatting with their regular programme seller, or scrambling from the pub at 2.59 p.m., the sudden noise from within the stadium a rabbit to a greyhound. I hear the tinny Tannoy, team line-ups being read out and Queen records muffling away-end chants. Finally, the smells are back: horse manure and Midget Gems, stale ale and cigars.

Wading in nostalgia, I think also of the club's history. None of the new hedges or walls remembers Alf Common, the first £1,000 footballer. His fee caused a scandal debated, no less, in the House of Commons, before he bedded in, scored goals and lost the captaincy for 'drunkenness and violent behaviour'. Nor do the smooth pavements recall that Boro's two greatest sides were stopped in their tracks by war: in 1914, a third place finish in Division One, in 1939, a team that had finished seventh, fifth and then fourth. Those 1930s teams brimmed with Ayresome angels. There was George Camsell, 345 goals in 453 for Boro, eighteen in nine for England (two per game!). In 1927, he'd scored fifty-nine in a season, only for Dixie Dean to break the record with sixty in the next. 'Typical Boro', the naysaying Teesside cynics in flat caps used to tell me. His job was made easy by wee Wilf Mannion, the Golden Boy, son of an Irishman who worked in the Bolckow-Vaughan foundry. Mannion's feet made the ball dance: Stanley Matthews hailed him 'the Mozart of football – stylish, graceful, courtly, showing exquisite workmanship with the ball.' But the double-glazing doesn't know 'Mozart', and nor does it swoon over Gentleman George Hardwick, the Hollywood-handsome Middlesbrough left-back who gave Total Football to the Netherlands. Gentleman George, then into his late seventies, once signed the autograph books of Chunky, Moustache and I. Underneath his signature in handwriting like my granddad's he scribbled: 'George Hardwick. Middlesbrough and Great Britain Captain'.

I turn left into Warwick Street, where those autograph days were played out. Still the bruised cobbles remain, but they lead only to a wooden garden fence, where the Ayresome Park Gates used to be. As I think back to Chunky and Moustache and me, two lads of ten or eleven years old begin to heckle: 'What you doing 'ere mate?' 'He's a paedo, int'e?' 'Aye, how, paedo mate, what you doing 'ere?' As I turn to leave I notice that one of them is white, and one Asian. How great that abuse of a stranger is helping the next generation to integrate.

Among grids of tight terraced streets once filled by matchday cars, three teenagers take turns to race on a scramble motorbike.

Much of the housing is boarded up, and the backstreet soccer schools of yore are sealed off by iron gates. 'Back Alley Improvement Team' say the signs fixed to them.

The streets without boards are inhabited by a large Asian population. Only four or five times watching Boro have I seen non-white fans – why do the club not embrace the people who live here, morally to show what a uniting force football can be, cynically because crowd sizes are dwindling?

Back on Linthorpe Road, I try to forget the past, but am frequently bombarded by it, both an upside and a downside of walking in a familiar place. I walk by the old site of the Rea family's cafe, where Brian Clough met his sweetheart Barbara, and past the elegant Swatters Carr Hotel. Ironopolis were founded there, and players of infant Middlesbrough used its dance hall as a changing room. It is now a Wetherspoon's, like so many historic buildings in small-town England. As is usually the case with the sachet-happy chain, a nod is given to local history – by the Gents' in giant lettering a poem reads:

Where alchemists were born
Below Cleveland's Hills
A giant blue dragonfly across the Tees
Reminds us every night
We built the world.
Every metropolis
Came from Ironopolis.

Linthorpe Road has become a trophy room of that great modern English obsession, eating out. Its retail spaces glisten with curry houses and pizza places, the spoils of a trend that continues amidst a recession. My favourite here is Akbhar's of Bradford; there is something wonderful about one post-industrial northern town exporting Asian cuisine to another.

I veer right by the world's first talking CCTV cameras. The police monitor the images they produce and can upbraid people from afar via a speaker. I've seen it used once, to tell off a teenage boy for dropping a leaflet, but have often thought how much it would enliven the town if the police took to commentating on people in the street: 'And the lady with the Poundland bags now. She's weaving in between the benches. Oh, and an audacious about-turn into Greggs. She must've smelt those sausage rolls ... Jimmy Armfield?'

Soon the street opens up into my favourite part of town, Centre Square. Though it sounds like a netball position, Centre Square is quite beautiful. The square itself ('the largest civic space in Europe', according to the council) consists of a dancing fountain and a well-heeled lawn. These are surrounded by the best and worst of local architecture, old and new. The columned splendour of the Central Library somehow looks comfortable next to Middlesbrough Institute of Modern Art, a giant, jagged and bold glass palace. Opposite, though, are the law courts and council offices, one of which is a bungalow dressed as a crematorium, on stilts. Everything is overshadowed by the town hall, part gothic grandeur, part Transylvanian castle and declared on its opening in 1887 to be 'in the style of the thirteenth century suffused with the feeling and spirit of the current time'. Today on Centre Square Emo kids mix happily with families – all are sat on folding chairs or blankets watching *The Grinch* on a giant screen. Picnics in the cold and scotch eggs through fingerless gloves. This is England.

With an hour until kick-off I walk underneath the meaty iron of the Albert Railway Bridge and by Bolckow and Vaughan's old flat towards a ghost town. St Hilda's, referred to by locals as

'Over the Border', was the original Middlesbrough. Its gridded streets housed workers, its main square their pubs and clubs. In one of its corners sat the Talbot Hotel, host of the alleged tripe supper that gave the world Middlesbrough Football Club.

St Hilda's is now a large piece of hilly grass occasionally punctuated by fragments of original road. Building-wise, all that remains is the crimson clock tower of Middlesbrough's original town hall, a spooky, lone relic, and a few blocks of adjoined, more recent housing. I walk towards it up what was once West Street, dodging debris left by recent house demolitions. Mayor Ray Mallon had determinedly cleared most of the area earlier in 2011; the last blocks avoided the wrecking ball due to the campaigning of their eldest resident. They seem to be clearing away old England, as if she was never there.

As I stand on rubble and glass, the silence is overwhelming. Everything is still, save for the town hall clock which, remarkably, still keeps the correct time. Outside one of the houses yet to be boarded then bulldozed, a giant St George's flag droops from a pole. There is so much space here, as is the case across Middlesbrough. So many boards and shells.

There is beauty too. I look down on the River Tees, inactive, but silvery and strong. Then there is the splendid Transporter Bridge (the 'giant blue dragonfly' of the Wetherspoon's poem), recently turned a hundred years old. This unique piece of artistry and labour is a symbol of identity for many here, and the fact it is surrounded by nothing but wasteland constitutes one of those endearing imperfections. In the other direction, the Cleveland Hills brood under a leaden sky, their unusual peak a Yorkshire Matterhorn.

I slip down imaginary side streets towards Middlehaven, the dock on which the Riverside stands. The all-new Middlesbrough College shines and looms. Could it be that inside its dramatic walls a new generation learns to make things as their forebears did? Beyond it, Anish Kapoor's 'Temenos' sculpture floats like a giant slinky or an open-ended condom, depending on your mood. These ventures and umpteen wooden walls of multi-coloured 'Middlehaven' branding do not mask the tragic waste of grand plans undelivered. This was supposed to be another New Town, a space-age land of quirky flats and floating restaurants. With barely a brick laid, the developers have bailed, leaving a Teesside mud steppe.

Perhaps a metaphor, in neighbouring Able Dock a ship slowly sinks. This is the *Tuxedo Royale*, once a Geordie party ship moored on the Tyne, then a pre-match venue in Boro's Premier days. Now she lists, her guts robbed hollow by local souvenir thieves. No one can now drink in her Bonzai Bar, nor endure her pre-game strippers (50p entry fee!). So many shadows of yesterday, some of them best forgotten.

In the distance, people drift towards the Riverside by stillborn dock water. An advantage of this sparse setting is how easily one can observe people going to the match as if they were in a giant, live Lowry canvas. I follow them, noting that none seem to be talking of football – has going to the football ever really been about going to the football? Eventually, we cross the oddly bucolic bridge that leads from one side of the dock to that which houses Middlesbrough FC's home.

Despite my love of Ayresome, we had to move here. Between the day I was born in 1981 and 1986, Boro slid down the divisions and into liquidation. A team of locals led by captain Tony Mowbray climbed back up, but that only allowed breathing space as Ayresome crumbled. Since Boro moved, we've seen five cup finals, European football and Fabrizio Ravanelli in a Middlesbrough shirt.

Half an hour before kick-off, there isn't an excitement about the place as in those razzmatazz early Riverside days of Ravanelli and Juninho, yet there is a calm buzz. This has everything to do with one man: Mowbray, back as manager, our manager. We identify with him, and him with our club and our town. He talks like us and dreams like us.

I meet my matchday friends Dave and Paddy beneath the feet of Mannion and Hardwick. Their action-curved statues act like brackets at each end of the Ayresome Gates, shifted here so that every time I pass them I'm reminded of Chunky and Moustache.

Inside the stadium, hundreds of people rush a final drink before forty-five minutes of abstinence. I queue up at the urinals where men converse with their backs to one another while pre-match beer passes through them.

I probably shouldn't still feel like this, but every time I enter the Riverside and see the green green grass of home I tingle. There really is no colour as vivid and no theatre as live. As a professional worrier, I relish what's about to come: an hour and a half when I'm not me and when everything leaves my head save for the football. Life becomes simple.

We file along the row and to our seats. As always, I bash the larger of my fellow supporters with my Man Bag. I still haven't learned that watching football is not a satchel-appropriate pastime.

Boro's recently reinstated and reassuringly shouty PA announcer Mark Page has had a career of Partridgian vicissitudes. In the early 1980s, he was plucked from local radio to fill the early Saturday morning slot on Radio One. Now, he is a star of Garrison FM, the British Army's premier station. Page's misdemeanours at the Riverside include the introduction of the God-awful 'Pigbag' as Boro's running-out music, the playing of Blur's 'Song 2' following home goals and the piping of recorded chants during a major European semi-final match (Steaua Bucharest, 2006. Seriously).

This may seem like needlessly parochial information born of petulance, and to an extent it is. However, it carries a wider importance – Page has played his part in the strangling of English football's atmospheres. He is part of the choreography of crowds and the stifling of spontaneous delight. When music is boomed out ten minutes before kick-off just as both ends should be bating one another and making themselves heard to players in the changing room, and when the full-blooded oral chaos after a goal is scored is lost behind 'Chelsea Dagger', watching football becomes a muffled, managed experience. No wonder football grounds are quieter now. An orchestrated atmosphere is a false one and very few of us want to be part of that.

To think that those around me – for it is a refreshingly young crowd today – have only ever known this contrivance is saddening. With oral expression suppressed by the Tannoy's onslaught, visual often takes its place. Chipping away at the Riverside's dull ten-a-penny architecture are legions of homemade banners. Above us, one reads 'Infant Hercules'. Behind the far goal is a silhouette portrait of chairman hero Steve Gibson with the words 'One of Us' next to it. Identity and belonging.

One exception to our sprightly neighbours is the old lady in front of us. She shuffles along the row at one minute to three, removes a large, crocheted owl cushion from her Tesco Bag for Life and plonks herself down. The teenager next to me is wearing dark red trousers. That this annoys me so much demonstrates that I am ready to turn thirty. He and his friend – thankfully sporting kegs of a less deviant hue – spend most of the first half talking about bands I've never heard of.

On the pitch, if and when it matters, a confident Boro move the ball about with grace. They are dominant, stroking it around as if imagining themselves in the early days of a better sport. Their passing style is comfort football, wholesome and reassuring. Key in this is their No. 10, part-plump, part-muscle, mostly a midfield tyrant. Nothing passes him. His partner in midfield grime, formerly ineffective and not unaccustomed to shouting at the crowd, has been converted into a bustling dynamo under Mowbray. This flying Scotsman is unashamedly old school, right down to the gigantic 'HEAD' holdall he carries into grounds on matchdays. Today, he hurtles into tackles at a speed that would make a fighter jet wince. When a Brighton defender blasts a clearance straight on to his back, the ball makes a bursting noise. The boy can play too, time and again fizzing it around or plucking a surprising turn from an armoury we had previously assumed to be barren.

Ahead of those two, Boro's Moroccan probes and picks away from underneath a straggly mullet. His abeyance of Ramadan at the start of the season doubled as religious education for many of us here, though I chuckle *and* squirm remembering that when I saw him play in August, a Boro fan near me started to sing: 'He's had nowt to eat/but he's fucking great/nowt to eat and he's fucking great ...'

The Moroccan's jiggery-pokery soon pays off as he plays a part in Boro taking the lead. A magnificent schoolboy scramble eventually sees Boro's squat Australian urge the ball into the net. Before and after the hateful music, our celebrations are loud, clear and symptomatic of a crowd that believes its team may be going somewhere. 'Twenty-five years since we nearly died,' we sing, 'Ayresome Park to the Riverside/Europe twice and we won the cup/with Tony Mowbray, we're going up.'

The stripes of Brighton are not having it, though. They awake and arise into the game, all short passes and cryptic manoeuvres. A forward buzzes about, his mane occasionally threatening to take somebody's eye out, and their enthusiastic young winger winds his way through a defence frequently paddling about upstream. When another Brighton player has possession, his right arm is constantly thrust aloft, a seven-year-old begging to answer a geography question.

There's an intriguing struggle between each side's Argentinian. Both are, in numbers of games played, England's most successful Argentines, and both are left-backs. It is reassuringly English that from the land of Maradona and Messi, our longest-lasting exponents are goal-shy full-backs. They are fiercely competitive with one another, not least in the quest to see who can roll their socks down the farthest. Despite their Latin American schooling, both are guilty of launching profoundly pointless passes forward. I'm reminded of a bloke I used to sit near when I had a season ticket here. 'Aye, hit it into the channel,' he'd say, 'the English fucking channel.'

As the floodlights blast into life – what is English football if not dark afternoons in the cold? – the half-time whistle shrieks. In the stand's concourse, it is dog eat hot dog in the race to the bar. Deploying a set piece straight from the training ground, we send in six foot-three Paddy to take away the man-markers, leaving space behind for a clear run on the till. It works a treat, and by 3.55 p.m. the three of us are sipping £3.80 pints of vile, heated bitter from plastic vessels. Our watching of the scores from elsewhere is distracted by the gratifying pursuit of staring at an old man failing miserably to poke a straw into a Capri Sun.

In the second half, Brighton's band of merry followers finally rouses with a quick burst of popular hit: 'You dirty northern bastards'. I do like a bit of regional stereotyping in chanting. A few years back, in the week when Newcastle was found to be suffering appalling levels of obesity, I thoroughly enjoyed our chants from the St James' away end of: 'Have you ever had a salad/have you fuck' to the tune of 'She'll Be Coming Round the Mountain'.

There's no such wit, alas, from the late teen behind us. He seems to be on day release from a monastery. I love a good expletive as much as the next twat, but this is proper, repeated nonsense which obscures the meaning of curse words that frankly deserve to be rationed and cherished. His expectations of a second-tier team are quite ridiculous. 'Fucking shoot', he cries when Boro are anywhere within fifty yards of the goal, 'fucking shoot, you useless bastards.' Am I mistaking passion for aggression? Was I ever like that? Would eighteen-year-old me hate me at thirty?

He does seem to be the exception, though. Although attendances have halved since Boro's early-twenty-first century peak, somehow the atmosphere is often better at games than it was then. It feels as if the club is down to a hardcore of deep, deep carers: those that identify most with the team. The drifters have gone; long live the belongers. The most heartening thing is that many of them are teenagers. One set has even formed an 'Ultras' group, the Red Faction, who've set up noisily in a corner of their own, moving the heart of the Riverside across the stadium. Undoubtedly their growing bond is accelerated by the fact that they're watching a team largely made up of players from the same schools as them, managed by a man who pronounces 'five' as 'fahve', just like they do. When I finish losing myself in today's game I realise that, against my fears, young people *are* finding the sense of belonging football offers.

Back on the field, in glorious Technicolor the Flying Scotsman is smacking away a helping Brighton hand like a mid-tantrum toddler. The Albion player had only sought to pull Boro's man from the ground to his feet. Knuckled Caledonian ire was probably unnecessary, but definitely funny. The two midfielders are grave robbers, taking the riches from Brighton attacks and covering one another's backs. Towards the end, one of them becomes involved in a touchline fracas with Albion substitutes. In seconds, his comrade is there, provoking a scene that will later be played out in drunken high streets across merry England. Pointed fingers, testosterone, men pushing, pouncing and punching for reasons they can't quite remember. Boro's midfielders: leaders of the pack … the pack coming for you.

Of late, the chants meted out by opposing supporters to Brighton have become a talking point and a reminder of football's inherent homophobia: 'Does your boyfriend know you're here' and 'We can see you holding hands' they sing. Offensive? Funny and a part of 'terrace humour'? Certainly the Brighton riposte of, 'You're too ugly to be gay' is. Unfortunately, my lot can't muster anything more than vintage number '(You're just a) town full of rent boys' today, boring and boorish from the Boro.

The whistle soars and we roar. Three points, that staple ingredient of a good weekend. Over another appalling pint in the concourse bowels, we watch one steward de-brief other stewards with militaristic seriousness. Never in the history of human resources have so many men in fluorescent coats listened to so few words of use.

The three of us line up by the statues of Wilf and George. There's Paddy and there's Dave and there's me. And, of course, there's Middlesbrough. Though personal, identity is nothing if not shared. Middlesbrough and football give us something to hold on to in an England of flux. The town, its history and its team are interlinked in themselves, and all three are constants of the England in my mind.

It is time now to visit an England I'm far less sure about.

Chapter Two
Sheffield

A woman sat by the window, glancing at the power stations and canals. Occasionally, she would turn to her husband and pass comment. When a young Yorkshire-Asian family got on the train at Doncaster, she grinned widely and fondly at their youngest member, a little girl with dark and wonderful eyes. 'I used to work in a nursery with girls like you, Love. Best times of me life.' Both the woman and her husband displayed Yorkshire Mouth, that local condition through which jaw lines protrude to allow proficient gritting of teeth. It is not an intentionally unfriendly look, more a contented 'seen it all before one', a happy, minor gurn.

Across the table from me, a boy of thirteen or fourteen studiously reads the Kerry Katona-clad pages of *Chat* magazine. This was the new Yorkshire: nostalgic but modern, traditional but progressive. Most of all, inclusive. It ladled warmth and belonging all over me. Despite my Teesside birth and Middlesbrough loyalty, this was the county in which I grew up. It makes for a strange, dual nationality only confused further by living in Scotland. When asked of my origins I reply, 'I'm a Yorkshireman, but I support Middlesbrough.' I belong to both.

The woman turned to her newspaper, read and then shook her head: "ave you seen this poor lad that got murdered. Eeee, there's some buggers in the world. They should string 'em up and throw away the key.'

I consulted the pages of my own newspaper. There was an article about Manchester City, '... a club where Harvey Nichols sends a mobile shop to the training ground and the menus are put together by Marco Pierre White.' To our left, the glass nipple of Meadowhall shopping centre stood pert. 'I do love Meadow'all,' said husband of String 'Em Up, 'It's got that smashing food court.'

Sheffield soon sprawled alongside both sides of the train, yards of metal shapes and dead chimneys interspersed with surviving industry, a key difference to Middlesbrough. 'Sheffield from the train', wrote H. V. Morton, 'one of England's saddest sights.' Morton was commenting on the city during its smoggiest period shortly after the First World War, and neglected to mention the seven rangy hills that tower over it with menacing beauty.

Under a high sun on FA Cup Third Round day nothing seems sad in Sheffield. Outside the station locals play in steely fountains with the kind of good humour that splashing freezing water on each other somehow brings. Kids roar about and couples kiss. We are all down by the railway station on Sheaf Square. It is so deeply and safely sunken into the valley and so well rejuvenated by New Labour facelift funds that one cannot fail to smile. It is homely, and I feel at home. The search for an alien, uncomfortable England is off to a bad start.

Up on high behind the station, trams slither under the watchful eye of the Park Hill flats, once dreamy 'streets in the sky', then harbingers of deprivation, now being re-jigged and resold. Shafted over and over, Sheffield is good at reinventing itself, it seems – clinging to the concrete sides of another tower block on the main hill into town is poet laureate Andrew Motion's love letter to a city of wild dreams realised. The walls are never boring here, nor the benches. Even the bollards are interesting. No swingeing cuts for architecture's swinging sixties. Instead they are reborn with quirky imperfection. Sheffield lives on and it doesn't really care what you think.

Now they *re*invent, but once they invented. Sliced bread was one of theirs. So were Liquorice Allsorts. Football, too, Sheffielders would say. By the door of the Top Nails Salon on pretty-bricked Norfolk Street a plaque celebrates Friday 22 March 1889, the day 'Sheffield United Football Club was born.' By that year organised football in Sheffield was already middle-aged.

Downhill streets speed me to where homes of football once were. The London Road area is now Sheffield's mouthy answer to Middlesbrough's Linthorpe Road. Food, food everywhere. Here you can eat as the Chinese, Mexicans, Japanese, Thai, Greeks or 'Africans' don't really (lemon chicken or cheddar nachos, anyone?). You can also drink within the cosy oaks of the Cremorne, spiritual – and once nigh on literal, so close was one of their early grounds – home of Sheffield Wednesday. This is now Bladeland. Owls enter at your peril. Walk left in the bar and young pup students analyse their Friday night out. Walk right and old men moan for South Yorkshire.

I sit at the bar and let local ale soothe and relax my brain to thoughts of football. How great that in Yorkshire they know how much it matters. How great that George Orwell felt moved to write of a visit:

> I happened to be in Yorkshire when Hitler re-occupied the Rhineland. Hitler, Locarno, Fascism and the threat of war aroused hardly a flicker of interest locally, but the decision of the Football Association to stop publishing their fixtures in advance (this was an attempt to quell the football pools) flung all Yorkshire into a storm of fury.

Many football firsts were smelted here. Sheffield took the old game of public schools and animal parts and moulded it into a sport. Then, when they decided to get London suits involved, with the Football Association they brought order and devised competition. Their 'Sheffield Rules' – a symptom of typical local otherness – heavily influenced what became the Laws of the Game. To up the sport's aesthetic appeal, the Sheffield Rules restricted hacking and handling by way of civilisation and allowed forward passes to make the game more attacking. The rules introduced corner flags, umpires, corners, goal kicks, throw-ins, crossbars, the half-time change of ends and the tradition of drawing cup ties from a hat. A Sheffield side taught London how to head the ball during a match at Battersea Park in 1866, much to the amusement of home supporters.

Organisational prowess fed cultural advances. Sheffield Wednesday's Jimmy Lang became, in 1876, England's first paid player. To get around the strict codes of amateurism, he was officially a cutler, though he spent his working day reading newspapers and drinking tea at the factory of an Owls committee member. Two years later, the country's first floodlit match took place at Bramall Lane in front of 20,000 Sheffielders. They loved a novelty match here: in 1879, a Sheffield XI beat the 'Zulus' 5-4 in a charity game aimed at raising funds for families orphaned by the South African wars. The Zulu players, it transpired, took not inconsequential fees to play, making them, perhaps, the world's first professional team. As if that were not enough to inflame the ire of the twenty-first-century humanitarian, the Zulu team comprised a squad of blacked-up locals dressed in beads and feathers and carrying shields. They even went so far as to make up Zulu names (Amaconga, Jiggleumbeano, Dubulamanzi, Umlathooef).

Sheffield also gave us printed fixture lists, football columnists, shin pads and the Saturday night sports newspaper. What bliss the latter used to offer before in-match iPhone updates and post-match screens in pubs, their back pages full of unknown scores, scorers and how many saw them; their front a real-time match report with goalscorers in capitals. Across towns they would be bundled over the arms of portly men in flat caps and sold from pillar to pub. And do you know what I find later, after the game, in a newsagent? Sheffield still bloody has hers, *The Green 'Un*. Oh yes, this is my England all right.

Sheffield holds numerous 'oldests', too. Not far from my barstool is Bramall Lane, home to football since 1862 and therefore the world's oldest ground. These bumpy streets of red bricks gave birth to Sheffield FC, the world's oldest football club. Across town is Hallam FC's Sandygate, the oldest ground in continuous use on earth. When the two young clubs met in that first match at 'The Lane' they set out to raise money for 'cottonopolis' poverty caused by the American Civil War. Instead, they raised their fists at each other, setting in motion internecine footballing intensities now well into their second century. 'At one time, it appeared likely that the match would be turned into a general fight', said the *Sheffield Telegraph* match report. Hallam's William Waterfall had run at Sheffield's Major Creswick 'in a most irritable manner, and struck him several times. He also threw off his waistcoat and began to "show fight" in earnest.'

In those young days, Sheffield was football's most fertile territory. It had an unparalleled, embedded playing and supporter culture. That meant early glory years in the Steel City, with not much else since. Between 1896 and 1907, United and Wednesday won four FA Cups and three First Division Championships. More than any other place, Sheffield explains how English football began. In recounting its story, one man who was there explains why it did so.

In 1901, the Blades' captain and greatest ever player Ernest Needham published 'Association Football', a whimsical ninety-page essay on football, the 'pastime that appears to possess a power that cannot be resisted.' Needham opined that this 'healthy and manly recreation' was a driving force for working-class well-being and sobriety. Football helped the non-playing public too, affecting the mental health of supporters as 'a wonderful stimulus to those suffering from depressed spirits.' His was a view displayed often by the Sheffield business families who were intrinsic in the foundation of the city's football scene; they, after all, could benefit from a healthy, distractedly contented workforce. Yet Needham's explanation of why football came about extended further. He believed that it met a core need of the English:

It is the true Englishman's love of danger which, rightly or wrongly, impels him to take part in a pastime in which there is a certain amount of risk; and the more risk, the more eager he is for the fray. It is only the 'namby-pambies' who delight in drawing-room games. We should not have heroes as Nelson, Wellington, and many others, if they had not 'faced the music,' so to speak. What Englishman with an ounce of pluck will not brave danger?

This was a patriotic game, fuelled by English needs and fuelling the nation's fighting spirit. The Sheffield Rules had made 'the game a display of skill, endurance and pluck' that excited:

… emulation in the breasts of young England. It has been epigrammatically said that 'Waterloo was won on the playing fields of Eton.' If this be true, and no one has ever questioned it, I venture to say that the country owes a vast debt of thanks to all true footballers, for they encourage the old combative spirit that has brought us always safely through, and they are fostering a succeeding generation of manly sporting feeling, and of grand physique. Almost might I say the hope of England is in her footballers.

Such views must not be written off as those of a moustachioed *Ripping Yarns* archetype, even if Needham played for Michael Palin's beloved Sheffield United. But, while Sheffield grew the game it was also cultivating a reputation as England's radical city. A pursuit that could keep steelmakers away from Marx was not to be sniffed at. If it could imbue a love of England and Englishness in them, then all the better.

Needham and the Blades' cause was abetted by the scintillating football going on at The Lane. In the years leading up to the twentieth century, English greats and ephemeral legends flowed through the place. Bramall Lane was an emporium of our game's early curios. Arthur Wharton, the first black British player, stopped off briefly on his journey from celebrated goalkeeper to a pauper's grave via syphilis. Wharton left before the collier triumvirate of Needham, Rab Howell and William Foulke led United to a title win in 1899.

Howell remains England's only gypsy international. A tiny right-half famed for playing without socks, Howell grew up in his tinker father's caravan close to where Meadowhall now hovers. When he was sold to Liverpool, goes the story, he simply hitched his caravan to a horse and scrambled across the Pennines. On the pages of a match programme published in the Blades' championship-winning year, Howell was described by a journalist as 'the happiest-go-lucky individual it has ever been my lot to run shoulders against'. 'Well, I am no chicken although I look like a lad,' said Howell, 'but I shall play a lot longer than most of them. You see, I never drink. I think I am thirty next.'

Howell weighed in at under ten stone. His goalkeeper William 'Fatty' Foulke is remembered for being double that weight, a real shame given his sporting aptitude. He did little to discourage the cult of caveman constructed around him. In one team photo, Foulke poses in apparent 3D, twice the size of everyone else in the squad. He displays the menace of a simple-but-strong film criminal who stands behind his mastermind boss and occasionally lifts people up by the throat. Foulke even seems to be sucking his own eyes in to make them more deep-set. The goalkeeper drank and ate with predictable aplomb, wolfing on one occasion the breakfasts of his ten teammates before they awoke. When playing, he was fond of hanging from the crossbar or lifting opposition forwards by their lapels and supporters by their ankles. Yet Foulke was also fond of making saves and leaping about his area, a colossus in every way. He even played first-class cricket for Derbyshire.

Foulke, Howell, Needham: what times in Sheffield, football's fatherland. What cheer when they brought the league championship home in 1899. All season, those inclined to red stripes had rallied behind their Blades in high numbers, home and away. As trains snaked out of South Yorkshire they sang their way across the country. One thousand at Goodison, where the Scousers pelted Foulke with stones, each bouncing off his girth. Sticks and stones. Two thousand at Notts County – the sport was young, but you could sniff history in the air. Women did not miss out. Already they saw the home games (season ticket admitting 'Self and Lady' in the John Street Stand = 21/-), but now they too went on the run and they too bought hats and scarves in Coles department store.

After the league was won United kept on going, for red Sheffield and for football. In four years, three FA Cup finals and once runners-up in the league. They kept on going when others thought perhaps they should not have, playing in the 'Khaki Cup Final' of 1915 as the sons of England headed off to Ypres, Somme and death. The *Sheffield Morning Telegraph* said United had brought shame upon the city. Thousands of Sheffield Pals battalion members were at the match, 513 died within a year. When the FA Cup trophy was collected for the final time, in 1925, United again brought national heartache to the agenda. Thirteen years earlier, goalkeeper Charles Sutcliffe had missed his sailing on the good ship *Titanic* due to flu. In the Second World War, Sutcliffe lost his winner's medal while sandbagging.

And then ... nothing. Nothing as the homes of football multiplied. By my 1981 anchor, United were missing presumed dead. Martin Peters had guided them into Division Four, a hero of England felled in Sheffield. Uneasy relationships between a steel-owning board (the chairman was a Tory! In Sheffield!) and out-of-steel-work supporters held. They chanted their support of the miners, but now of manager Ian Porterfield too. The Tory chairman knew all about club and community, and did what he could to bring the two on to speaking terms. Nothing, though, melted hearts like the goals of Keith Edwards. Brilliant, boyish, arrogant and, oddly, born on Teeside of ICI stock, but missed by my own imploding club. Forty-two goals from Edwards, ninety-six points from the team. Champions. Champions again.

The peace was volatile and challenged by rioting, political and otherwise. The Blades Business Crew, purveyors of casual violence (but they were well dressed! They *never* hit normal fans!) owned the streets – these streets I stroll down today.

After the terraces that bricked over football's maternity wings, the main stand of Bramall Lane hovers into view. Like the Park Lane flats, it is a Soviet masterpiece of concrete – brutalism with a club shop. Pillars rise above its roof like stretched gravestones and random bits of window prod outwards. The mind expects antiquity and the eyes receive a poke. The here and now is brought even closer by banner images on each car park lamppost of a tragically deceased former Blades manager. Five weeks before my visit today, Gary Speed was found hanged in his garage. So quickly does football go from history and mattering to frippery and not.

On the game rolls. On and on. The Magic of the Cup is in town. Part-time visitors Salisbury City are here in the ancient home of football. They have borrowed Swindon Town's team coach for the forage north. There it sits by the Legends of the Lane Lounge, squeezed in front of a St John Ambulance. City fans loiter and take pictures of the Soviet stand. Two thousand are here from Salisbury today. They don't often get half that at home. Full-timers will be shaking their heads as they queue and employing particularly obscure chants to alienate the Johnny Come Latelys. Eventually and secretly they will love the way the city has got behind their City. Yesterday, the press handcar trundled into town. Chairman William Harrison-Allan (there's a proper chairman's name) said it all: 'The formation against Sheffield will be 9-0-1 I expect, but it's great fun ... I'd love a draw against Sheffield United – you wouldn't need to get me a car to go home, I'd run down the M1.' Eighty-four rungs on England's ladder separate the two clubs, but we all know that this sport is for dreaming.

In the ticket office queue, I take in local sounds. There are 'reights' and 'nowts' and dialogues about a recent signing's arse size. Everyone seems to pronounce Salisbury 'Salsbury', as if elongating the 'a' would compromise their Yorkshireness. The Soviet stand is officially called the GAC Stand. 'What's GAC, mate?' I ask a steward. 'Not a clue, pal. I'm from Barnsley.'

Scattered flowers on the grass verge up to the Kop are part of the Sheffield United Memorial Garden. 'To Our Dad', most of them read, or 'To Our Dad, The True Blade'. Their cellophane flutters in the wind and people stop to remember. Some probably imagine that one day there will be flowers for them here too. It is where they want to be, where they belong, in life and death.

The electric turnstiles bleep us in, a mass of denim and Christmas gift hats. A shabby, but modern sign, aged perhaps with tea like an infant's treasure map, offers welcome to 'The World's Oldest Professional Football Ground'. I peep through to the empty Kop, closed today due to the small attendance anticipated, but still atmospheric, ominous and mighty. People sneak in a crafty fag then run up to their seats to sing about cigarettes. The music strikes up but is, brilliantly, cut in time for an entirely arisen home end to belt out their anthem:

You fill up my senses
Like a gallon of Magnet
Like a packet of Woodbines
Like a good pinch of snuff
Like a night out in Sheffield
Like a greasy chip butty
Like Sheffield United
Come thrill me again

The tune is John Denver's 'You Fill Up My Senses', though *his* lyrics feature forests, mountains, springtime and a calm azure sea. I prefer the Sheffield depiction of life's pleasures. It speaks of a northern hedonism that I like about England, as compared to, say, an American's slightly spiritual and wholesome devotion to open air and space.

The choir sits and leaves Bramall Lane itself to exude atmosphere. Whatever the architectural butchery outside, sitting here and looking at this age-old pretty green is a rush. For so long, people have played and watched sport here, not only football but also cricket, and even baseball. Several generations have come to escape real life, all of them looking in the same direction. That continuity breeds a sense of belonging whomever you support. Ultimately, we as football fans share the pleasure and the pain of our game. It is a key part of our own version of England. As there are so many of us, it is a key part of England as a whole, too.

Bramall Lane is an all-seater stadium, but alongside heritage it still has enough rough edges and oddities to be special. Giant crutches keep the Kop roof in place, and other scattered pillars make for a communal experience of thousands craning their necks at once, a tennis crowd only with more use of the word 'shite'. It is also unfailingly, blaringly red, from those pillars to seats, walls and roofs. Dusky in-ground lights bounce off surfaces and enhance the feeling that you are part of a bonfire in a skip.

Our FA Cup Third Round begins. Teenagers around me discuss their real preoccupation: the Football Manager computer game. One has even signed Messi for the Blades ('But I've still kept Chris Morgan'). 'Two pound yer programmes,' squawks a man in a bright coat walking up and down the stand's steps. 'Two pound yer matchday programmes. Just two pound. Two quid.' At this point, one in two males in the vicinity howl variations of the question, 'How much did you say they were, mate?' We are all highly unoriginal. We all think we were the first bloke to go into Poundland, pick up an item and say 'How much is this, love?'

The Salisbury fans – far away in the low-ceilinged away end – make disjointed noise. Around forty of them sit separately from the main body of supporters, and I wonder if these are the regulars,

sat apart in their morally superior ghetto. We all see the same
game of kick-and-rush, clear and dart. Every now and again, the
Blades remember how easy football can be and pass their way to
superiority. Against such relatively unfit opposition, it is a rare
chance to be easily the best lad in the playground. A throw-in
allows time to notice the two advertising hoardings facing me.
One is for Fantasy Island, Lincolnshire's premier family theme
park. The other is for the Samaritans.

When my neighbours turn to the real world they have a
surprisingly good line in old-fashioned 'dad at football' speak. ''e
runs like 'e's got a Farmfoods freezer on his back. Ay! Farmfoods!
'Urry up.' Eighteen minutes in, a United goal interrupts the pursuit
of low-end supermarket-based abuse. Salisbury retaliate by
entering the United half for the first time. They remember how to
make runs and angles for each other, and even how to pass.
Corner-kicks are eked out of nothing and the City followers arise
and yearn. One corner acts as a summary of the rest, outswinging
as it does with absolutely no adherence to the basic laws of
trigonometry, and starting a home attack.

The sharp-tongued teen next to me appears to have a favourite
boo boy too. The victim seems like an able enough full-back to
me, and if nothing else is the first Haitian international I have ever
seen in action. Yet to teenboy he is hilarious. It actually crosses
into nastiness, though I don't think racial, and I ponder again the
anger of youth as witnessed at the Riverside.

Half-time brings a tight squeeze into the stand's contracted
stomach. Old men in possession of classic Yorkshire Jaws parade
up and down the end of each queue for food and drink tutting and
shaking their heads. This is *their* stand. *Their* concourse. Just who
are these interlopers? Those that do make the finish line can
choose a Steak and Stone's Bitter Pie. There *is* character and

region to be spotted in football ground catering, which surprises and pleases me. In these little ways can we keep our corners of England familiar and particular, should we wish to.

When the second period gets underway, Salisbury tear into United and dash about like purposeful sheepdogs. United retort by sending on their ex-England centre-forward, now large of breast, but still full of huff and puff. He scurries around effectively, a titan among plodding ogres. A City midfielder takes umbrage and jackknifes his opponent, a scalp to tell his mates about. Unfortunately, it is like taking cheesewire to a steak, and the forward gallops away. 'Who are ya?' sing the United men.

Their team make it 2-0 when the teenager's Haitian bête noir and another beanstalk forward combine to force an own goal. The City defender who plunges the ball in is guilty only of trying too hard. The same forward later bundles the keeper into his net, ball and all, though the Sheffield Rules rule no longer and the tally remains at two. Today he is a hero. By the season's end he is in prison for rape. Frequently, the ball balloons, pings and pinballs about the City box as tired legs push clearances on to clumsy knees. Eventually, the future jailbird coerces another own goal. Shortly afterwards, the previously silent man three seats to my left darts out like a tracksuited jack-in-a-box and hurls a quite incredible string of abuse at the linesman. It is ferocious and pent-up, as if the two are old friends and my neighbour has been holding something back since 1987. Meanwhile, my younger surrounding comrades are now fixed to their iPhone screens, no *Green 'Uns* for them tonight.

Towards the end Salisbury score the goal of the game, a thumped effort from distance. The City roar is strident but regretful. For a few minutes their team pile forward inspired by a floppy-locked substitute, a rock star of a footballer. Could his be the story? *Maybe, just maybe.* Then the whistle goes. A 3-1 loss. The first city of football claps the Salisbury yellows from the pitch. *If only, if only.*

I walk back into the black Sheffield night. The tram up to Jarvis Cocker's place is empty and seems to have the voice of Sean Bean. Sheffield is glammed up tonight. She glints terrifically as we rise through hilly housing estates, a flickering mass with no perceptible end. I walk from Manor Top along Mansfield Road to Intake, where Cocker spent his youth. Cocker is important to Sheffield's story because music is, but he is also important to England's. It is, after all, one of the great stereotypes of our nation that it produces eccentrics, though they usually have to be of a certain social class to attain the label. I pass a model railway shop and then Intake Fish and Chips. Intake is not quite inner-city Sheffield, but not quite leafy suburb. It seems to be on the frontier boundary between working-class city and factory-owning country.

Cocker's old place is badly lit, large and set back from the road behind high bushes and bulky walls. As the trees lazily sway in the winter wind the house has an arch creepiness to it, as does the smoggy limestone Methodist Church next door. Turn left on the main road at the house's front and you find Sheffield. Turn right, it's the south, escape, and stardom. The shops that nuzzle Cocker's old home are, in their names, aptly wry and faintly Royston Vasey. There is Short 'n' Curlies hairdresser, 'air Barbers, A&E News and Snakes & Adders – 'The Right Lifestyle For Your Reptile'. Not all of them can have been here when Cocker was, but they still help explain him, Sheffield, his, and to an extent my England.

After two decades of struggle, Cocker's band sprung on to the national consciousness in the mid-1990s, Michael Jackson's warts and all. Theirs was an England of bus shelter sex and happenings in town parks. As much as anything Pulp created English fiction and characters rather than singing truths, whether in their songs or their personas; a local criticism of Cocker's 'Common People' lyric was how fabricated it all was given the sizeable house in front of me tonight, and his somewhat bourgeois upbringing (siblings named Jarvis and Saskia, anyone?). But imagined or not, its template was of an England not completely unrecognisable to me. As Cocker told *Select* magazine, it was a country of 'chips, the Peak District and cul-de-sacs.'

Across from the Cocker house I enter The Ball Inn. It is a large black and tan mansion of a pub, and surely the place to garner proud local tales of its former neighbour. Conversation above the jukebox is, though, impossible. I sit by a man feeding his baby dry roasted peanuts and sup up quickly. At the bus stop a dolled-up woman in her fifties tells me that this is a fantastic place to get the bus 'because they're all eight minutes apart, just enough time to bob in the chippy for a portion.' The 42 fills up as we head from high on Cocker hill down into town. Saturday night is here. 'Single into town', says each passenger that boards. Aftershave boxes perfume for attention.

I alight at Haymarket in search of music. It matters here. It's not quite football, but it matters. The story is well worn: Joe Cocker, the New Wave movement (Human League were Number One on the day I was born), Pulp, Richard Hawley, Arctic Monkeys ... All are resolutely Sheffield (the wryness, the quiet assuredness) and resolutely England (the peculiar sounds, the particular lyrics). They are the Sheffield poets who have often determined how their city is seen and the international artists taking their England to the world. I walk by the Boardwalk, where The Clash made their debut supporting The Sex Pistols. It is now boarded up and for sale, fly posters masking its spit-stained walls.

I walk to Coles Corner, title of a Richard Hawley album and according to him a major reproductive organ:

> Sheffield's couples, lovers, friends, mums or dads or whatever, would meet there. I've always found it quite a romantic notion – how many kids in Sheffield are knocking about as a result of a meeting at Coles Corner?

Coles department store is gone now. Gone are the matchmakings. Gone too is the sports section where those United fans of yore bought red and white things for forays afar. Down a dark street The Grapes glows golden. Here the Arctic Monkeys played for the first time. I settle by a fire in the snug and listen to a man describe Huddersfield Town striker Jordan Rhodes as 'the Clive Allen of League One'. He is sat among work colleagues for whom football is a recurring conversational topic, despite the efforts of the only woman present. This is not a sexist thing; she seems determined to change the subject to terminal diseases, and no one is really up for that on a Saturday night.

Back in the Saturday night streets of Sheffield I look for legendary home of synth pop, The Limit. I reckon it must have been just about where Nando's now stands. Furiously reacting to this steamrollering of England's cultural prestige, and as an ardent anti-chain restaurant socialist who regularly moans about the crass homogenisation of Britain's high streets, I take the only option left to me. My half chicken, rice and chips, washed down with a glass of house red, is delicious.

I sit, the man alone in a chain restaurant with nothing for company but a plastic bag containing Haribo sweets and a local paper. My window perch makes for widescreen HD viewing as a Saturday night unfolds. Everywhere outside there is flesh and laughter. Sheffield is smiling at itself, all preened and up for it. The police get kisses.

On the next table to mine a real gone kid of a drunk refuses to drink water when offered by his girlfriend, and then launches into a tirade about her friends. Student flatmates embark upon the early stages of an argument that I predict will sprout and last long into the morning. 'No, no, NO. Look, Tom. What about those case studies. Those fucking case studies.' Ah Nando's, or to its friends, 'middle-class McDonald's'.

Outside, waiting for the tram, there is undoubtedly an amiable feel to proceedings. Drunks even stumble politely. Lasses slur and giggle the night away. A scruffily dapper young lad who is probably in a minor indie band takes an old gal by the arm: 'Come on, my love. Just me and you on the Costa del Sheffield.' A fat woman somehow trips up on a lamppost and dissolves into a guffawed chant of 'I'm from Chesterfield. I'M FROM CHESTERFIELD.' It is not the Saturday night of Bravo TV documentaries showing sick-strewn streets run by spitting, spoiling lads. It is one of exuberance and gentle hedonism. Like a gallon of Magnet. Like a packet of Woodbines.

Breakfast in the Hillsborough Hotel. A cider expert from the Campaign for Real Ale inspects his condiments and slurps tea. I take my table behind him and am soon eating a gloriously English breakfast. Henderson's Relish, 'The Yorkshire Sauce', seems like a fitting accompaniment. It is only available round here and Sheffielders are rightly proud of its cheekily spicy ways. For over a hundred years it has spiced up dull fare and been mopped up by post-fish and chips slices of soapy white bread. CAMRA man is having none of it, bathing his plate in HP Sauce, a clear outsider.

He is here because The Hillsborough, a prepossessing Victorian pub and inn, is on Sheffield's real ale circuit. From miles around people pile into the city to tour twelve designated pubs by tram, friendly Hillsborough owners Helen and Andrew tell me. Many are young. Indeed, many real ale *brewers* these days are young. What a surprising turn of events, that local bitter should become a trend with the achingly Guardianista name of 'craft beer'. That is certainly something fresh about this England I am returning to. It is neither a small quirk nor a fad, and comprises one of very few native industries on the upturn. The microbreweries and beers, in their names and labels, usually tap into a cherished slice of England local to them. A pint of bitter, then, is a nourishing beacon of identity; drink rivers full, for you are preserving what makes us.

Regretting not being quite alcoholic enough to have one last pint of Hillsborough ale at 9.30 a.m. on a Sunday, I bid Helen and Andrew goodbye and head for the tram. 'Two pounds ten please, love', says the male conductor. I had forgotten this was supposed to be true of Sheffield, that men called men 'love'. May that never die out. This method of transport is key to making this city the social, approachable place it is. Cars are banned from so many streets, so life has not been privatised.

Scotland seems to be pursuing me today. The newspapers contain more ramblings of independence, and the man stood over me on the tram delights in giving his view to a travel companion and anyone else within unlucky earshot: 'Let 'em go. It'll get rid of the chip on their shoulders, bloody Jocks.'

This morning, with trams clacking about underneath Park Hill flats and a Sheffield Wednesday-blue sky, it feels like a vibrant post-Communist central European city. All it needs now is Ryanair flights and the stags and hens will swamp in. The city is by no means artistically beautiful, but she is captivating and I can't keep my eyes off her. She has an air, a buzz of things happening, of people getting on with each other and with life, whatever is thrown at them. The landscape helps – to be pitted at the drop of a valley like this makes the place insular and conceitedly riveting. Sheffield is in its own world, a great English republic.

Down bonny lanes and ginnels I walk to Paradise Square, occasionally tripping over empty bottles of WKD from last night. I take that back about Sheffield not being a comely lass – the square is a gem. Cobbles and old gas lampposts are surrounded on all four sides by adjoined high and handsome Georgian houses. It is, naturally, hilly, a sharp curve running from top to bottom, a dishy face clinging to a crooked body. The square is silent today; save for birdsong, bells and some Auto Windscreen repair men sawing glass. Most of the buildings are now occupied by law firms and accountants. One is a retirement and investment planning company, which seems far too long-term and un-hedonistic for Sheffield. These walls, however, whisper rebellion and revolution. On a picnic bench between numbers seven and nine I sit and read accounts of when 20,000 people gathered here in the name of Chartism.

Sheffield had been a centre of English radicalism long before the Chartists took root: 50,000 protested against Manchester's Peterloo Massacre, and when the military demanded 'God Save the King' be sung in theatres, audiences jeered their way through renditions. The people of Sheffield did not like any authority but their own. In 1837 they formed a Working Men's Association. A Female Radical Association that thought hard and fought hard came soon after. Both groups quickly became involved with the Chartist cause, led in Sheffield by Samuel Holberry. Though only in his twenties, Holberry inspired a campaign of church occupations and firebombing. Thousands supported him and gathered frequently here at Paradise Square to roar for social change. In January 1840, Holberry plotted with Chartist leaders in neighbouring towns to begin a revolution that would spread outwards. But the plotters had a traitor in their midst, and as their scheme got underway soldiers swooped. Holberry was sentenced to four years in prison. After a constructed campaign of ill treatment he died, aged twenty-eight, of consumption.

Successfully suppressed, Chartism withered. Sheffield's rebellious streak found different channels. Trade unions were of constant, over-arching importance, and gave others the confidence to rebel. Throughout the nineteenth and twentieth centuries, various rambling groups asserted and exercised their right to roam, most famously at Kinder Scout. These were often impoverished steelworkers who regarded the surrounding Peak District as their playground. In 1851, the Sheffield Female Political Association held its inaugural meeting. It was the first Suffrage group in England. (Take that London feminists, says Sheffield; take that Pankhursts over the Pennines.) Sixty years on, Sheffield women were still fighting for their liberty and fraternity. In 1911, twenty-one-year-old Molly Morris took charge of the local Suffragettes. Molly chalked the streets, fundraised, spoke at meetings and blew up postboxes. Violent, perhaps, but by 1929 Sheffield had elected ten female Councillors. Molly would later marry Jack Murphy, a Sheffield trade union and Communist Party behemoth. Together, the two travelled to Moscow following the Soviet revolution to meet with Lenin and his cabinet.

While the Communist Party had significant support in Sheffield, it was Labour who came to dominate city politics. Throughout the 1980s, the city repeatedly showed Thatcherism the back of its hand. Under the tutelage of, remarkably it seems now, David Blunkett, the Socialist Republic of South Yorkshire installed its own economic system to save the steel industry she at Number Ten sought to kill. They hoisted the Red Flag over the town hall and declared the city a nuclear-free zone. Even the buses cost nigh on nowt. When Maggie visited, it took 1,000 batoned boys in blue to keep the mob off. National authorities and agendas won in the end, but by 'eck what a fist they gave it here.

A hulking jeep pulls up and parks next to me in today's Paradise. Its driver, a man in a Barbour jacket and khaki chords, beeps the beast locked and leaves her to sweat, tick and cool. My wistful bench reading is over. Back by the cathedral, which teeters on the more depressing side of Gothic, if that's possible, an occupation is underway. A tented community has taken up residence in the square outside. 'If not us – Who? If not now – When?' reads one of their many signs. Given the Chartists' penchant for being church nuisances and displaying such catchy slogans, could this be a re-creation, the left-wing version of those blokes who on a weekend dress up and run about in potato fields pretending to be Yorkists? The cathedral bells shake the ground and smoke out the tent dwellers. Bearded men and attractive nose-studded women emerge, yawn and smile. Another day and the world still needs saving. These folk are members of the Occupy movement, an organic protest group that refuses to let rapacious capital off free. They, too, are heirs of both the Sheffield Chartist tradition and the English radical tradition of trespassing or camping on stuff to make a point. Their presence here cheers my Sunday morning no end. Still we protest in England, still there are people that defy agenda and apathy to make a stand.

As I am reading an article on the side of their main tent about Wayne Rooney entitled '£10m a Year for Kicking a Ball – This Can't Be Right', a drunk intrudes the camp. He sings the Mamas and Papas' 'California Dreamin'' and then announces his intention to burn the church down on behalf of the protestors who are, apparently, 'sound lads'. The campers engage politely with the drunk to remind him that theirs is an alcohol-free zone. Marvellously, he shakes hands, apologises and then parks himself down next to the camp fence to finish his bottle of cider.

I continue on to the Peace Gardens, apt after that fine display of conflict avoidance. Water laps down cascading fountains dedicated to Samuel Holberry. The gardens, more a calming civic square, are overlooked by Sheffield Town Hall, which resembles an officious stately home with a clock tower. Once again families stamp cold water on to one another and fill the tongue-tied air with giggles. I continue through the Winter Gardens, a giant oval percolating clammy air. There are more gigglers, here: nervous young daters, old-time couples laughing over the same stories retold. Determined businesswomen set up their infant enterprises that sell sandwiches and, of course, cupcakes. Is England becoming a nation of beer and sponge? I hope so. We *are* virtuous, Mr Shakespeare, but we want our cakes and ale.

Via contented landscape gardens lapping at two theatres and the giant car battery sticklebrick that is Sheffield Hallam University, I arrive back by the station and endure a severe attack of dreamy goosebumps. Sheffield has done that to me. The trigger now is a wall poem I had missed yesterday by the Bard of Barnsley, Ian McMillan. 'The passenger now leaving platform five,' it begins, 'arrives in a place of shining steel/And it makes that passenger glad to be alive.'

There is just something *about* Sheffield, and therefore *this* England. The architecture is mixed and sometimes ugly, but its situation takes one's focus away from that. 'A dirty picture in a golden frame' said local resident John Ruskin. But as well as its bonhomie and welcome, it is the city's resilience that I am particularly taken by. Because where post-industrial towns like Middlesbrough seem to have given up, Sheffield has not. It has retained industry where possible, but failed to mope when those forces no one asked for made it impossible. Give them a monstrous 1960s tower block, and the people paint it pink and call it a cultural centre. Don't believe me? Sheffield now has the most artist studios of any place outside London. No one has given up. Indeed, even this current recession doesn't seem to be biting, perhaps because, as one man in the Cremorne told me, 'We had nowt in the first place'. There is a happiness about the place – that Woodbine hedonism – that does not scream like there is no tomorrow in a Mancunian way, but has a cracking night out while it can. It is the contentedness of rain on a tent roof rather than champagne and dancing. No one is grinning ear to ear, but they are smirking that nature has given them these hills and this city. The wit is sharp but not sardonic or cynical.

There is enterprise in Sheffield. It is Our England, modified. Think of Chartism as the Occupy protest, the Park Hill rejuvenation, or, even, Jarvis Cocker inspiring the Arctic Monkeys. History and the present are interwoven; how good England was and can be, instead of bemoaning the state of things. I am contractually obliged to write it, but football was vital to this. Playing such a role in its invention and early growth created an ethos among Sheffielders – conscious or otherwise – that what they said mattered, and that their actions could change England. That optimism is retained in the way the city is today. This England I have come across resembles the highest ideal I built in my Caledonian exile. Next stop, Luton.

Chapter Three

Luton

Pity Luton. People only ever pass through. It is a commuter train station of a town. Every year ten million people come within fifteen minutes of its centre yet never think to drop in. Luton is a discarded great-aunt with Alzheimer's we keep meaning to visit. The trouble is, people think she stinks of piss.

I am popping in, and from the airport at that. The driver of the number 61 looks a little confused when I tell him I want to go into the town centre and not alight at the airport's railway station for a train to London. He is positively discombobulated when three German backpackers board and demand transport to 'the centre of Luton Town'. From the window the grey horizon of tarmac and sky is broken only by grey factory buildings in-between. It makes a change from the scarlet rust of Teesside and South Yorkshire, I suppose.

One of them is Home of the Vauxhall Vivaro, a reminder that the company once employed 30,000 workers here. From everywhere, people were drawn to Luton and the work it offered. A decade ago, the main Vauxhall factory closed. Working-class work wound down another gear and the melting pot began boiling over. Vauxhall's demise brought the death of its social structures – the clubs, the societies, the outings, the football teams. Those people from everywhere needed something to belong to.

We splash on, making the satisfying noise of bus tyre on wet road. The *Daily Express* and *Star* printing hangar is sleeping now, awaiting the new poison-arrow words and pictures that will arouse England in so many different ways tomorrow. Chevrolet and General Motors look silent too, but do hint at weekday work. There are no north-eastern-style gaps here, but then the south-east has always had a better PR department. Just like Teesside, the public sector is Luton's biggest employer. We plunge past the Sicilian Cafe, its Budweiser sign flashing, and the University of Bedfordshire's visual timeline of architectural horror schemes into view. The latest effort – Jenga comes off worse in a barney with a full cement mixer – is, at least, unique. The *Sunday Telegraph* once asked if this was the 'worst university in Britain'. It is easy to sneer at these Cornflake-box polys, but it is often they who give access to a family's first university attendee, and they who prop up wasted small-town economies.

The bus drops me outside the back of something, but then, as I later find, a fair proportion of central Luton seems to be the back of something. Slightly befuddled and wondering if jetlag is possible from an Edinburgh to Luton flight, I find myself in a courtyard full of industrial bins. They seem to man-mark me and I am only able to escape with a deft drop of the shoulder. When I emerge, the rain is doing Luton's concrete no favours. Mascara is running all down her face. There are spots and sites to cheer. The Hat Factory is a smartly adapted old industrial unit now comprising an arts and entertainment venue. I think of chancing the cafe, but am put off by frequent mentions of jazz and contemporary dance. Plus, Luton is not really open yet, so I perch on a wall and read about hats.

Luton exists because of hats. Before migrants arrived to make things for roads, they arrived to make things for heads. Some were troubled souls, driven to the workhouses to make headwear they would never wear. From the 1600s straw boaters were Luton's number-one export. Over the next couple of hundred years, women and children used their bare hands to plait straw and were paid by the hat. The Plait Mistresses built a cottage industry in their hovels. Its spoils symbolised their town. Nowhere else did the police sport straw helmets, nor the football crowd boaters.

I walk on by Polish lads in baseball caps, up early to beaver away and send a few quid home. Towards The Mall a concrete labyrinth of stilted walkways leads to the Holiday Inn, a groaningly tired tower block stocked with guests who thought they had booked a hotel in London. In the 1990s my guidebook, *The Changing Face of Luton*, had confessed of its 'dismal' subject: 'It is easy to identify the town centre as a problem area, being one which encapsulates Luton's difficulties with its self-esteem as a whole' and gone on to list previous descriptions of the place: 'a dirty town' (1782), 'a poor town which evinced marks of decadency' (1828), a place where 'no lady dares walk the streets after dark' (1846), 'an urban smudge amid the green of Bedfordshire' (1989). The same work, though, encapsulates in a line the genetics and genius of the place when it offers that 'Luton was not an attractive town, but it was a place of opportunity, drawing in thousands of hopeful people.'

The Mall itself is awakening garishly. Shutters roll upwards and shop staff arrive and greet one another groggily. Not so long ago, The Mall was an Arndale Centre. If these places are the children of the swinging sixties then it says little of their parents. Only one of Britain's twenty-two former Arndales is outside England (Aberdeen), and eighteen are in the north. The Arndale scheme represented a vision of a New England, and is thus worthy of mention. It was a utopia built on shops, a consumerist Jerusalem rising from bulldozed streets. If you build it, they will come and buy stuff. As a concept, it worked – it is an idea of England that prevails; only now the Jerusalems are out of town and include household pet megastores. By the time us Children of Thatcher were looking for places to hang around, Arndales had mostly been renamed and lingered only as cultural references. And when I say 'cultural references', I mean 'mentions on Corrie'.

The bright blue frontage of a favourite bijou deli of mine – Greggs – beckons. Now that their range extends to sausage sandwiches, there is no reason, other than morbid obesity, not to purchase all three daily meals from their be-capped servers. As I lumber about The Mall eating microwaved meat from a brown paper bag, I am embarrassed to recall a Greggs encounter more southern than even this. I had become lost in old London town prior to Christmas, and not a little unsettled. When her azure façade came into view and my eyes met her pasties, I felt the kind of homecoming comfort that greets an Arctic explorer when he returns and hears someone moan about the weather. Oh faithful Greggs, there you were in London, just ready to hold me as I now hold you.

As I leave The Mall I hear two men enthusiastically debating the assassination of John F. Kennedy. The burghers of Luton, it seems, are not afraid to embrace the current affairs agenda. I emerge on to George Square, a hotchpotch of regeneration schemes. There are fountains in its centre, largely populated by rainwater, and a large pole that seems to bear two solar panels and some upturned bells. To the left, the faux-marble giant tree house of TK Maxx leads around to the firm and fair town hall. The far side is lined by a sliding scale of Victorian shops, which is brutally capped off by a forbidding multi-storey car park. Next, a couple of chain bars in 1990s rotting lemon colour fill one side, before giving way to the library and theatre. The library and theatre building also contains a blood donor centre, which, hearteningly, is packed with givers. Theatre posters advertise visits by Lutonian genius John Hegley, and 'Cinderella: The Second Coming – A Naughty Panto For Big Boys and Girls'. Intriguingly, a plaque on the side of the library erected by the African Caribbean Community Development Forum commemorates 'all slaves who suffered and died in Bedfordshire'. I leave George Square in search of legendary arson.

Luton's current town hall is a thing of beauty, though admittedly it stands next to some pretty ropey competition, a puma among pugs. It resembles a traditional junior office of government, one that deals in wars with minor African republics or regulating car washes. Doe-eyed windows surround an ornate and pillared portico, before two hidden tiers recline. These seem secretive. Perhaps this is where the Lutonian authorities prepare for chemical warfare with Dunstable. A banner hoisted by something called the Love Luton campaign hangs above the main door and heralds the town's bid for city status in 2012. Just when any normally pleasant art deco building might stop, there is a chunky but graceful clock tower. It looks like a monumental brick sculpture of an old-fashioned police box, standing vigilant and proud over Luton's main shopping street.

Adding to this scene of stony reverence, in the town hall's lap a magnificent war memorial steals the eye and speaks to the heart. Carved on to its plinth in an understatedly poignant font-size are the words: 'Greater love hath no man than this/that a man lay down his life for his friends'. Not his country, note, his friends. Many of those friends are listed around the statue. Names, names, names; people from Luton and England. This particular England, War Memorial England, is not necessarily as patriotic as it appears at first poppy-wreathed glance. It is about lost people, united. United with people from everywhere.

The friends who came home never forgot. They did not need a plaque to remind them of that greater love possessed. What England had put them through, and the deaths she had sent their friends to, shook them. So in Luton with fire they came and burnt the town hall down.

It happened on 19 July 1919, under a year since the people of England were left to their uneasy peace. After the war, Luton's veterans, Luton's *friends*, had formed into two organisations, the Discharged Soldiers and Seafarers Federation (DSSF) and the Comrades. Both resented how government had disregarded servicemen since the conflict ceased, and each disliked the other.

Saturday 19 July had been designated Peace Day. A march, led by the mayor on his Throne of Peace, stuttered through town, heckled at every turn by the ex-fighters and their other friends, those that were not there, and did not see, but cared. Festival floats rolled sadly on and bunting sagged in the rain. 'We Do Not Want Processions, We Want Work' read a banner strung across the road by the DSSF. When the mayor read a proclamation from the king, shrill jeers drowned him out. On he shuffled in his robes to the town hall and safety. The seventy-year-old doors of oak harrumphed closed behind him. He could breathe. He could curse the ungrateful people of Luton. How dare they not celebrate victory, how dare they boo England's king?

Then they came. The mob of democracy. At 3 p.m., kick-off time, they began to gather. First it was the ex-servicemen, then their many supporters. When the women and children joined in, the mayor knew they were not for turning. Loudly the crowd demanded he address them. Quietly he moused from a back door. The police in their straw helmets made by locals formed a line. The people crawled through it to make speeches. What surnames they had, Goodship, Good, Quince and all. Each spoke of the injustice done to them and to their friends. Piffling war pensions, no jobs, the wounded left for dead in dirty houses. Now, 10,000 were here to listen and roar.

The straw police collapsed and a sub-mob raided the town hall. They tore flock from the walls, lights from the ceilings and threw lampshades and chairs into the street. The police fought back and forced them out, but on went the speeches. Harry Miles, Bolshevist recipient of the Military Medal, offered to lead the revolution. A workers' Soviet in Luton for the people.

When the pubs opened, the numbers dropped off. When they closed, they grew again. Bricks, iron bars and bottles had been added to their armoury. On the hills around town, flares were lit to signal Round Two. George Heley, a seaman with HMS *Violent*, took on the police, hitting one on the jaw, one in the stomach and, when floored, one privately. Around the side of the town hall, they broke into its food store and burnt ration books and coupons. In charged the fire brigade.

The emergency services fought with the men from the services. Gentlemen, we have ourselves a riot. From the shattered windows of Herts Motors a man emerged with dribbling petrol cans. On to the town hall went the petrol. Up went the town hall. Looted perfume and potions were added to the blaze. Just after midnight, the town hall clock's face melted away and fell into the street. With the building beyond saving, stalemate prevailed between rioters and protectors. Still, on they looted, this time S. Farmer and Co. Music. Gramophones were liberated, grand pianos pushed into the street. A pianist appeared and within minutes hundreds were singing 'Keep the Home Fires Burning' and dancing the night away to show-tunes, their backdrop an inflamed orange sky. At 3 a.m., the troops came – their friends. They would not fight their friends and so ended England's first peace riots.

Of the twenty-eight men and women sent for trial at Bedford Assizes, most had a military background. Where they did not, they had a friend or family connection, or just wore a soldier's tunic and cap for the fun of it (mad Maud Kitchener, a machinist, who got six months in prison for 'inciting riot with obscene language'). There did not seem to be too much regret. The following summer, on their holiday travels Lutonians sang, 'We're a jolly lot of fellows yes we are/For we come from Luton Town/ Where they burnt the town hall down ...'

The town hall incident is important. It reminds us, a few months after shattered glass on the streets of London, that burning and a-lootin' is not new, that the 2011 summer riots, though far different in participant motivation, were not the rotten fruit of a New England, but an uncomfortable tradition. It is also important because it represents the distortion of an England we thought we knew. War Memorial England was a reverent place that quietly and mawkishly mourned the passing of a generation. It was patriotic and occasionally proud of victory. But we, Thatcher's children and our parents, created that England. Real war memorial England is often none of that. It is angry, its memorial the burnt down town hall. It is angry at war and waste and people with money sending those without to die. It is rebellious. Luton's act, disregarding the appalling damage caused, spoke for a nation united in unrest. Luton's War Memorial England, I find far easier to relate to.

I turn around from the modern town hall, built on ashen soil in 1936, to peer down George Street. A tracksuited man in his thirties jogs backwards, facing a motley crew of twenty-or-so kids in bright bibs. They strain to keep up, each with a smile of helpless and breathless humour. Rarely has such ecstasy been witnessed in this section of Luton's main pedestrianised zone. They have the

right idea for it is mercilessly cold today, the kind of cold this
northerner presumed impossible in the beautiful south. I clamber
up and down the modestly inclined side streets that filter from the
main drag and give a flavour of Luton's current DNA. On the first
the Lebanon Grill is neighboured by Polska Chata. Up from that
pair are The Flame gay bar and the subtlety titled Cheap Adult
DVDs (does that mean the adults are cheap or the products?). The
parallel street hosts Bangladesh's Sonali Bank, advertising in its
window today's taka rate, and has a Caribbean food caravan at
its foot. Marvellously, alongside curried goat and jerk chicken
this claims to sell 'Raps'. Back on George Street, the stylish
premises of Polskie Delikatesy Smaczek are busy doling out
evocatively scented bread and exotic sausages to a mixed crowd
of Poles and native foodies. Onwards from there a remnant sign
describes an event last September: 'Taste of Luton Food Festival –
Celebrating the Food and Culture of Luton'. In Middlesbrough,
Sheffield and now here, food offers a passport to integration and
understanding. We should not be surprised. When the Portuguese-
Jewish helped to establish London's fish and chip trade, it aided
their assimilation no end and bred tolerance from others. England:
where tikka masala heals racism.

Among the foul and shabby concrete of Old Bedford Road
everyone seems to walk alone. There are no couples or gangs of
teenage friends, though it *is* shortly after 9 a.m. on a Saturday
morning. The River Lea, the lifeblood Luton was founded on and
then built over, is clogged and shallow. Litter blocks cause it to
eddy in places, which I suppose livens proceedings a little. I turn a
corner. The houses smarten up, streets widen and a sloped green
common offers breathing space and pensionable trees. In Luton's
salad days this route – from the town centre to Wardown Park –
was known as 'The Monkey Parade'. Young pups would throw

on their handbags and gladrags and walk up and down eyeing up suitors. Marriages were made here, Luton's own version of Coles Corner. I enter Wardown Park by an anonymous gate. What a place. A garden of Eden, of England.

We do parks so well in this country. Their very Victorian reason for existing, to provide leisure places for rich and poor, seems still to exist. Of course, the rich now would more likely prefer a weekend in their Cotswold retreat, but the point of a democratic open space remains. Albert Park in Middlesbrough is hemmed on two sides by housing estates that time forgot, but is undeniably beautiful and can lift any spirit. Wardown Park in Luton, though surrounded largely by mock Tudor houses, is the same. Recently spruced up, it doesn't half look grand for its age. Ducks waddle and float contentedly on its boating lake, oblivious to the toddler attempting to hit them with a stick. Cyclists, joggers and dog-walkers crisscross one another with hearty 'Mornings!' bellowed. We are surrounded and walled by naked trees and we could be part of anywhere's winter. One of them has a notice pinned to it. 'Budgie found in Wardown Park, Sunday 22nd', it says, with a number to call.

I pass the frilly Daisy Chain Wall, a hundred years old and stretching out luxuriously, and enter Luton's town museum. It is hosted in an old stately home and creaks with experience accordingly. Portrait-lined walls lead to snug exhibit rooms. The atmosphere is still, calm and utterly comforting. There are no blaring noises and the only interactive experiences come from the happy nods and glances of other visitors. One of them, a young mum, remarks to a curator: 'Wow, I've not been here for years.' The curator replies that 'Oh, it's changed a lot' though I don't really believe her. One room is crowded with artefacts of the Bedfordshire and Hertfordshire Regiment, an Aladdin's Cave if

Aladdin were slightly too obsessed with military regalia. I learn two things that I like: that in the Second World War Luton formed 'Pig Clubs' which gathered metal under the slogan 'saucepans into spitfires'; and that during a 1917 munitions strike union meetings were held at Kenilworth Road, my footballing destination this afternoon.

Upstairs in the Luton Life section, locals Robert Wilkinson, Philip Harman, Bob Ireland, Larry McGrattan and Verna Ible respectively talk about the 1920s, the Arndale Centre, Scottish immigrants fighting Lutonians, and arriving from Ireland and St Kitts. It is a shame their memories are only recorded, as I would love to have met them. 'I know lots of people say horrible things about Luton,' says Verna, 'but I always defend it.' Putul Islam adds: 'When you talk about Luton you are talking about English, Bangladeshi, Pakistani, Irish, Scottish – everybody. We feel this is our home. Lutonians are multi-coloured, multicultural.'

Beyond the voices of Luton are the hats, floating like camp body-less legions. Relief comes from The Plough, a replica of a dark oak Victorian bar torn down, inevitably, for the Arndale, and a fine display on the town hall riots. One of the cases includes singed and salvaged legal documents, now the shape and colour of cartoon toast, a policeman's straw helmet and the XII from the fallen town hall clock. I still get a shudder when I get as close to history as this. If anything, that feeling only increases with time. These cremated items make English history, or the aspects that appeal to me (rebellion, setting fire to things, funny hats), easier to grasp and relate to. Continuity equals identity. It's not unlike supporting a football team. Surely we should all have our own period or theme as we do a team. Perhaps yours is represented by the two framed photographs of Miss Electrolux factory 1976 and

1985 on the wall opposite the riots display? Look how pleased you are, Lorraine Sibley 1976, with your bonny smile and sash. See how the men on the production line gawp at you, Helen Drewell 1985, with your perm and trophy. Alas, a lass, those days are gone. As a museum placard near you says, 'Luton business is now more office-based'.

I leave Lorraine and Helen because I have spotted something all museums should have – cases containing football memorabilia. As far as The Hatters of Kenilworth Road are concerned, it's all there: photos of the jubilant League Cup winning side of 1988; a 1959 FA Cup final programme; a piece of Astroturf ('Many famous players will have walked upon it').

The Hatters are not a young club, though their history tends to be obscured behind Eric Morecambe, those pieces of Astroturf, David Pleat skipping in a Del Monte suit and hateful ID Cards. They are of a finer vintage than that. Luton Town were formed in 1885 and made their own bit of history a decade on when striker Frank Whitby became the first player in southern England to be paid. For decades they bobbled around, providing recreation for the hat and motor vehicle labourers of the town. In days of sepia and obligatory moustaches their supporters were a sight to behold – looking at old crowd pictures, it is difficult to spot a single fan not sporting a straw boater. They were still wearing their boaters when miraculous Joe Payne sprang back to life.

Payne was transported to Bedfordshire from Derbyshire coalfields in the early 1930s. On Good Friday 1936 he was left for dead. Disregarded, forgotten and fighting for a place in the reserve team, Payne had only recently returned from enforced loan exile with Biggleswade Town. Not once had the mining man dug his way into the Hatters first team. England froze that Easter, the coldest for thirty years. By Easter Sunday it was clear that the aching limbs of Luton's goal-getters were not to be healed in time for the following day's match with Bristol Rovers. 'Who shall save us from the evil of an underwhelming performance?' asked the directors. From the dark emerged Joseph Payne. 'He's been playing centre-half for the reserves all season, but maybe he could save us, maybe he could score?' And so it was that on Easter Monday the resurrection of Joe Payne occurred.

Payne scores his first after twenty-three minutes and goes into half-time with a hat-trick. His fourth comes on forty-nine, his fifth – a controlling nod with the forehead, a smash into the roof of the net – on fifty-five. Two minutes later the double hat-trick is his and soon after the seventh and eighth. Twelve days earlier, Bobby Bell of Tranmere has scored nine. Nine? Pah, says Joe as he rattles another in. Four minutes to go. Can Joe do it? *Can he become a record breaker?* Pah, says Joe again, from his position on the muddy floor of the penalty area. He turns on his backside and diverts the heavy ball home. Joe Payne 10 v. Bristol Rovers 0. The resurrection is complete. Payne is re-born. 'There was football drama in excelsis at Luton yesterday,' says Tuesday's *News Chronicle*, 'What a debut! It was a debut unprecedented in the long history of soccer.' The next season he scores fifty-five times in thirty-nine games as Luton win Division Three. Soon, England sniff and Chelsea pounce. Illness, injury and war hold Joe back and his career dies aged thirty-three. No one ever beats his perfect ten.

The Hatters' maddest period began in the Brylcreamed surroundings of 1950s English football. In 1955 they launched themselves into a brave new world of Division One football and board promises of a stadium fit for 35,000 Lutonians. 'We will get a lot of the support which goes to London at the moment,' promised the chairman. Town finished tenth in their first year, their attacking football winning luscious praise. They were fighters, too. Before a match at Birmingham, their coach crashed and span off the road. By 5 o'clock, the shaken players had won a point.

For a couple of years Luton built patiently and bedded down with the Establishment. In 1957-58, it was they who finished directly above stricken Manchester United in the season of the Munich Air Crash. That year the Hatters were the bane of golden Wolverhampton Wanderers, beating and drawing with the champions. It all became too heady for the Bedfordshire boys. They had tasted champagne and wanted more. More, more, more. The board broke free of frugality and threw the cash around. Down Division One they fell, the price of compromised principles. Belief in youth faded, belief in high wages shone. Oh for another Joe Payne, another resurrection. The moneyed boys were only good for one thing, the FA Cup, that glamour puss of a pursuit. In 1959, Luton reached their only ever final.

In the run up to the match, Luton – town and club – did not believe it could lose. Town had hammered opponents Nottingham Forest 5-1 a few Saturdays earlier. Local businesses contacted Kenilworth Road to book the FA Cup trophy for their post-final window displays. But, as the big day approached, Hatters in posh hats did not see fit to send their players to a hotel, far from the maddening crowds. As the clock struck midnight the night before the game, full-back Ken Hawkes was answering his front door to Lutonians desperately seeking tickets. The Hatters in bowler hats who selected the team did their bit to beckon defeat, dropping Gordon Turner, the hotshot hero of the fans, the reincarnation of Jesus Joe Payne. Even the FA helped Luton lose the game before 3 p.m. came, objecting to acting manager Tommy Hodgson's outsize straw boater. On the pitch, the mental and physical tiredness of the players was married to complacency and they lost

2-1. Forest triumphed with ten men after goalscorer Roy Dwight was stretchered off in the first-half much to the horror of his nephew Reg, later Elton of Watford. Luton were scathed and scarred by what happened at Wembley. The next season they were relegated, and within six years had sunk to Division Four. FA Cup hangover pains had turned out to be liver disease.

By the time my 1981 mooring came around another resurrection was underway, its unlikely creator a pinch-toned man from, of all places, Nottingham. David Pleat's Luton strolled to the Division Two title in 1981-82. The manager's grasp of basic arithmetic helped. Before the pack had found their calculators Pleat had grown an attacking squad capable of exploiting the new three points for a win system. Draws had been robbed of their value. Win, win, win, loadsamoney, win, win, win, was in. The club, headed by a Thatcher-mad director then chairman (and take that any way you wish) – David Evans MP – embraced the cut-others'-throats philosophy. The following term in Division One, Pleat refused to defend. When his side won at Maine Road to preserve themselves and relegate Manchester City (survival of the fittest, Mrs Thatcher, survival of the fittest), much of football rejoiced.

Turning from the case of Kenilworth jewels I descend shrieking stairs to the museum shop. Tending to its neatly stacked shelves and obligingly wiping dust from the book I buy are two museum workers. One is a middle-aged woman touring a marvellously Cockney accent, the other a stylish man in his mid-twenties who should really be the shy guitarist in an Emo band. Both are bashfully friendly and charmingly proud of their workplace. When they hear I am from elsewhere they scramble for an old photocopied history of the museum, which I later notice contains notes added in biro. An expensive interactive guide available for iPad download this is not, and all the better for it. We move quickly through the issues affecting Luton: whether the Hatters goalkeeper should be dropped, the rebranding of the Arndale, the English Defence League. 'Immigration and racism are only a problem when the EDL decide to march,' says Emo guitarist. 'We have our ups and downs like anywhere, but generally it works.'

Ah, the English Defence League. I wondered when they might crop up. This, after all, is where they first protested, where they first donned their Stone Island cagoules, where they first caused fear and loathing. They started as the United Peoples of Luton, and their particular brand of incendiary street hate was moulded by a local tanning salon entrepreneur, Tommy Robinson. Robinson gathered a ragtag platoon of refugees from far-right parties and football banning orders, often both. Their work began when another reasonable, measured local group, affiliated to Al-Muhajiroun, took to burning flags in streets and celebrating the deaths of British soldiers. Both groups seem to be part of a New England that depresses me: angry, Intolerant England. The England in my mind always had its moaners and its reactionaries, but never were things so venomous, so full of hate. Where I imagined anger it was a uniting, solidifying factor – the miners' strike, the anti-war movement or, even, here in Luton the Peace Day Riots. Never was it so divisive. Always it was about people from everywhere. Perhaps I am too simplistic about all this; perhaps my intolerance of intolerance ignores genuine concerns, often working-class ones. Perhaps in this case distance is not the place to write or judge from. Fuck it, though.

When I read that the Lutonian trend of wilful disharmony and manic street preaching is historic, I do not know whether to take comfort that perhaps these times of ours are not as grimly novel as they seem, or be depressed that nothing changes. Toxic voices scarred Luton life way before Robinson found his megaphone or

minority barkers of a distorted Islam emerged. In the late nineteenth
century it was the Reverend James O'Neil's turn. O'Neil used a
gang of loyal disciples to ensure mob rule in a career of fractious
meetings, and was once charged with assaulting his churchwarden.
He presided over a town that had long uneasily tried in the name
of harmony to restrain the most extreme of its people from
everywhere, those that turned free speech into a bad thing. A
worker at the Chase Street Mission spoke of the prevailing
rambunctiousness, commenting 'the work was hard and very
rough ... those who attended having the freest idea as to their
liberty of speech and conduct.' It is possible to see friction as part
of Luton's historical DNA, then, but it is also possible to see it as
part of present England's uneasy truces and states of anger. Most
of all, then and now, it demonstrates that those who shout loudest
get heard, no matter that they represent only the few. That is an
England worth trying to change.

In a cafe not far from the park and its museum I sit and talk
with three old ladies. Each woman is speckled with gentle facial
hair. They share a pot of tea and tell me about the way things used
to be. This soon becomes a triumvirate rant against anyone who
does not look like them. It is as if their earpieces are not helping
them hear, but allowing Alf Garnett to feed them a script. 'Oh it's
changed. Yes, for the worse. Much worse. There were no, you
know, *black faces* in them days. I've nuffink against them, but
they're, you know, *different*.' So is it the few shouting loudest, or
is this the majority view? It probably comes close to the mutterings
of the many, but not for a second do I think these are vitriolic
views. If only people actually mixed here those views would
disappear, so they cannot be that entrenched. These are fears of
difference and a refusal to reap the rewards of being a mongrel
town – when I ask, these women have sampled nary a speck of

rice from Luton's incredible menu. Theirs are views that have long been aired in Immigration England. Indeed, two of the women I speak to have Irish surnames and one Scottish; Lutonians probably spoke of their relatives in similarly hostile terms. 'Anyhow,' one of them finishes as she shuffles between tables towards the door, 'it's not as bad as Coventry.'

As we crawl towards the far end of town my taxi driver asks me why I am here. I have barely finished explaining before he offers his view. 'It's generally fine here. The likes of the EDL don't speak for the town. Or the mad Mosques. They're a tiny minority of … well, I won't swear as I'm at work.' After he has taken me for the kind of fare that makes a Yorkshireman who lives in Scotland come out in a rash, his parting words are, 'I've lived here all my life, and most of us get on.' He has dropped me at a local community centre. Inside the locals are partaking in 'participatory democracy', voting on which projects should receive council funding. It is either an inspired way of guaranteeing community ownership or a sly method of passing decisions over funding cuts to those that will suffer from them. Either way, it is tremendously good, noisy fun. Young boxing boys bob and weave between the pensioners of the Evergreens group, their white hair providing a cloudy skyline. A pair of teenage girls requiring £500 for their hospital music project canvas for votes, and a children's martial arts group show a little old man karate chops. It is a vision of what Luton could be. The boxing club impresses me most. Through his Polish translator their Ukrainian coach points me to the man in charge, a Luton Asian with a robust south-east accent. As a chubby Irn Bru-topped boy of eight or nine jabs with dangerous proximity to his crotch area, he tells me how the lads that attend his club come from every background possible. 'If they can punch and behave, we don't care what they are.'

A cheery chap called Malcolm comes over. As a native of South Shields he is as exotic as anyone here. He came to Luton forty years ago to labour on building sites and never returned. Now, he runs several community groups. After a good chat about how appalling fish and chips in Bedfordshire are ('curry mind, is another matter') Malcolm invites me to a Crimestoppers meeting the following Tuesday night. When it suddenly occurs to me that he thinks I am a *Secret Millionaire* I head for the exit, stopping to sign a Luton in Harmony pledge on my way out.

After the tatty gardens and fried chicken depots of Dunstable Road it is a relief to arrive at Luton Central Mosque. Its dainty minaret pokes out above houses to my left, just as the floodlights of Kenilworth Road do to my right. Temples, temples, everywhere. The mosque is situated in a leafy street of withdrawn houses. Its sudden scale hits me in the face as if my rowing boat has crashed into a hidden cruise liner. Men wearing startlingly bright white scarper into the building, late for prayers. One gives me a smile and the universal eye-roll of a man being late for something. There are probably people in Luton who fear this building, both its insides and its imposing frame. Indeed, when it was built enterprising racists hung a pig's head from its crescent moon (no perpetrator was ever caught). I think it is spectacular. I think it brings life and drama to a timid street in a town short on architectural ambition. But as I am essentially hanging around in a mosque car park staring at people, I move on to the main drag of Bury Park.

Bury Park is an England I have never seen before. It does not look like the north, east or west. It does not even look like the south. It is fervidly different and, well, *foreign*. Shops battle and their hawkers howl to see who can sell the very brightest products, from fabrics to fruits that look to me like GM experiments. Jalabi mountains that Willy Wonka would find excessive cover entire windows and street grills add a delicious smell-track. I peer in at the Luton Halal Meat Centre. Eight women stand with their backs to the windows, their heads covered in a variety of shawl designs and colours. Each emerges laden with a blue plastic carrier bag full of fresh meat. Not a single shop unit lies unoccupied, an impossible phenomenon in most towns. England bemoans the demise of her high streets, but here they thrive. Here Tesco Metros are unheard of. It is just a shame that the same English who reminisce about butchers, bakers and candlestick makers are not here. The only other white faces I see are those of bargain- and stomach-hungry Poles. Shopping is a social occasion about talking on corners. Unexpected items in the bagging area do not give you that. Perhaps the people 'from here' are just jealous.

As a naive idealist I am stunned by the extent of wilful segregation in Luton. I think back to Sheffield. On Saturday there I saw multicoloured couples and nights out, on Sunday a posse of faiths being pursued individually, but in harmony: Catholic, Muslim, anti-capitalist. I remember a man in his twenties on the way to chapel opposite the Ruskin Gallery. A sari-wearing toddler ran into his path and fell. With a smile that suggested his day had just been made, he picked her up and returned her to her parents. Laughs were shared. All that seems to be shared here is suspicion, some of it mutual, most of it enmeshing people from trying anything different.

Just off Bury Park a wooden board advertises Beech Hill Conservative Club. As I walk in I am rebuked: 'Woah, woah, woah, come back here.' Suspecting that they have scented a lefty I crawl back to the door expecting to be slung from it. 'That's 50p, sir,' says the doorman. My coin hits his empty mini-safe with a clang, causing the four or five Lutonian Conservatives present to look over. Even the Queen's portrait seems to scowl at me, while David Cameron looks on incredulously in a large framed photograph above the bar. This England lives cheek by jowly jowl with Immigration England. We are but a row of houses from halal meat and Urdu bookstores, many of them staffed and frequented by sons and daughters of Her Majesty's Commonwealth and His Cameronsty's free market. I pass through a darkly beautiful snooker room, its giant oak tables charismatic and steady. In the back lounge, Hatters fans in orange, black and white talk about the Conference play-offs between sips of wildly cheap and decent beer. Perhaps this Conservatism thing isn't so bad. In one corner, lads and dads play pool. In another, lads and dads stare silently at a Liverpool v. Manchester United FA Cup game disfigured by player racism. The lads and dads are in their fortnightly process, phoning in the rituals without any effort, comforted by routine. It is their identity, just as those over the wall in Bury Park have theirs. Rarely do the two mix, despite the fact that they have much in common. I am startled when a man of Asian appearance in a spark-bright Luton top walks in and engages in Party chat. This is my prejudice; tell me yours. We are all guilty.

I sidle through Bury Park and a boisterous mosque charity appeal to the street that takes me to Kenilworth Road. Out of one world and into another. The ground sits at a right angle to back-to-back lanes of terraces so that one of its stands appears at the end of each. A grotty alleyway is all that stands between. As I file along it I notice flyers on lampposts that read: 'You Are Entering a Sharia Controlled Zone. Islamic Rules Enforced'. They contain red circular No Smoking-style graphics promising 'No Alcohol',

'No Gambling', 'No Music or Concerts', 'No Porn or Prostitution' and 'No Drugs or Smoking'. To escape the complexities of these posters (Who? When? Why?) I remind myself of a joke from my schooldays: 'I don't swear, I don't drink, I don't smoke. Oh bollocks, I've left my fags in the pub.'

This tunnel of doom leads to Kenilworth Road's main entrance. It is a Portakabin village that defies its scales of grey to flow with matchday buzz. No matter the surroundings, this atmosphere seems to doughtily survive outside football grounds. It is the equivalent of cockroaches after a nuclear attack. Behind glass screens in the ticket office, sharp women offer giggly service, clearly enjoying their work. With an outsize ticket ensconced uncomfortably in my wallet, I walk around the ground to the Bobbers' Club supporters' bar. Its door is next to the away-end turnstile and opens to a wee heaven under the stand. A formidable Yorkshirewoman takes my entrance fee (50p again) and directs me in. Beneath the sloped contours of the terrace above fans pack in, pausing occasionally to tell each other stories about the photos on the walls. I perch next to three old boys, hoping to hear yarns of yore. Alas, they are talking at length about double-glazing companies, which fits entirely with my lazy prejudice about the house-proud south-east. I think of a wartime Cockney evacuee to Luton quoted in a history of the town: 'Heaven preserve me from ever becoming like Lutonians ... All they think about is their homes. House-proud, that's their trouble.'

Behind us, an excitable man-child is parading up and down shouting the names of Luton's centre-halves over and over like a weird train. With his poetry recital shortly to move on to full-backs, I exit. 'We're here for Pat Butcher's funeral,' shouts an Alfreton lad on his way in.

Eric Morecambe, whose lounge I now pass, would have approved of these surreal offerings. Perhaps it was he, while a member of the board here, that designed the main stand. After heaving my way beyond the turnstile I become lost in a warren of steps, corridors, bunkers and walls until somehow I am back in the open air. The architectural plans must resemble an Escher drawing of a scrapheap. I eventually find my wooden seat, again among teenage fans. For the third match in a row I feel like a particularly uncool Fonzy, destined to hang around with high-school kids.

Happily I seem to be in the 'loud' end of the ground, though these things are always relative (happiness and volume, that is). Those around me seem fixated with Watford, which I suppose is novel. They scream songs of steaming in and Boxing Day scraps. I am definitely in my thirties now, because some ditties offend me. 'He's gonna die,' they sing to the tune of *The Red Flag*, 'He's gonna die/Elton John is gonna die/Twenty years of HIV/Elton John is history'.

Discarding the feeble rhyming scheme, I think again about Poisonous England. Football is part of the disease and its infection has spread in the span of my lifetime. Toxicity has been fanned by the rise of the internet messageboard. There was always rivalry and there was always scrapping, but rank hatred? I am not so sure. Though inexcusable, casual violence all of a sudden seems aptly named. David Pleat once recalled that many of the good luck letters he received ahead of Luton's Maine Road judgement day came from Watford fans. Inside thirty years, that has become unthinkable. I have yet to see a dark face in this Luton crowd. I was ready to argue that football could be the very thing to bring Luton together, but how can anyone feel welcome in a venue that wishes death on pop stars?

All around us at Kenilworth Road is the neon branding of Stelios's orange and white army. The stands are festooned with Easyjet destinations, which must act like word prompts to a bored supporter's wandering mind. Behind a goal Alfreton's hardcore stand with their backsides rested on seatbacks, the Bobbers' Club below them. Many appear fixated with the stand to their left and opposite us. This entire side of Kenilworth Road is a tunnelled double-glazing showroom stretching the length of the pitch. Behind its conservatory doors and windows televisions can be seen blaring *Soccer Saturday* to corporate attendees who would rather watch others watching football than watch it themselves. It is raised slightly, to accommodate three rows of half-empty seating at its front. Behind it run the streets of Bury Park, with the minaret of Luton Mosque viewable beyond a floodlight.

In mosque-white shirts and red bottom halves, Alfreton defy divisional mathematics to emerge from the traps faster, stronger. Their right-winger G-clamps the touchline, stretching Luton wrack-like. He slides his tiny frame between opponents, an Oliver Twist squeezing sprucely through the crowds after a pocket picked. At the back, a centre-half who once scored an own goal from thirty-five yards gallops around calmly snuffing out home advances, his stride as pronounced as a cheetah on stilts. There is a defiance about Alfreton's early play, a prickly undercurrent perhaps best explained by the fact that while they have eighty-nine supporters present, 5,569 baying Lutonians are here. Unfortunately, unexpected away-team dominance makes for giddy mistakes. The right-winger's dribbles start to trundle out for throw-ins and the goalkeeper brazenly hoicks a series of back-passes straight to his Hatters counterpart. Each time he runs up to take a goal kick he is confronted with a sort of 'wwwwwooooooooohhhhhh' noise. This turns to a 'You'rrrrrre shiiiiiiittttt' when he makes contact with the ball. This, I think, I have never witnessed outside lower division football, and I spend a good few minutes contemplating the cut-off point (the top half of League One, I decide).

Luton harass their foes into a glut of corner kicks. Repeatedly, their own No. 11 curves crosses in artfully, prompting the Alfreton keeper to nervously hot potato the ball. 'Non-league,' sing the fans around me, 'You'll always be non-league.' They are not, you will have gathered, the most forward-thinking, positive of supporter groups. In fact, it takes them half an hour to muster a chant championing their team rather than upbraiding another. Where I sit the crowd is almost entirely made up of males. 'Lino you're a cunt, lino you're a cunt' sings a man to my right until said lino helps in the award of a dubious penalty. When the referee points downwards to the glory spot, the people around me are divided. Some celebrate as if a goal has been scored. Others shake their heads, as they already know their team will miss. They don't miss – 1-0.

With the ball still rippling the net my teenage associates flee towards the neon snack bars of jumbo hotdogs and stone cold chocolate. At half-time I chance upon the Nick Owen Lounge. Somehow, I had forgotten Owen's chairmanship of this, his beloved club. His lounge is, appropriately, not unlike an old breakfast TV set. It takes the form of one room in an oddly triangular shape, with a bar at its centre. Owen's set designers have opted for Dulux's Nineties Dentist Reception range. I ingest a Guinness while a man with a ponytail shouts 'You're shit and you know you are' at a bar-girl. A fuzzy screen brings us images of Luton arriving back on the pitch, and the match recommencing. Very few people move. Conversation surrounding me remains unencumbered by the match everyone is nominally here to see. Topics include holidays ('Bloke in the next room was a Scot, so obviously I got on with him.'), Tesco alcohol offers and future away-day arrangements. A hat-trick of matches and I am still to hear anyone present talking about the football.

I leave them to it and decide to sit in a different part of the stand for what remains of the second half. Things feel happier here, with the women and children around me very unlikely to sing anything about Aids. Our seats are backless and there is nothing between us and the sky. I sense the contentedness that being outside and wrapped up on a cold winter's evening brings. In front of me, a dad rests a son on each leg. We could be at a bonfire or a fair. 'FACKING WAKE-UP CALL, LUTON' shouts the dad when Alfreton nearly score.

After its early promise of craft and guile the game is now about graft and bile. Heavy-footed players labour about and tackle spitefully. The main noise is that of 50-50 ball thwacks, the abiding image of players' visible, choking breath. This is ugly football under the orangey glow of Kenilworth Park. A few rows back a man rants: 'He's got his hands all facking over him, the cu–... Hello, John speaking. Oh hello there, sweetheart.' His ringing phone has curbed a swearword and shown Non-Football Him, a him concerned about picking something up for tea on the way home. When the call ends and Football Him reawakens, a vocal campaign against an Alfreton player's hair is the upshot. 'Who cut yer 'air? Stevie Wonder?' After he reads that the player's surname is Jarman I am delighted by his intensely parochial response. 'Jarman? Fancy getting named after a leisure complex in Hemel Hempstead, you ponce!' A gloved finger taps twice on one of my giggling shoulders. It is a lady in a fluorescent coat. 'Excuse me sir. Me and the other stewards, we've seen you writing on your pad. Are you press?'

'Er ... no.'

'Well if you want to write you need a press pass.'

'I need a press pass to write notes on a pad?'

'Yes. What are you writing? And are you writing to be printed?'

'Eh?'

'What are you writing about? We need to know.'

I could carry on typing out this dialogue. I could tell you how I refused to tell the steward what I was 'up to', about how she informed me that they needed to know as 'people can be nasty about Luton. People write bad things.' However, I'm getting aerated just thinking about it. Is this another England – Paranoid England in the town where 7/7 began? Or is it an inappropriately officious woman? Or is it just funny? I expect to turn around and see a bunch of stewards laughing out the words 'Haaaaa, got you mate!' Instead, I turn and see a bunch of stewards staring determinedly back at me. Oh the damage I could wield with my 99p pad and chewed biro (lidless). They have basically foiled a terrorist plot. They are heroes.

Only the wonderful words of Luton fans can rouse me from my stupor. 'We're not a once great club like we once were,' I hear one say. His friend goes on to construct the following sentence, a masterclass in inclusivity: 'I wanna go up as much as the next person. You. This man in front. Him. This lady down here. Her behind us. Her there. Him with the trousers.' The match finishes and half the ground jeers their team off. They have won 1-0 and are fourth in the league.

Back in town a genial Eastern European girl directs me to the station. I find it exciting that Luton is full of people from everywhere, and always has been. I think it gives the town a heartbeat. If you accept change and renewal as the lifeblood of a place, Luton is in good health. So much is about perception: if you like difference then this is the place for you. If you don't then at one end of the scale you moan in a cafe, but get on with things and at the other you join a violently divisive group in some shape or form. Somehow it all, in the main, holds together. I think England should be about more than holding together. It should be about mixing together. This is never easy: who is capable of approaching a group of blokes in Bury Park and saying: 'Excuse me. I'm white; you're Asian. Let's integrate'? Instead it is done in subtle ways, in food, in football, in young people boxing together. In his charming account of growing up a Luton Asian, *Greetings From Bury Park*, Sarfraz Manzoor attests to the power of football as a uniting force. Manzoor remembers how, following England's victory over Argentina at World Cup 2002, he and two other Asian friends piled into a bar to celebrate:

> When 'Three Lions' began playing on the jukebox, the entire bar, packed with whites, blacks and Asians, sang along. I sang too, with as much passion as I could muster. The louder I sang the more confident I felt in wearing the flag of St George; it felt like it was my flag too. The search for an identity I could feel comfortable with had, I believed, reached its destination.

This imperfect game of ours will not change the world, but it does have some answers.

Chapter Four

Ipswich

Middlesbrough, Sheffield, Luton. All complex, all noisy. The former's sad and deafeningly silent spaces plagued me, the latter's disharmony induced upset and anger. Sheffield stooped and thrilled, but even subtle hedonism is unsustainable when you're a miserable sod. I needed peace, most of all from my thoughts. So many versions of England speeding through my head and shouting for attention. It was time to find Quiet England. Suffolk called.

In my head, Ipswich whispered along softly. On Saturdays it was populated by country squires and farm labourers, all up in the big town to return library books and buy stationery. Errands were run in my mind's Ipswich, its spacious streets pounded by friendly, ruddy faces. If you are going to imagine a place, you might as well ramp up the stereotyping.

This imagining extended to, or was perhaps caused by, Ipswich Town Football Club. They had always been gentle, nice, dispassionate. For the neutral they were a club who neither whipped-up fervour nor raised hateful hackles: the tinned tomato soup of football. Town hushed their way through, occasionally flickering but mostly toiling. Always they were there, a sturdy rung of England's ladder.

I had a vague notion, too, that Ipswich was a 'family club'. This had nothing to do with foam hands and face paints, and everything to do with who, in their past, had governed them. Ipswich's origins have a familial, cosy feel. They were established by patrician aristocrats as another resource to enrich the town.

Into the big town from the country came the Cobbold family with errands to run; football clubs to found. A brewing dynasty, a land-owning machine, good Suffolk stock quietly improving the locale – that was the Cobbolds. For over a century, their Etonian Lords, Ladies, Knights, Right Honourables and dishonourables ran the show. In the 1870s, Thomas Clement Cobbold started the Ipswich Association Football Club. In the 1980s, the Cobbolds were still there. What fun they had, in from the country to run the Town. 'You ask what constitutes a crisis here,' said chairman Patrick Cobbold in 1982, 'Well, if we run out of wine in the boardroom.'

Cobboldian eccentricities seeped through to their club, many with an agrarian tint. In the 1920s, they employed a groundsman who kept chickens, goats and sheep in a Portman Road stand. One match was abandoned due to a pitch-invading plague of rats. This was no knockabout Wurzel Gummidge FC, though: Town were a finely supported force of the amateur game. In 1936 chairman Captain Ivan Cobbold led them to belated professionalism, aristocratic sensibilities of fair play and no wages giving way decades after they did in Middlesbrough, Sheffield and Luton. Their first game in the Third Division (South) saw them take on Tunbridge Wells FC. Their last saw them crowned champions.

Captain Cobbold closed his club down during the Second World War. Respect for conflict returned no reverence for life: in 1944, he was killed when a bomb struck the chapel in which he prayed. His seventeen-year-old son John became the man of their houses, and then Town chairman when only twenty-nine years old.

John Cobbold, the man who put the 'port' in 'sport', is the Cobbold most remembered and revered. Hilarious, charismatic and secretly, allegedly gay (imagine Suffolk whispering), for a long time 'Mr John' was the boozy oxygen of Ipswich Town FC.

His organism, the club, breathed in everything Mr John ('Sir' was too stuffy, he felt, 'Mr Cobbold' too deferent) had to offer. The mindset was straightforward ('One's object in life should be to make people happy and have a good laugh'), the philosophy sharply egalitarian: 'The most important thing for a director is to have a really good rapport with every single member of staff at the club, from the manager all the way down to the person who sweeps out the gutters.' Presiding *über alles* was the grand matriarch, John's mother, Lady Blanche, daughter to the Duke of Devonshire. His brother Patrick was always there, always pouring the drinks and plotting the way. This context made Ipswich into a family as tightly effective as a mafiosi version of the Waltons.

Perhaps Mr John's Ipswich family success came from classic and clichéd English notions of fair play and upper class paternalism. His stewardship went beyond sport. More likely though, I think, it came down to this fact: he didn't actually like football. 'I will confess I am not particularly keen on the game,' he wrote in his autobiography, 'Indeed, I remember saying that I would not cross the road to watch a football match – unless, of course, Ipswich Town were playing.' As such, Mr John was removed from impassioned engagement and all the reactionary decisions it can provoke. Not once did Cobbold presume to know better and interfere with signings, selection or tactics, and Ipswich did not sack a manager until 1987. Indeed, on the one occasion Mr John was given a scouting brief, he availed himself of copious boardroom whisky and filed a full report on an absent player.

Somehow, wilful indifference bred an uncanny knack for spotting great managers. Once he had blooded them, Cobbold nurtured close relationships with his coaches, half a father, half a brother, fully avuncular. In 1957 the youngest chairman in football appointed the newly retired player Alfred Ramsey as his manager. Ramsey quickly won Division Three. At a celebratory party, Sir John found him under a table singing 'Maybe It's Because I'm a Londoner'. After three years' patience and persistence, Ramsey produced another title, Division Two, and a superlative follow-up: the 1962 Division One championship. They had conquered England. After the last ball had been thumped, crowd and players danced, delighted and disappeared. Ramsey stayed behind and walked a solo lap of honour, Portman Road empty, but for an applauding Mr John.

When England called for Ramsey, Wor Jackie Milburn stepped in, but walked away again, fortune always hiding. A few years on, the north-east sent another missionary: Bobby Robson, Mr John's soulmate. The two guided one another over stony ground with steady hands. Fruitless years soon gave way to bounty. At the 1978 FA Cup final, Town's Roger Osborne socked a left-footer beyond Arsenal and promptly fainted. Still though, the trophy was dressed in blue. Mr John, Bobby and the boys sang all the way home. Next stop, greatness.

Bobby's team played champagne football for their champagne chairman. You drink it, Mr John, we'll play it. Dutch sorcerers Arnold Mühren and Frans Thijssen plied the team with zippy passes and twisted opponent blood into a curdle. Young Terry Butcher refused all entry, and Johnny Wark prompted and picked, a midfield drumbeat. The bonhomie of Mr John masked a ruthless winning machine of a club. In the tunnel at Highbury, an Arsenal chaplain remarked 'May the best team win'. 'Fuck that, Reverend, we want to win' retorted our John. Ipswich were sticklers for the Top Five and European football. Mr John filled his boots and embraced the bright green liqueurs of continental destinations. His club crept under the Iron Curtain, to Lodz with its food shortages and Leipzig, where Mr John sat among thick-coated

Soviet generals, each of them a Town fan for the day. When Cologne visited Suffolk, he invited their wigs to the stately family home and plied them with booze. By midnight, they were blindfolded and bashing one another with a folded-up newspaper. The playful club was a successful one, snaring the UEFA Cup in 1981. Ten thousand East Anglians flocked to Amsterdam for the final, opening their own blue light district. They charmed the city with their impeccable ways, doing the family proud. Where English fans usually elicited batons from European law keepers, the children of Town induced a letter of congratulation from Amsterdam's finest.

As I was being born, though, the Football Association was eyeing up the family silver. When another vintage season, 1981-82, ended Bobby Robson left for Wembley. Mr John had once more sent a son to fight for England. Cracks appeared in the family. They expanded into chasms when, a year later, Mr John suddenly died. 'He was too young and too good to die and it is a sad and heavy blow to me,' said grieving Bobby Robson. 'His death is also a dreadful loss to the club. He could turn disappointment and disaster into humour and laughter. There was always tomorrow as far as Mr John was concerned.'

And so to Town I go, to trace a crayon across the bark of the family club. The alarm wakes me early, before even Suffolk farmers have stirred. At the airport – to get to Ipswich from Scotland on a train requires a problematic change at Bratislava Parkway – sore eyes squint at neon screens. Dixons is packed with the kind of man who needs to buy a scart lead at 5.45 a.m., while prohibitive queues in WHSmiths lead me to pay for my newspaper in the honesty box. When I worked in WHSmiths as a teenager, one of my jobs was to empty this vessel of change. The floor staff knew it as the 'IOU jar' so frequently did we find scrawled notes bearing the acronym. Other payment methods included Deutschmarks, McDonald's vouchers and a safety pin.

'Oh my God, my, my God, oh my God' cry the girls in the security queue. They are wonderfully archetypal trust fund students. Rosy-cheeked and Ugg-booted, all have a luscious and scruffy surfeit of mousy blond hair, and hoodies sheathed by gillets. 'It's so not funny being up this early,' says one. I am sure the others agree but nodding would take too much effort and involve breaking their ridged stoops. I would like to pass comment here on the continuing importance of social class in England, but there is every chance that these are the daughters of Highland lairdship or the united sisters of Harris Tweed. I like them. Their caricatures perk up the 100ml maximum process.

The flight peaks early on when an air stewardess scolds two French garçons for talking through the safety mimes, even if they are frequent fliers. After that, I am left to luxuriate in the hills, dales, streams and retail parks of England sliding into view beneath me, and the pilot's voice. This begins at a high pitch, but decreases to a low one as his sentences progress, much like a balloon being let go.

At Stansted, I board the coach for Ipswich. Whitney Houston has recently died, but her caterwauling is immortalised on Heart FM's 'Whitney Day', streaming from National Express speakers. By the end of the journey I emphatically do not want to dance with somebody, unless the foxtrot brings deafness.

We pass through Braintree, a pretty hive of cottage terraces topped by a dome-headed library. At its centre is the Essex American Hall. We are close, of course, to the border with Suffolk, where 80,000 American troops were stationed during the Second World War. They brought their ruptured society with them. Fights between troops resulted in designated 'white nights' and 'black nights'. In Ipswich, some pubs were declared 'exclusively for coloured troops'.

Braintree's outskirts field small factories that are still clearly in use and add to the feeling that this is a model railway town. Colchester is stirring bonnily too, its circular castle a postcard-perfect English relic. Garden St George flags quiver as we whoosh along, signs for Colchester's new Weston Homes Community Stadium in blurry brown. Wherefore art thou, Layer Road where Leeds United were slain?

There are signs too for Copdock and Spiral as we approach Ipswich. Suffolk is the county of Snape, Shimpling and Rishangles, of Boulge, Iken and Eye. These place names conjure a whispered poetry perfect for the tranquil England I am seeking. After a tantalising striptease view of Portman Road the coach drops me at the Cattle Market Bus Station. It is immediately serene. When a lady trundles by on a mobility scooter it seems like a raucous, unnecessary intrusion.

At the Tourist Information Centre, housed among the fairy tale beams of an old church, two helpful ladies try and remember the name of a pub I've asked about. 'Has its own brewery, does it? Oh. I think I know. Paula, what's that pub down the docks where they have the beer and such?' I am never to find the pub. I continue along narrow, quiet streets. There is no traffic here, just the clops of feet and murmuring voices. I sit on a tomb behind a church requisitioned as a cafe and inhale the tranquillity. The sounds here are sounds that have gratified the air for centuries: feet and voices and even, when the hour strikes, church bells. Ipswich feels like a permanent, constant and confident England.

Crooked buildings of bright colour and groaning beams culminate in Ancient House. The plasterwork beneath each window depicts the continents of the world, fifteenth-century style: Europe is an elegant lady with an open book, Asia a palm tree with a lady lying beneath, Africa a naked man on a tree stump and America the same in a headdress.

By H&M a dad stops his teenage son and points at the man bearing a 'McDonald's This Way' placard. 'If you don't start trying at school that's what you'll end up doing,' says the dad within earshot of the sign man. This tale is played out on the site of the Chaucer family boozer. In the thirteenth and fourteenth century the writer's family ran a tavern here. He would later satirise the port of Ipswich's 'fork-bearded' merchants, placing them on horses defending the River Orwell. Chaucer's relationship with Ipswich numbers one of its many insistently English credentials. No town has been lived in by English-speaking inhabitants for a longer continuous period than this one. It was here that two great pushers of an idealised England, John Constable and Thomas Gainsborough, lived and worked. Even Lord Nelson bought himself a house in Ipswich. It is also the home of the world's first motorised lawnmower, and what is more English than a Sunday spent with a Flymo? From the quiet contentedness of its aged streets to these heritage yarns, it is the most English place I have been to so far. That does not necessarily make it the one that most embodies what England is.

I walk by the Admiral's House, former home of Wellington's naval friend Benjamin Page. My guidebook teaches me that after an illustrious career at sea Admiral Page retired here. The peace of Ipswich that he craved was frequently interrupted by a rowdy watercress salesman nicknamed 'Must-Go'. Page paid him a 'pension' not to sell outside his home. Along from the Admiral's House is the Ipswich and Suffolk Club, a protracted and ancient maroon building, part-stately home, part-egregiously Mock Tudor golf club. I have always found the world of private members' clubs intriguing, and not only because I am convinced that they are fronts for Masonic Lodges or sex clubs or Masonic Sex Clubs. Judging by its website this version does sound vaguely welcoming though one wonders how much to the denizens of the building opposite, which houses the Bangladeshi Support and the Zimbabwean Women's Resource centres. So many Englands, and this just on Tower Street, Ipswich.

Around the corner P. J. McGinty's pub is home to one of the town's most celebrated ghosts, a monk who enjoys walking through the fireplace. From its earliest days Ipswich was home to various breeds of friar. In the twelfth and thirteenth centuries mendicant monks walked the local streets begging for money in return for prayers (it beats '50p for a cup of tea', I suppose). When they left, the Franciscans became dominant. As disciples of St Francis they embraced the rule of poverty, excluding all else. This was especially hard on their feet, for the rejection of shoes meant everything became caked in what is euphemistically referred to in history books as 'street waste' (*trans* shite).

By a sign that promises Ipswich Polish Club is 'coming soon', I cross to the former Packhorse Inn. This heroically leaning and blisteringly elegant old house is now a solicitors'. It had the same use in 1936 when Wallis Simpson bobbed in to confirm her divorce. Papers signed in this typically quiet Ipswich street changed England. There is no time to ponder the magnitude of what took place here as I am drawn to a poster over the road. It is a noticeably bright advert for 'An evening with Tough Talk'. 'Tough Talk' is apparently 'made up of a group of men with backgrounds of ex-bouncers, ex-football hooligans and ex-East End hard men who have turned their backs on the past.' Instead, 'The group have found the message of hope in Jesus Christ' and now travel around 'performing power lifting demonstrations as a backdrop to telling their amazing stories.' It is very much what He would have wanted.

I carry on and am duly stung by the unexpected beauty of Christchurch Mansion and park. This, an open, council-owned stately home lolling amongst stunning communal land, lifts Ipswich from 'pleasant' to 'ace'. When England takes its heritage assets and makes them public like this, it too is ace. The mansion itself is imperfectly beautiful, chiselled together in bricks of various shades of cerise and charmingly asymmetrical having been built in the sixteenth century and often beavered away at since. In front of it is an oval lawn on which this morning kids race about. Beyond them, giant oaks perform a guard of honour around a sweeping and bumpy park of hills and ponds. The park is home to the town's war memorials and gives them the reverence of space and silence. In Ipswich, war memorial England is of the more traditional, weeping type.

A curator heaves Christchurch Mansion ajar and welcomes me inside. The scent is overwhelmingly evocative – fusty books, thick varnish and Worcester sauce. Perhaps the shop is burning Olde England-scented joss sticks. I read how Christchurch is another part of the Cobbold family silver, polished on behalf of the town. In 1895 it was due to be demolished. Felix Cobbold, a banker, stepped in and bought the place under the proviso that it opened its hefty doors to the public. Christchurch, the wet dock, swimming baths and Ipswich Town, all fed by Cobbold money sent from civic duty. Nowadays, English sons of money cart their spoils from this country to the tax vaults of others.

Upstairs the corridor floors groan and are angular enough to make me feel drunk, which is an added bonus. The walls of one room are covered entirely in panels that bear Latin slogans and surrealist fairy-tale illustrations. Another, The Chamber, is so full of varnished wooden items it looks as if a class of Jacobean CDT pupils has just left.

I leave this deeply special, garishly English place and walk back by bumfluff trees towards town. On an adjacent road the Friends Meeting House seems to double as a taxi rank, unless cab drivers here are chiefly Quaker and so instead of boring you with their opinions sit in silent contemplation for the length of your journey. The houses are large in this neighbourhood, withdrawn from the road behind generous gardens. I imagine that the illustrious of Ipswich once lived on this street, men like a doctor I read about. I remember the doctor because he once caught a man stealing vegetables from his garden. The local version of law and order back then – the nineteenth century – seems to have been a 'wise man' named Old Winter, so the doctor sent for him. Old Winter used white magic to punish miscreants and bewitched the thief into spending the night sitting in a cabbage patch. Elsewhere, he coerced one man into walking in circles for hours on end, carrying the firewood he had stolen.

Eventually, I come to a columned archway and hear the busy voices of market traders beyond. The archway unfolds into a compelling scene. Beneath blue and white canopies stallholders bawl about bargainous fruit and veg, about leggings and tights, about fuses and drills. Customers peruse and chatter ('Oh look, Mary, thems got those slippers you liked') while a man in fluorescents snaps litter from beneath their feet. One stall proffers a surfeit of oval, circular and oblong breads and pastries that my nana would have called 'right fancy'. It is run by two urbanite young men, members of a growing population who see bread and brewing as art forms, and charge accordingly. Food in England has become middle-class pornography. More traditionally there is Billy's Meats, a butcher's van from which a man in a red and white-striped apron calls out deals from a headset microphone. The van is festooned in boards proclaiming deals and tailed by a sizeable queue of customers. Billy has his patter and he is going to use it. 'You ask I serve, you don't, it serves you right. Who wants a dozen sirloins for twenty quid? No, how about thirty quid then, your call. Look at this, my love. Marbled, caressed, a specimen, a fine specimen.' The scene is flanked by Ipswich's Town Hall. It is impressive but neatly proportioned; there is no call for ostentation here. No one would ever think to burn it down. As its modest clock is ticking on I decide to head from the town to the Town.

At Portman Road they are unfurling match day. The PA man is testing his apparatus, and grills sizzle as raw patties hit the burger street stalls. With their teeth, programme sellers remove the plastic taping around their bundles and apply their fingerless gloves. Stewards are briefed and distributed to their four corners of the ground.

From town, you first see Portman Road poking out between two saddening office buildings over a roundabout, and it lifts the soul. Its curving yet jutting angles resemble a dexterous cat's arm. Floodlights rise from its roofs on iron tripods. It consists of two older stands and two newer, the former wearing the words 'Ipswich Town FC' in a classic and proud typeface. I loiter by the Cobbold Stand, whose rib-caged and organised 1970s appearance reminds me of the more artistic elements of Communist architecture. That sounds sarcastic, but is meant as a compliment. The early risers start to trickle in, ambling towards informal meeting places where semi-strangers gossip about full-backs. Many congregate by the statue of Sir Bobby, others twenty metres along from him by Sir Alf. I wonder if these reflect Tractor Boy Ultra factions, and in north-eastern solidarity perch by the iron

Robert Robson. His right hand is aloft, pointing to the position in between the front two, pointing to glory. Men who should know better but happily don't and boys who never saw him but feel they did queue up and offer a kissed hand to his solid feet.

I hear the Town Crier before I see him. 'Ladies and gentlemen. Welcome to Portman Road for today's match with Cardiff City Football Club,' he says through a megaphone. 'Hooray, here 'e is!' whoops one of the burger men, familiar warmth in his voice. When I turn I see that he is a gentleman in his fifties wearing a white Town T-shirt, a beanie hat on top of a deerstalker, tracksuit bottoms and snow-white trainers. The megaphone he holds is small in size and plays bursts of calypso music in between his proclamations. He scuttles up and down the length of the Cobbold Stand for at least half an hour, welcoming those present, giving an update on Town's form and belting out homemade topical chants. Of the thousands that walk past him few are surprised. Most smile and some wave at him. This Town Crier is patently part of the furniture, part of the matchday carnival of ritual.

Behind the Sir Bobby Stand, I pause by Sir Alf of Sir Alf Ramsey Way. Above him a giant mural of Bobby in his pomp grins down. Standing beside Alf at a certain angle it appears as if the two are in conversation, talking Town, talking times in the sun. Some say English management's finest sons did not get on. I say they would now; they would now with Town and time to heal them. Alf died here, Bobby died with here wedged in his heart.

A fried onion perfume hangs as I pass a twenty-something lad distributing tickets to his mates ('You get them and I'll square you up on Saturday'). I heave my Cobbold Stand turnstile and enter the 1970s. Beyond concrete stairs men in suede and fur jackets stand by corrugated Perspex. This is a time-warped concourse, untouched since Bobby. I buy a bottle of Aspall's cider and marvel at a price list that includes whisky and brandy, surely tip-of-the-hat tipples to Mr John. A couple in their sixties kiss and embrace with an exhibitionist passion that screams 'affair'; very shocking at the family club, but the guts of Portman Road are a fine place to hide. There are ruddy-faced men with shovel hands wearing cords and Barbours. They stand reading attendances from the programme's statistics page, always my favourite feature.

When 'Sweet Child O' Mine' ends and the Cardiff City fans begin to sing, I turn a corner and climb some stairs into the light. The Lincoln green in front of me is fresh and stirring, the people in their stands a theatre of intrigue. May nothing stop the feeling a first visit to a new ground gives. The rain swishes and bounces as the groundsman stabs a last-ditch pitchfork into his turf. After a medley of stadium classics ('The Boys Are Back in Town', 'Simply the Best' ...) and a club song that begins 'I've never felt more like singing the Blues/When Ipswich win and Norwich lose', Town and City players trudge on to the field. It is regrettable that they enter the fray in this way. Long gone are the Saturdays of teams galloping into the coliseum, revved up and sky high on nervous energy. Departed is the anarchy of them blazing kamikaze warm-up shots into the huddling masses behind the goal. As befits the mollycoddled game these days, their entry now is organised and functionary. The spontaneity and the jubilance of expectancy have departed. It has been replaced by a stage-managed handshake parade, probably on the advice of sports scientists and crass marketing men. The choreographing of pre-match fan behaviour is transposed on to the players. Everywhere, breathless excitement has been turned into stale air. 'I remember when they used to sprint on,' says the man in the seat behind mine. 'Of course, it's all about political correctness now.'

With the coin spun both teams retreat to their halves and embrace in eleven-man huddles. I think the purpose is to impart last-minute words of inspiration and share shouts of 'grrrrrrr'. It is more interesting to imagine that the footballers are debating Hegelian dialectics. Once the game has kicked-off a disappointing hush envelops the stands. Everything – the rain, the setting, the clacking of wooden seats – is in place for noise. All that can be heard are the barks of growly Welsh voices and the occasional clap of gloved hands. For a change I am by far the youngest person in my seating block, and one of only a few not wearing a waxy jacket. Many are still living in a past from long ago. Two seats along from me a nasal Suffolk voice says, 'I wish we could find another Bobby Robson, another Johnny Wark.'

Down on the pitch Cardiff spark. They are due at Wembley next week for a League Cup final tryst with Liverpool and play with chutzpah. Their busy right-back raids forward incessantly and I am surely not the only person in the ground wondering when they last saw a grey-haired player. His left-back teammate struts around like a Siamese cat based on Liam Gallagher. When he is forced to run it appears as though he is hopping among fire. At times he seems to fly in an upright position, like a Tomy Supercup Football figure. On the front-line a skin-heided Scot jerks in and out of the home offside trap. When not snared and flagged he is a nippy whippet. His style of play and bareback aggression invites fouls as snow invites footprints. At one point he wins a free-kick and then daggers the ball with his eyes, as if it has offered him outside.

As the first half motors on, Town craft matches City efficiency. Where skin-heid wishes death upon the ball, the home side smother it in kisses. Passes are tip-tapped together, and gentle feet dribble softly. Important in this is their centre-forward, a lanky doodle-do-er with a persistent side parting. He ensures that Town's caressing is not just foreplay, busily directing proceedings and irritating Cardiff with ceaseless running. His speedy partner up top is addicted to blood-curdling challenges on opponent defenders. It's the kind of nastiness and immediacy that Town, the nice club too often stuck in yore, need.

Beneath the mossy roof of their characterful main stand, Town's heavily Liverpudlian manager folds his arms and thinks something very, very Scouse. As he peddles backwards to the dugout Ipswich burst free from a Cardiff attack and score. Inevitably, the brash chirp of 'Chelsea Dagger' drowns at birth any long-awaited din from the home crowd. When the game renews Town become commanding, their crisp pushing of the ball occasionally mesmeric. Still home crowd smiles do not come, and nor are voices raised. What finally gets them going is a thudded, studded ground-based contretemps between forward and foe, followed by a City middleman running the ball out of play. In their thousands the people of Suffolk rise and jeer. While England and Ipswich roar for minor violence and opposition mistakes, we will never be sickly purists like Spain and Barcelona. I like that. Sheffield still rules.

The visiting Welsh are forced to respond with a constipated 'Que Sera Sera ...' and prolonged barracking of Town's winger ('One lazy bastard/there's only one lazy bastard'), a former Cardiff loanee. With gallant strides the high-rise No. 9 responds by repeated drifts through the City defence. Towards half-time things dampen down. Player shouts can now be heard, a hollow thrill. When a crisp packet tries to make a tackle the referee purses his lips and blows for tea.

Epic rain shatters the half-time ceasefire and I take shelter by a pie stand that has run out of pies. The second-half, we hear, is to be delayed as a linesman is injured. 'Must've got a tooth stuck in a biscuit' offers a steward, his bright orange sleeves pulled long over frozen hands. The Ipswich team emerge and slop about in the mush for a full five minutes before Cardiff join them and the game breathes again.

Bolshy and buxom, Town's choppy striker cares not about the weather. He thunders in Ipswich's second goal, the net sploshing on impact. The Cardiff fans turn poisonous on a man once the hero of the Taff. 'Wanka, Wanka, Wanka' goes their war chant. Despite the pleasantry of Portman Road, the game's poisonousness breaches and pervades.

The family members in the stand now react to their brethren on the pitch. Each pass is cheered, a football fiesta in the rain. Portman Road at long last imitates a degree of the exuberant days of Mr John. Half the problem though is that all todays are measured against yesterdays. That is the thing with families. Always harking back. Always sharing the same old jokes and the same old regrets.

Town's busy side-parted forward does not respect the past. He is an irreverent little brother. With a quarter of an hour left he squeezes the cheekiest of goals into a mousehole spot. Town three, Welsh nil. In the flecky Suffolk rain people drift away to their Saturday evenings. Home from the football, the win will spur their night and make the weekend. Tomorrow, the papers will make congenial reading. The pleasure of victory lingers.

By the Sir Alf Ramsey Stand, Chunkys and Moustaches wait for autographs. Despite all its distortions, I feel part of something permanent. This small glimpse of England makes for happiness in sodden Suffolk. After much ado I am on to something.

I cross the Sir Bobby Robson Bridge and check in to my chain hotel. The production-line room is smart, but as with all of these places it can feel like sitting in a furnished storage unit. I head downstairs for a pint and bamboozle the barman with my Scottish tenner. For a while he stares at it disbelievingly, as if I have just passed him a human foot. Then he accepts it anyhow. Supping up I do a strange raising of the eyebrows at the barman which I instantly regret and leave. He doesn't mind, though; with my strange illegal tender I have glossed his shift with surrealism.

From a dim street by the River Orwell Portman Road can be seen. Her floodlights close down: one, two, three, four, as I look. They leave behind them the tasteful 'Ipswich Town FC' yoke neons. This is one artful arena. I turn a dingy corner and am pleasantly affronted by moody lights shining high on a disused dock building. Every ten seconds they alternate in colour: blue, white, red, blue, white, red goes the rhythm of the night. I approach and read that this is an art installation named 'Light Waves', and runs every night from dusk until midnight. It is funded by the local council. For all the tutted grief councils get, it seems that in the Englands I have seen so far they propel much character and culture, even if it is sometimes forced or miscalculated.

Light Waves marks the start of The Waterfront, Ipswich's placid and wistful dock area. Sailing boats gently bob as the Orwell ripples, moonlight showcasing raindrops. There is a faint angina beat from the surrounding bars, doosh, doosh, doosh, none of which I will be entering. I scuttle over tired train tracks that once carted lime from Casablanca, timber from Canada, wheat from Philadelphia. Lights draw me to a glass cupboard where a building's window should be. This, it seems, houses an ingenious mini-museum. The window museum has been set up, I read, by Ipswich Maritime Trust, and is England's only such portal. Its orderly objects represent a 1,300 year-old port that made Ipswich matter from Domesday to D-Day. This wide-open slew of water invited invasion from Romans, Vikings, Angles, Saxons, Normans ... anyone with an atlas. Of all brutal incomers my favourites are the Wuffingas because they sound like hairy characters from children's television. The port was advantageous too – the ease of building and accessing the Thames made it 'the shipyard of London' by the seventeenth century, and in the Second World War sloops, minesweepers and trawlers were refreshed here and sent back into battle.

As night-out heels clip clop towards Jägerbombs, I drift by the University of Suffolk's ample glass temple and towards the town centre. The Spread Eagle glows golden on the corner of pretty and dead streets. In its window is a poster with mugshots of twenty or so people who are barred from all pubs in Ipswich. I enter just as a man is reproaching the barmaid with the sentence, 'Since I went to the loo my stool has been removed'. 'We always clear the bar when there's a band on,' she contests, fighting a smirk. The band – two midlife men – approach the stage. Both have limps. Their first number ends abruptly when the drummer/singer hits a duff note, but the covers soon flow. Smokie. Check. Journey. Check. Robert Palmer. Check. Pocketing my notepad and pen I walk in front of them in order to leave, slightly worried that they think I am an unimpressed A&R man.

After visiting in 1722, Daniel Defoe wrote that provisions in Ipswich were so reasonable 'that a family may live cheaper here than in any town in England for its bigness.' It is pretty obvious to me that he must have been referring to the 90p Store ('Everything 90p'), which I spy shortly after leaving the Spread Eagle. I continue down Dogs Head Road and pause to survey an Ipswich pub on a Saturday night. This corner bar can be seen in profile, yellow light from the street, Hopper's 'Nighthawks' in Suffolk. In a side-room two men sit silently on separate tables. Both have an arm outstretched cuddling their pint, and an eye on the boxing contest blaring from the room's corner television. The main bar hosts a dozen or so people, most of whom are staring fixedly at another covers band as they plough through Cameo's 'Word Up'. A bunch of link-armed women with Hellraiser hair slow down, glance in, and move on. Their big laughs warm the air. Everyone is chasing their Saturday night.

I walk down Silent Street, renamed, so it is said, when all of its inhabitants died of the plague. Its delicate mix of Georgian and Elizabethan buildings seems transcendent and surreal, England channelled through a Dickens film set designer from Arkansas. At the silent foot of Silent Street a bronze Cardinal Wolsey stares at me like skin-heid staring at a football. Thomas Wolsey was the son of an Ipswich butcher who for a while in the sixteenth century ruled England by proxy. Henry VIII devolved the irksome business of government to Wolsey, who initially won his trust by efficiently organising a royal feast and pageant. The next time you organise a finger buffet, just make sure the Queen is watching. Far from giving Wolsey – probably the most famous Ipswichian – celebrity status, the locals called him 'The Butcher's Dog' and subscribed to the view offered by his biographer that he was 'the haughtiest of men in all his proceedings that then lived, having more respect to the worldly honour of his person than he had to his spiritual profession.' They're not much better these days – until the statue was erected in 2011, he was commemorated by Cardinal Park, a leisure settlement counting KFC, a Harvester pub and the Liquid/ Envy nightclub among its tenants. After capping the night two or three times over I take the long walk home, passing the Rasputin Eurofood shop on my way. The rain has stopped on Portman Road and Sir Alf is speaking to the moon. Ipswich's England has been a pleasant one. There is a permanence about the place, from footsteps and voices in the street to autograph hunters at the stadium. It is not a backwards idyll of farmers buying batteries, but there is a sense that Ipswich is a destination for the area rather than its own metropolis state. In from the country they still come. There is an ethereal beauty to life here. It is like watching a dream you cannot influence. I retire to my room with a pizza, fall asleep in my shoes and snore away the night in quiet, quaint old Suffolk.

Part Two

In the Spring:
Hornets, Os, Seals and Railwaymen

Chapter Five

Watford

For too many of us, Graham Taylor is 'Do I not like that' and Elton John is Princess Diana's funeral. Both are caricatures created by the press and upheld by the public. To think of them as such is not only mistaken, but detracts from a time when the pair pulled together and changed football.

Reg Dwight had stood and watched football from the rusting shackland stands of Vicarage Road. He even had a favourite spot – a piece of old terrace between the Rookery End and Shrodells Stand known as 'The Bend'. When Reg became Elton and sang to the world, riches accrued allowed him to move to the directors' box. Watford were a Division Four club, their stadium a corrugated waste ground. There hung over them an amateur ethos that made for a deteriorating, if charming, club. Watford's full-time non-playing staff numbered only three: one manned the Pools bureau, another was a groundsman and the third calculated and paid player wages, sold tickets, ran the press office and performed all general tasks.

Elton needed help. In the summer of 1977 he called Don Revie. 'Graham Taylor at Lincoln City,' the Middlesbrough alumnus told him, 'he's the man you want.' A manager at twenty-eight, Taylor had taken his Imps to promotion the season Elton arrived at Watford, 1975-76. Twice along the way they thrashed Watford. Enticed by a five-year deal making him the highest paid manager outside the top flight, Taylor chose Hertfordshire life. Early on, the new manager asked Elton for his aims. He replied: 'I'd like to get into Europe.' They agreed that it would take ten years and a million pounds to get there, and then revealed their 'impossible dream'.

One by one, Taylor's players attended introductory meetings in his office. He sat on a giant, raised chair, each of them on a small one, looking up. His message was simple: the manager was on the way up, and only they could decide if they wished to join him. Taylor installed a new code of discipline among his squad and asked that they move to the area. All were informed that they would be expected to perform several hours of work per week in the local community. He instinctively understood that to move Watford the club anywhere, he needed Watford the town's backing. Taylor and Elton set about giving them a more amiable place in which to watch football. They oversaw the patch-up and re-paint of Vicarage Road and scrapped the perimeter greyhound track, a source of distance and distraction.

Taylor set about instilling a playing system and culture fit for their refreshed, ambitious club. To escape the fourth tier they would blitz it: attack, attack, attack. They would be direct, but not aimlessly long-ball. Each man would know his space, each teammate where to deliver to him. The key would be getting the ball to centre-forwards who could hold on to it (gifted big-man Ross Jenkins and young rocket Luther Blissett), at which point six or seven others would attack, a ravenous pack. Each man had to be athletic to pull his weight in the machine, and focused on the explicit plan set down for him. It worked: high-tempo Watford became champions at Taylor's first attempt. That year they won and scored more – and lost and conceded fewer – than any other team. The following season, 1978-79, Taylor's system did the trick again. Watford were promoted. Between them, Jenkins and Blissett scored sixty-five times in league and cup. They even won at Old Trafford in the League Cup, and lost only to Clough's Forest, soon European Champions, in the semi-final.

In two years Taylor and Elton had built a swashbuckling, vibrant club. Going through a chaotic time in the fickle world of rock 'n' roll, Elton revelled in its structures and its avuncular manager. Taylor was one of the few 'no men' in his life – he banned Elton from giving freebie tickets to players and, when he showed up at the training ground in flares and platforms sent him home ('We're a football club here. We have standards and we have a dress code'). In return Elton often lived dreams that first entered his head while stood on The Bend. He travelled on the team bus, watched training and had his hero players round to the house, albeit to sing on a record. Where before the town had been drifting from its club, Taylor and Elton's endeavours won them around while success made them smile. Watfordians already knew Elton was one of their own; when Taylor refused a roof for his dugout until the Rookery End had one too, they knew they had another.

The town's loyalty helped Watford through two consolidation seasons in Division Two. The plan had not stalled, but the club had got ahead of itself. Now, Taylor revised his playing system to once more begin the move onwards and upwards. The basic ethos would be the same, but with added science and better players, produced by a lively youth system and Elton's generous pockets.

Still Watford would keep it simple. The game was not about avoiding defeat, but about winning. Attacking play, forward passes, Luther or his rock Jenkins holding up. The yellows streaming towards them. An avalanche, a charge. Pressurising as high up the pitch as possible. Knock-backs, through balls and arcing centres. Thumps, larrups and bullet headers. Goals, goals, goals. Open play rehearsed, experiments learned off by heart and repeated on the pitch. Taylor souped-up a dossier of diagrams, statistics and patterns sent to him by Charles Reep, 'the human computer' whose theories had helped inspire Wolves' Golden Greats in the 1950s. Reep had watched hundreds of matches at every level, identifying the areas from which most goals came. He claimed that on average ten shots equalled a goal, and so twenty were usually required to win a game. Taylor disagreed on some of the finer details, but put into practice the basics. By his own calculations, goals came from first-time shots and re-starts, with the far post being a fertile area to attack. Though we remembered them from the credits of *Match of the Day*, there was only ever one scorcher or full team move for every fifteen or twenty tap-ins. Most goals had few passes behind them. Taylor's Watford, then, would fully embrace quick, sometimes long-range, accurate passes 'for' not 'to' a teammate, and, in short, crosses and shots at every possible opportunity.

At the start of the 1981-82 season, the system was in place. All it needed was fireworks – step forward John Barnes of Sudbury Court FC, seventeen years old, dancing feet, swaying hips, cushion chest. His debut came in the season's opener at Stamford Bridge. The Shed made monkey noises; Barnes made goals in a 3-1 win. On the other wing, starboard to his port, was Nigel Callaghan, a homegrown virtuoso with pinpoint feet. The two helped the Watford machine move up a division, second behind Luton. On promotion day, Elton walked off stage in Norway to listen to a phone held up to Watford Hospital Radio's commentary. Afterwards, he spoke with every player. 'You've made my dreams come true,' he told them all.

When their first season in Division One started, football's puritans panicked. Watford were uncouth, 'wild dogs' who would be found out in the manors of the aristocracy. They even had the temerity not to give individual Rolls Royce opponents time on the ball, snapping at them hungrily. Theirs was throwback football and could only finish in relegation. They finished second and qualified for Europe. The impossible dream had taken only six years.

Thirty years later, grey skies garnish Watford Junction station with slow fat rain. It gloops down and settles on its office block walls like sap on a tree. Remove five Bourbon biscuits from their packet, lay them on top of each other and you have an accurate model of Watford Junction. One function of a railway station is to set your expectations of a place. A station is the handshake you judge a man by, in this case limp beyond recognition. It is probably best that you do not make eye contact with Watford Junction.

A London bus hurtles by, splattering this canvas with much-needed colour. I walk down a long, spirit level-straight avenue of taxman call centres and oil company headquarters. After waiting an age to cross the inner-city motorway that strangles Watford town centre in a noose, I walk by the proud New Palace Theatre, twice-domed and steadfastly glamorous. On Watford High Street pigeons gather on and around an old lady who feeds them Mighty White bread. The lady's lipstick circles her chin rather than covering her lips, and her eyes are narrated by tears-of-a-clown eye make-up. Somehow she is stalked by a strange prettiness, Judi Dench plays Edward Scissorhands.

It is pleasing that town centre eccentrics survive artless, monochromic English high streets. Watford High Street and Everywhere High Street have a Revolution, a Poundland, a Greggs and so on, but only Watford High Street has its pigeon lady. Similarly, only here will you find the toothless busker whose voice douses the heinously drab Charter Place centre in feeling. With his eyes closed he sings soulfully, from the heart. Elton lives on. In front of him, children climb and bounce on marble elephant and hippo sculptures, while escalators churn dispirited pensioners towards retailopolis. This is the land promised half a century ago.

The developers wore suits to transmit seriousness and hardhats to win the high opinions of a working-class town. It was the 1960s. Anything was possible. Their plan involved charging at local streets with a planet of a wrecking ball. Where stood ancient pubs would stand stuff to buy. When their blueprint was unveiled, the *West Herts Post* raised a glass. 'The face of Central Watford will change dramatically during the next five to seven years,' they cheered. 'By that time it is hoped that the borough will become the Croydon of North London.' The future. Car parks! Shopping centres! Easy access for cars! Overhead walkways!

It took time, but the men with the plans, their offspring and their council cousins pulled it off. One result is the tarmac piping that courses cars through Watford's veins. Another is the indoor market I enter. The market's interior seems to be both dimly lit and garish. From a pitch-black background, interrogation spotlights hone in to resemble approaching UFOs. Its brown tiled floor is shiny like wet pebbles and well pounded by Watfordians. At the market's front are stalls selling balls of wool, greeting cards and handbags, plus family butchers and greengrocers. Behind a busy curtain Tina Tarot and Peter Healer do their things, which include 'Healing for Mind and Body, Spirit Vibrations, Putting Light in Dark Corners,' and 'A Psychic Experience, Only £5.' The rear section of the market houses a less professional breed of stallholder. They embrace a more bric-a-brac approach, which means a table of dolls that are at best petrifying and at worst racist; hippyish tie-die prints and the unavoidable cupcakes. It is hard to taste the future here, but perhaps that is because the air weighs thick under colliding scents of raw butcher's meat and sizzling canteen bacon. What you can taste is atmosphere, life, a real England busying itself in small-time commerce.

Back on the High Street, Saturday is stirring. Shopping bags and husbands are dragged in and out of faintly attractive buildings and lanes. I walk downhill and spot the familiar motifs of Transport for London plastered on Watford High Street Overground station. London tentacles stretch into Watford and endanger its identity.

Beyond the Overground station is the town museum, a stunning Georgian house, all bricks and windows. Its polished exhibits tell of a town once knee-deep in ale and paper. Lead characters are Benskin's the brewer and the Sun Printers, both town empires and employers who moulded what Watford was. Benskin's faded away as old Watford died of 1960s aspirations. Sun hung on long enough to be merged into oblivion by Robert Maxwell. The town supported other industries along the way, many ploughing peculiar furrows that make particular history, history that helps sustain identity in places like this. Dr Tibbles opened a cocoa factory whose products, says one town history, 'contained a fair amount of cocaine.' Despite his narcotic tendencies and a catastrophic fire at the turn of the century, Tibbles was placed in charge of regional munitions during the First World War.

As in all small-town museums in England, as in all small towns in England, the wars we fought feel uniting yet unique. Which part of war memorial England am I in here, I wonder, when I am in one that hides away its lists of the fallen in a faraway dead end of an under-used museum? Here I am in a non-room the colour of a sticky plaster walled by plaques for 'The Employees of Scammell Lorries Limited Who Laid Down Their Lives in the Second Great War' and crying panels for 'The Men of the Watford and District

Post Office Who Fought in the Cause of Freedom'. It is neither Lutonian rebellion nor Ipswichian reverence. It *is* saddening.

Back in the thoughts and streets of today I walk to the pub behind Sky Blue lads jiving in a Coventry burr. Only football takes chain gangs of men from one provincial town to another, and only football brings them back each year till relegation us do part. A postcard advertisement in a newsagent window next to my pub of choice shouts at me. 'Stunning mixed RACE mature Lady Fun MASSAGE', it reads, and I shake my head at such haphazard use of capitalisation, noting her telephone number with a view to a condemnatory call later on.

Inside, pub hubbub conquers the thick stench of fried food. Friends and acquaintances greet each other – the ritual recommences. Since their heyday Watford have usually treaded the safe waters of England's second tier. This year has been the same; next year will be the same. Such stasis is a fine exemplar of the comfort of football and the belonging repetition brings. It means calm supporters and a club that chugs along, offending no one but the foul-tempered, ill mannered of Kenilworth Road.

With others I make the 2.40 trudge to Vicarage Road. I pass behind the One Bell pub and its adjacent, solemnly pretty church. This should be a place to linger and think for the visitor to Watford, but its rotting tombs are fenced off by crude silver barriers and chains. Such brash security seems to hush the visitor and usher him on – nothing to see here, just heritage and the dead.

I fall in behind supporters walking two by two – hurrah, hurrah. There is much evidence of traditional dress: white trainers, fresh jeans, official club merchandise coats and holdalls bearing flasks. Police huddle and chatter while fans leave the Fry Days fish shop stooping over their chips, swerving to avoid the folded arms of the law. The streets leading to the ground host an unusual array of outlets, a bizarre bazaar. One contains A Different Sauna, Beavers Strip Bar ('Fully nude and topless lap-dancing. Air conditioning.') and XFC Fried Chicken. The next has a shop that sells gravestones and mirrors, and one that claims to be the local bevelling specialist, a competitive market I am sure.

Vicarage Road appears suddenly, hemmed in as it is by a ramshackle collective of yards, houses, garages and allotments. Such a packed-in area forces a pounding pulse, the intensity of matchday squeezed into electric existence. The community club forged by Taylor and Elton lives on. This is resolutely still its town's club. As they pass the Bill Mainwood Programme Hut, people nod and wave and promise to pop in after the game. The conservatory door of the sallow bungalow that hosts the Hornets Shop claps open and half a dozen young fans spill out, Merchandise one, Pocket Money nil.

By the bright orange Coventry City team coach (registration 'KOV 1') and beneath a barbed wire CCTV camera, the electric turnstile files me inwards. At long last I am in the Rookery, once a roofless hovel, now a steep, deep and comfy structure. The Rookery's concourse is like the minimalist garage-bar of a gadget man millionaire. Flat screen televisions alternately flicker *Soccer Saturday* and an England rugby match, while neon blue computer gadgets glow, new and yet somehow already obsolete. Lager is sipped from plastic bottles; giant hot dogs test gravity to the full.

Near the Rookery's summit I take my seat and drink in the view – a compelling one above the twenty-two men in shades of yore, old Watford yellow and dreamy Sky Blue. The goal-net shimmers breezily way below awaiting, *hoping for*, action, a state shared by the unfinished concrete apartment spaces that fill a corner to the left. Its crude beams and dark gaps bring to mind

Spanish stories of empty development. It adjoins the Rookery to the main stand, which in turn leads to Vicarage Road's third complete enclosure, where visitors sing. What flows from there, on the opposite touchline to the main stand, is unique.

There are in total three different enclosure remnants in Vicarage Road ghost village. Together, they resemble an amalgamation of tax year-end local authority projects. The first and smallest is a square segment of tiered concrete speckled with gravel. It is the size of the foundations for a small semi-detached house. The second is larger and steeper, and looms behind a poled canopy that shields the dugouts. It is veiled by a giant grey modesty screen, leaving romantics to imagine the memories that rest beneath, and those less that way inclined to wonder what grotesque beast sleeps under the duvet. The third ghost is of a curtailed seating area, this time with roof included. It is a quarter of the pitch's length and proffers fading plastic seats to its front and wooden benches behind. Here no one sits but the Gentlemen of the Press, their laptops space age, freakish and not completely immune to poltergeists.

The three stands are the giant shrapnel of other times, *materiel* that fell to earth when Watford burst skywards. At such breakneck speed did the impossible dream happen, there was no time to anticipate Hillsborough horror. So quickly did Watford fall from the stars afterwards, there was no money to build towards the other Taylor's dossier. Thus an entire side of the ground consists of condemned terraces and paddocks, inadvertently creating a museum to better times.

Vicarage Road's dead side means crowds are pushed together, a community upheld by necessity. As such even low crowds do not vanish among seas of empty seats, as at the Riverside, though today's attendance is healthy in any case. Once *Z-Cars* has faded it is loud without being noisy. Proximity and community force naturally reserved supporters to interact, to be the crowd not the attendance, even if that only means clapping in time. Poked along by their unremitting midfielder, captain and headband-wearer, Watford charge into their opponents, a buzzing, heady squadron. They are direct and full on, as if the grass still echoes the instructions of Graham Taylor. Coventry's No. 30, a centre-half, is a one-man barricade. He is an oak tree, but with slightly better heading ability. Time and again in the first twenty minutes he is also a Newfoundland dog diving underwater to haul up the ball from the riverbed. Watford continue to batter and prise the castle door, Vicarage Road denizens roaring their approval like drunken sailors. Chances beg, the crowd rising as one then sinking at different rates. A goal must come. A goal *needs to* come.

It is nearly half-time when I realise this game is going to end 0-0. I am staring at a mascot, Harry the Hornet, who is rubbing a large Guinness top hat on his crotch. Watford have choked and frozen. Coventry are in the game, but that means little. When sky blue backline thumps reach their forwards, the ball bounces off the backs of their knees or hits a shoulder. It is like watching a toddler play swingball. Their fans, on a rare day out from staring at the relegation zone in the paper, are undeterred: 'While we sing together/we will never lose/BLUES!' Proceedings today bring to mind a newspaper report of yesteryear. When in the early 1900s a goat meandered on to the Watford pitch, the *West Herts Post* reflected that it 'in certain actions, spoke eloquently of its disgust for the whole dull and uneventful proceedings'.

The home side lapse backwards. For long stretches headband-wearer and his midfield colleagues collect the ball from centre-halves and hoist it forward, forlorn fishermen casting a line into the same barren part of the river. 'Give it to him, give it to him,' screeches a young supporter behind me, 'he's so open.' A man in a cloth cap glances over his shoulder and seems to tut with his eyes. All the time drummers at each side of the Rookery tap out the game's faint heartbeat.

The whistle blows. High-tens at half-time for Coventry's No. 30, breathing hearty gasps like a dad on a first New Year's resolution jog. Magnets on pitch diagrams for the home team. 'You run there. He runs here.' Where's Graham Taylor when you need him? For us there is the raffle, won by ticket 0001. 'Amazing,' screeches the PA man. 'Just amazing.'

In the second half the ball frequently takes to the sky, as if trying to escape the match and stadium. My mind wanders. What if, in games like this, a second ball was introduced after sixty minutes? What if ballboys were allowed to join in? Why does anybody want to be a linesman?

The home fans avoid existential questioning, as they are not hundreds of miles from home watching a dire 0-0. Besides, they are performing an instrumental version of 'Ring of Fire', en masse and on repeat. I start to feel tired and prickly. For the first time, I slightly lose interest in the Englands and the English football I am trying to find. Watching my own team gives me time to escape thought. Watching others is giving me too much time to think.

I try to concentrate on the good things. Perversely, I appreciate the way in which Coventry punt, brick and scoop every ball they are fortunate enough to be near. They are surviving, last gasp and death defying. It is anti-Barcelona stuff, but as I am growing sick of hearing about Messi and the toe tappers, I like it. It is the dark side of Watford's 1980s version of the game, one I have grown fond of.

I am less fond of how vitriolic crowds now seem to be, individuals at Middlesbrough and Sheffield, large numbers at

Luton. Here, when the referee points his arm in a direction the Rookery does not like, hoarse yowls of abuse follow. It is not the language; because I still believe swearing has a grand place in football. It is in bit part the loss of the humour with which supporters formerly rebuked referees, but more than that it is the sheer individual venom and the way it climaxes into a collective baying mob, a million teeth gnarling. In this is a crowd's energy wasted. Put together at a corner kick it can beseech the ball into the net.

'Wanka, WANKA, WANKA!' peaks the chorus. Like so many supporters, Watford's sing in an exaggerated version of the local accent. Football breeds a higher, intensified identity. As Coventry continue to paw at the cliff edge, the home side remember how to pass. At one point they nearly score. There are six minutes of injury time, an unfair purgatory. Harry Hornet looks at his crotch. Now Coventry almost score. Again the fans rise, again they fall. The final track of their dejection is the sound of seats thumped upright and mumbled goodbyes.

Back in town, St Patrick's Day bunting points out all-day drinkers like arrows. On the flyover that scythes the High Street into two portions are the coats of arms for Watford's twins: Mainz, Nanterre, Novgorod, Pesaro and Wilmington. Somewhere at a Beavers twin-club in Germany, France, Russia, Italy and Delaware, a man wearing a Guinness top hat is peering at air-conditioned tits over the rim of his pint. Underneath the flyover a gorgeous busker stuns the air with her radiant voice. I put coins in her guitar case, praise for the beauty, praise for the singing. An English rose in a faraway town melts the heart and stings the Yorkshire pocket.

I haven't smelt damp booze nor had my shoes stick to the floor in some time, so I head for Wetherspoon's. It is named The Moon

Under Water, presumably after George Orwell's essay about the perfect pub where, 'In winter there is generally a good fire burning' and the garden has 'swings and a chute for the children.' In Watford's version men with fading Irish accents toast the Fields of Athenry and sing of taking Kathleen home. As I open my Official Matchday Programme a Watford Irishman, not a day over eighty-six, falls backwards on to the wall, then forwards on to the table. Glass shatters. Blood curdles. No one acts so I walk into the street and give a policeman something to do.

I leave most of my pint – a sin, a sin – and check in to my hotel. 'Do you want a room on a lower floor, or a higher one, sir? It gets very noisy up high on Saturdays.' Dazed and confused I take a lower room, eat a pasty in it while watching *Take Me Out* then head for the bar. There a marvellously camp man from Head Office teaches two Polish barmen about customer service. One is blindfolded and told to buy a glass of Coke from the other. He does so, but then decides he's been short-changed and shouts at his colleague. 'I gave you a tenner. This is change for a fiver. A FIVER.' 'OK, Pavel, let's go again and this time you thank him and you walk away.' 'But I am customer. Customer is always right. Customer is always dick.'

The firing gun has spoken and Saturday night in town begins. Beneath green, white and orange balloons outside Malloy's Bar men hold pints in one hand and gesticulate wildly with the other. Girls shiver behind folded arms in the long queue for cash. There seem to be arms and legs everywhere, heels and straps too. Dance-music beats compete like fairground soundtracks and bouncers nod along, preparing. There are eight or nine pubs and clubs to be stumbled between and outside most promotion staff hop around dishing out flyers. 'Foam party tonight, mate' a terracotta lady outside Paparazzi says to me. She then looks me up and down and revokes the offer. Gangs of lads and gaggles of lasses cast their eyes around and talk of eating being cheating in the pissed-as-a-rat race. A short-sleeved lad in his early twenties taps me on the shoulder by Rehab Bar Lounge Club and points at his friend: 'Whatever you're writing in that notebook, put down that he's a cunt.' Watford High Street on a Saturday night is a Greek island resort under shivering skies. It is the Bravo TV event Sheffield was not. Everything is pumped up, high on cold air and booze, but the mood is good. Steam pours out of ears and evaporates into the sky. For all of these people, young in an England of high flux and low employment, Saturday night is required. It is impossible to be angry at a place that has such relief-valve functions, impossible to be dismayed at England with its hair down.

On Sunday morning, the High Street breeze blows stale alcohol, and men in fluorescent donkey jackets push around WKD bottles with large brooms. Live Christian rock booms from the Centre for Missional Leadership, exorcising the echoes of last night's noise. After passing Watford's serene town hall I try and fail to find the Grand Union Canal, ending instead in middle-class suburbia. For an age I walk tree-lined avenues in this expansive, expensive settlement. Houses with names like Elm Cottage and pretend timber beams sit among ferns and lawns. On each drive are two or even three cars. Lonesome joggers pound away the hours, while mums gaze from bay windows awaiting their Mother's Day visitors. Garage lights illuminate tinkering; ajar shed doors highlight pottering. On a few separate occasions the scent of sausages wafts strong. Most gardens are neat, tendered, sources of pride. Some are scruffy. There will, I imagine, have been neighbourhood meetings about these. So quiet is it here that I can make out tennis balls being thwacked on a court a hundred metres away.

When I think of southern England – and we shall come back to exactly where and what that is – I think of areas like these. I think of good people, but people whose spaced-apart properties and removed lives breed Little England thoughts. I think of the kind of people who wrote the following two letters, printed in the local press a half century apart, in 1938 and in 1993:

Sir –

I am glad to see the subject of Sunday washing raised in your paper. At one time in this part of the town people used to put their washing out on Monday and Tuesday, and then no more was put out until the next Monday and Tuesday. But now it is put out every day of the week, including Sunday. Surely housewives can do all their washing on six days of the week and leave us free from this disfigurement on Sundays. Sunday is so much more enjoyable if we make it different from other days.

R. I. K

Sir –

We are a heterosexual family of five, no gays or lesbians, no one cheating the state with false claims, no unmarried mothers, or so that it sounds more respectable, no single parents, with the result that there are no bastards in the family, nor are there any intentions of having any under the circumstances described. Could you kindly inform us of our rights, entitlements or any freebies to which we may be entitled. We all pay taxes in, then sit back and watch it being handed out to those who claim incessantly, with no contributions being made …

C. M.

I am probably wrong, my assumptions lazy and hurtful. Those who people these houses may well be tolerant and liberal; things have changed since 1938 and 1993 (and what an angry, scapegoating time the latter was, when you think back. I can remember, as the son of a single-parent family, being made to feel second-class.) Yet whether I like it or not, it is an England that existed and probably still does in some form and from behind the primroses of areas like this one. As such it is discernible and valid and worth writing of here. I do not have to like all the Englands and should stop trying to do so. But what I like in Watford are the people of the High Street, the pigeon ladies and the psychics and the good-time Saturday-night kids. They are a lively England, rushing with passion. I leave them now and head for starry London town.

Chapter Six

Leyton

In the dead, dead station in the dead of night I board the train for London. N-n-n-n-n-n-night train/stopping off at/Carlisle. The inside of my carriage, the one containing the cheap seats, the equivalent of the *Titanic*'s lowest cabins, has a golden hue. It is the nocturnal cheddar yellow of a children's moon, the colour accompanying Jesus on a tacky illustration at a souvenir shop in Knock or Lourdes. I take my reclining seat and try to tune out the white noise of an American lady in sunglasses chomping on a Walker's Grab Bag.

It is hot in the golden carriage. Stifling. My dreams get more disturbing each time I wake from half-sleep and then roll back to slumber. In one, Graham Taylor is teaching me how to wrap text on a spreadsheet. Senses are dumbed down, but the mind heightened. I can't be entirely sure if I am awake, asleep or even alive. Aside from the heat and the crunching American (a *Twin Peaks* gargoyle likely to eat my head, I decide), the carriage's constituent parts and geography add to my mind's crisis. As I am on the last-but-one row of seating, when I turn around the entire carriage seems to stare at me, even with eyes closed and drooling mouths open. Many are wearing eye-masks, but in such a sallow light they appear as giant bumblebees. The seats, curtains and walls are a mix of light purple, medium purple and dark purple. On the wall ahead of me is a disused flat-screen television. This will obviously come to life when everyone else is sleeping, speak to me and then pull me inside it.

As the conductor checks my ticket I ask whether the heating can be turned down a little. 'You'd only be cold, son,' he replies. I walk up the carriage with the aim of tutting at buffet car prices. Unfortunately, I learn, someone with my type of ticket cannot go beyond the 'vestibule area'. I stare through the window at four people having a rare old time. I am jealous not of their whisky and wine, but of the idea that they may have air conditioning. I retreat from the Advance Purchase Berlin Wall, pondering whether the class divide is a better metaphor.

The train hulks, moans and stops dead. In the silence many shades of snore can be heard. Staff run around, as much as you can in a train aisle. A female employee with spectacular nails rushes behind a closed door. Two male colleagues follow. I drift off, believing myself to be a character in *Carry on Sleepertrain*.

Shortly before 1 a.m. the train violently shudders at the very thought of Carlisle and shakes me awake. For some reason I wave at Carlisle station's nightwatchman, who northern nods back, a little perturbed. Try being on here, mate. An hour later and I am still awake on a cloying, baking sleeper train. I am rattled and berserk. Tomorrow is the first Easter since my daughter arrived and I am going to watch Leyton Orient. *I'm not really here*, I think, *I'm not really here*.

As I rest my head on a train door window a voice asks, 'You OK there, sunshine? Can't sleep either?' Helen is a Zimbabwean in her seventies. She has a walking stick, which she occasionally hoists as a rifle to emphasise her point. She loves cricket and the stick is raised often when on this topic, even becoming a bat for the re-creation of an Andy Flower six. She lifts my dark, homesick spirits immensely; her wicked cackle a surprisingly hypnotic night lullaby. Suddenly, the carriage door slides open and a skeletal old woman appears wearing a scowl that would make a tiger cry. 'Do

... you ... *mind?* I bought a reclining seat and all I can hear is *you two*. Now will you *please* be quiet.' Though we savour the precision (not just any old seat ...), Helen and I have been bowled out. We tiptoe back to our seats giggling in silence.

A form of sleep takes me as far as the bourbon biscuits of Watford Junction where, given how discombobulated and timeless I am, I picture another version of me watching a lady feeding the pigeons. We slurp into London Euston and the train howls painfully to a halt at 7 a.m. Helen and me catch one another's eye and chart the progress of our capturer as she walks by the window on the platform. 'What a bat,' says Helen, 'Let's wave', and we do. 'May I never be a bat. Kill me if I am.'

Euston is a spoil tip of concrete and communist pillars. I love it. Everything is straight, even, smooth and grey. It is exactly what I need after a beguiling night on the multi-coloured sleeper train. There is real air here too, and my face retracts several shades of red. Things, I think, are getting better; then I thwack my knee on a shelf in WHSmith.

Like most walking northern stereotypes I over employ the 'loves' in response to cold London customer service. Among sour faces in a chain cafe I watch people flock home to the shires from whence they came, for Easter. England spends so much of its time flowing into London and couriering all resources there, yet so many Londoners strain to get away when it matters.

In the cold sun I walk towards St Pancras and fail to resist its unobtainable beauty. The station – and doesn't that word undersell it – is almost completely empty. I feel that once more I am dreaming. Light drops in and shines the heads of the couple embracing in giant sculpture. It pours through the centres of five giant brass Olympic rings suspended from the roof. In my ragged mental state it is almost too much for me, this beauty a terrible beauty.

London is the quietest I have ever seen it, yet where this silence would turn other places beige it animates England's capital. There is so much more time and space to inhale the nooks and crannies of its buildings, to let your mind conjure and be enraptured. Like many people, I have in the past employed the sentence 'I 'ate bloody London.' This morning I disagree with this, because London without people in it is a city of fairy tales. There are no traffic jams in *Peter Pan*.

In Andrew's Cafe on Gray's Inn Road pop goes the radio and hunter-gatherer men tap along. 'Two bacon rolls, darlin', one with brown, one with red.' 'Hash brown roll please, sweet'eart. And a sausage one for 'er.' A Kurdish waitress, exquisite like St Pancras, brings me a full English. Where dead London streets refreshed the mind, this fuels the rest of me. I am ready for my journey to the Orient, or so I think.

On a Tube carriage lightly sprinkled with tourists a pinstripe-suited gay couple read a newspaper together. They laugh at the same jokes in a loved-up way. As they reach the end of the newspaper one half of the pair looks away and rolls his eyes in a way that seems to say 'you and your bloody football.' After a lengthy spell of turbulence beneath the streets of London I step off the train at Stratford. I aim to begin my Oriental walk with a viewing of the Olympic Park, neighbour to Leyton. Stratford station belches me out into the glossy metal world of the Westfield Shopping Centre. A good rule in life is never to trust a place whose floor you could eat your dinner from. Floors like Westfield's are so hygienically sparkly that they become like ice reflecting a staid, lifeless world. In places like Westfield, joy must be taken where possible. For that reason I snort objectionably when I see Nosher's, and guffaw immaturely when I read a sign that invites me to 'Enjoy a Nosher's Experience'. The vivacious life of language and dialect and smut cannot be conquered by sheeny shopping centres.

I ask a South African woman for directions to the Olympic village. 'Well, you have to leave here!' she snarls, scoffing, as if I thought javelin events would take place in Waitrose, discus in Boots. I then ask a staff member at Stratford International station the same question. 'Dunno, fella.' 'But isn't this the station for the Olympics?' 'Dunno, fella. I just work in the station.' We are I realise, standing beneath a giant directions sign that reads 'Olympic Park'.

I turn and survey the Olympic skyline. First there is a fifteen-foot-high mesh fence that stretches into the long-distance, then a marquee island shanty town where those allowed through the mesh will pay high prices for sustenance. Beyond the gated community and as at Middlesbrough's Riverside is a gigantic Anish Kapoor sculpture, this one like an upright coiled serpent. Finally, there is the Olympic Stadium itself, a silver bowl clasped by white stanchions. I am at once gladdened to be near England's newest stadium yet appalled at how removed it is from its community. There are literal barriers here – it is the antithesis of a town's team building their ground among redbrick terraces. Even when the Riverside was springing up from dockyards we visited nearly every week; we could smell the wet cement. No one is excitedly watching outside Westfield. The only watching being done is by a team of G4S security guards, prowling like uniformed kerb crawlers in a patrol jeep. Above, a helicopter loudly circles in the velvet-blue sky. For a place soon to be at the centre of the world it is incredibly lonely. I think they should bus in the Watford pigeon lady to colour the walls.

I tramp onwards, the Olympic fence always at my arm's length. In places further on it has an extra, electrified tier. A side road hosts the Olympic Park Vehicle Screening Plaza, an immense linguistic mixture of security procedure and glamour. I come to a viewing platform set back enough for the whole Olympic Stadium to be consumed. A shoal of French schoolchildren swing from fences and look bemused at a poetry installation. This shack brings much-needed context and reminds the viewer that London was not born yesterday. A poem by Lemn Sissay salutes the striking Victorian match girls of the nearby former Bryant & May factory:

> In tidal shifts East London Lampades made
> Millions of matches that lit candles for the well-to-do
> And the ne'er-do-well to do alike. Strike.

Sissay's words bring atmosphere and make sport feel a bit trifling. When the Games begin, army snipers will be sited on top of the Bryant & May building. I continue along a raised track, the stadium to my right, a warm-up track to my left. A man in sunglasses and what can only be described as a purple leotard rollerblades by. I say 'knobhead' a little too loudly.

An hour later, I am still walking. London looks so much smaller on a map. At first the canal I keep stumbling by seems cute, its colour chocolate. Now it looks like sewage. It is I realise, the Lea Navigational Canal. If I fall in, I may end up back in Luton. An information board tells me I am close to the building where once Matchbox cars were made. Why was everything *once* something in England, I wonder yet again? Why is it nothing *now*, nothing but posh flats or Tesco Metros?

The board designates the happy fact that I have arrived at my target destination: Hackney Marshes. Hackney Marshes was a phrase, an abstract concept for those of us who grew up in

Elsewhere England. It was often used by pundits ('You won't see defending worse than that on Hackney Marshes') to signify the game at its rawest grade. Players had, very often, 'started off at Hackney Marshes and then come through the ranks'. In my youth, I pictured a giant football factory with a thousand stars in stripes or hoops passing and hoofing. The 'marshes' element meant that these many players were fighting for the ball, and for the attention of watching scouts, in a deep green bog. It was mystical and brilliant. Even on a dead day I find that in reality, it is exactly that.

It is mystical because when I imagine the goals gone by here I am awestruck. It is brilliant because of how it looks. Even to describe in basic terms what Hackney Marshes is portrays its majesty: it is a whopping field with eighty-eight football pitches. The white markings of pitches stretch to what seems like the other side of earth, their goalposts like toothpicks. The grass is green like the inside of a lime, with stud mark acne and goal area bald patches adding theatre. On each goal frame are the sticky tape remnants of a thousand nets hung. Today the pitches are piercingly silent. When Sunday comes they shall ring to the barks and hollers of kickers and dreamers. This is an open-air temple.

I turn and watch a large dog nuzzle a plastic football down the left-wing area of pitch S16. He, his owner and me have this netherworld to ourselves. London in space again. Beyond the trees that enclose the Marshes in one direction can be seen the City skyline of Gherkin and wheel. In the other is Leyton, The Orient. I emerge out of the forest and into the frying pans of Lea Bridge Road. This takeaway-decorated stretch is just about the top boundary of Leyton, until 1965 an independent Borough, and before that an Essex town. Leyton is enriched by the bordering Hackney Marshes woodland that I have just walked through, and a collection of similar green spaces. Less enriching is the shabby state of Lea Bridge Road; though it does buzz along, paved golden by the many different lives lived here. It helps that all of the shops, takeaways and otherwise, are independent, albeit ramshackle rather than chic. In ten minutes I pass Baps and Bloomers (snigger), Küçükyapalak, Polski Sklep Zosia, Mr Gr8, Kozn Continental Foods, the Karabacak Social Club, Percy Ingle Bakers, Nigeria's Cargo Force and the Indigent Muslim Trust. No matter how long I stare at this last one it still appears to read the 'Indignant Muslim Trust', possibly because I want it to – I like the idea of an irritable charitable organisation: 'Oh, have your bloody grant then, I don't care.' The Lagos Island Restaurant – a not entirely successfully disguised house with a sign on it – offers 'Buffet!! Buffet!! Buffet!!' People talk on corners and it seems as if they are mixing here, if not directly then at least in buying things from one another, and sharing all-you-can-eat Buffets!! I wonder if they know that here once stood Mr Schubert's German bakery, one of many in Leyton stoned during the First World War. Lea Bridge Road also houses the area's other football club, Leyton FC, born in 1868 but 'resting' since a series of events – not least the imprisoning of its fraudulent chairman – pushed them into oblivion.

The call to prayer fuzzily sounds and crisply clad men speed-walk to the Jamia Masjid Ghosia mosque. There are smiling stragglers, as at Luton. Outside, the loudspeaker atop a maroon 4x4 vehicle competes, its message demanding votes in the Greater London Authority elections for the vehicle's passenger. After my hushed morning the din startles me, woozy and teetering on the brink of a return to deliriousness. Was it really today I waved at a man in Carlisle and talked about Zimbabwe?

The refined poise of the Bakers' Almshouses soothes me. These neatly adjoined cottages surround a heart-shaped lawn. They were built for destitute or diseased bakers in the 1850s. Local comedian and writer Meera Syal opined that: 'Not even snowfall could make Leyton look lovely.' This collection of buildings begs otherwise, though they are, admittedly, in the minority.

What happened in Leyton is a story of social class. Cast in a narrative familiar to so much of England, the town was made by the railways, though to a different pattern from elsewhere. Before tracks and platforms it was rural, a provincial settlement of mansions for the richly retired and aristocratic. *White's Directory* of 1863 called it: 'A large and handsome village, with many neat houses embowered in trees.' Shortly afterwards, steam arrived. City merchants identified Leyton as a dormitory town. The wealthier long-term residents began to move out to the country, in search of what they had first found in Leyton. As the railways spread further and fares became affordable, on their land grew terraced housing for working-class Londoners. From Leyton, they could travel to the docks and domestic servitude without having to face the rotten existence of slum dwelling. The railways, in opposition to elsewhere, did not bring people to work in Leyton, for there was little industry. Instead, the town provided a base away from the hoot of the factory whistle. Between 1861 and 1901, Leyton's population swelled from 4,800 to 98,900. The masses had blown in, and they had built a pie and mash shop that specialised in live eels. Earlier middle-class arrivals reacted by following their predecessors out to the sticks and Home County lives. Later, a similar trend saw many East Enders of old migrate to Essex, chasing after the county their town was no longer part of, to be replaced by those I see before me today. Now, scarves and voices of The Orient can often be seen and heard in Essex, and when rumours surface of club plans to move stadium – the county, not London, is the mooted destination.

Tiny gardens nudge the pavement in the squeezed terraced houses that remain. There are thousands of them, their host streets cambering off lengthy Lea Bridge and High Roads. In one of the houses on one of these streets was born 'the imperishable boy' soldier, Jack Cornwell. Cornwell was fifteen years old when he joined the British Navy, in 1915. A photograph taken at the time shows what you want it to: the hero, a determined, serious young man; the teenager, yet to shave, stroppy shoulders, fear masked by folded arms. What we are assured of now is that no boy aged fifteen should be sent to war.

The same war that took Cornwell took Orient men too – forty-one players and staff – the largest contingent of any club – served in the Footballers' Battalion of the Middlesex Regiment. Leyton Orient were consumed by the conflict at home and away: an anti-aircraft gun kept watch from the terraces of their Spion Kop; at war, three of their players died.

George Scott came from the coal pits of Durham and died in the cesspits of the Somme. A versatile forward loved for his bandy legs, he was in the footballing form of his life when that bullet struck Archduke Franz Ferdinand. He knew the French, he knew France; he had played for London against Paris not long before. Then there were his pals, Richard McFadden and William Jonas, teammates, bestmates, deathmates. Jonas had the looks, McFadden the brains. Jonas had the girls, McFadden the goals. So many love-letters went to the former that he had to place an advert in the Orient programme demanding they stop. So many times did the latter score, big clubs, even Middlesbrough, fluttered their eyelashes at him. On a forever Orient corner of Flanders Fields, Jonas, another County Durham lad, and McFadden, from Cambuslang, sat together, shaking in the trenches. An Orient programme clipping from 1916 tells you what happened next:

On the morning of the 27 July 1916, the two of them were trapped in a trench near the front. Jonas turned to McFadden, shook hands with him and said, 'Goodbye Mac, best of luck and regards to the lads at Orient.' Before he could reply, Jonas was up and over.

No sooner had he jumped out of the trench, he was killed. On 24 October 1916, McFadden, his partner on the field and in battle, was also killed in action.

I think back to Luton, where they burnt the town hall down, and I understand the anger of those who nowadays are referred to as 'normal people', those who struck the matches and chucked on the petrol. A Leyton boy dies at sea, and his tragedy becomes not a metaphor for the futility of war, but a jingoistic jamboree. Star Orient players are sent to their pointless death. All's fair in sport and war, and they *did* get a telegraph from King George ('Good luck to Orient FC, no football club has paid a greater price to patriotism'). It is a wonder town halls still stand, here and everywhere. I ponder whether similar events today would reap a Leyton or a Luton. Reverence and rebellion, those two strands of war memorial England, again come to mind. Just as England seems ready to admit mistakes and march against war in great numbers, military muscles are flexed and to question whether the meaning of Poppy Day has been lost is to kick someone's granddad in the balls. In an England of flux the fighting past is a surety.

When war took Scott, Jonas and McFadden, their club was just under thirty years old. Its origins were familiar – men of cork and willow desperately seeking winter entertainment. Fellow members of the Eagle Cricket Club had shoehorned into captain Pomp Haines' house in the 1880s. One of them, Jack Dearing, suggested the name Clapton Orient. 'Clapton' came from the area west of Leyton in which their team would play, 'Orient' from Dearing's employers, the Orient Steam Navigation Company. Eagle members agreed to the 'Orient' part of the name as it would reflect their origins in the East End of London, and add an exotic mystique. 'Clapton', a label courting undesirable connections, was voted down and Orient FC came into being. At the turn of the century Dearing, a key player and influence, told a club meeting: 'With Clapton now being considered a good district socially, the name would give the club more respectability'. They became Clapton Orient, and moved to Millfields Road, a 40,000 capacity ground nestled next to Hackney Marshes.

Early days were spent in the London League, home to Thames Ironworks (later West Ham United), Millwall Athletic and Queens Park Rangers. As Sheffield's professionalism annexed the south, Orient took the plunge to pay workers for their labour in 1903. Propelled by the schmoozing and influencing of Leyton bigwig Horatio Bottomley, the Os were granted league status two years later. They finished bottom and sent in the cavalry, supporter and army Captain Henry Wells-Holland, to plead for their survival. 'I beg you to extend to us the benefit of the First Offenders Act,' Wells-Holland petitioned, 'after all, it has been our first year in the league. We will do infinitely better this forthcoming season.' It worked, just, and the Os stayed in the league by one vote. Their history was to become pockmarked with such near misses and wiped brows. Wells-Holland's promises were not completely hollow. That 26,000 people saw them defeat Arsenal a few years on from his statement says that much.

Funds have forever been scarce at Orient. Their geography is a killer: Spurs to the left of them, West Ham to the right, they are wafer-thin ham between chunky rustic bread. Early on they rented out Millfields Road for boxing and baseball. In 1908 3,500 people watched the British Baseball Cup final there. Nachos and flat caps. Their surprisingly strong royal links have helped in the form of donations. In 1921 the Prince of Wales took in an Orient match against Notts County, becoming the first royal to attend football. He sat beside Orient director and Labour top brass Herbert Morrison, who I hope lectured him on the offside law and the advance of democratic socialism. Football had the power to not only level a royal, but to make him feel inferior – many in the crowd laughed as he craned his neck to converse with Notts keeper Albert Iremonger, six foot-six of pure Nottinghamshire breeding. However, one was obviously impressed; the Prince's brother George, future king, came for a look a year on. When later Orient had slid into their default position of dire finances, George sent a healthy donation that helped save the day.

Whatever fate befell Orient, they littered the game with characters and were often witness to some of football's key events or hosts to its greatest sons. There was Dave 'Buck' Brennan, a swashbuckling half-back known across the land for wearing a skull-cap during matches and Ike van den Eynden, a Belgian signed in 1913 and barracked by Hull City fans as 'slant eyes' in an early example of racial, and racially confused, chanting. When the great Herbert Chapman's damned Leeds City visited, Orient haggled the kick-off time and scored three goals in a pitch-black second half. Chapman seethed. Newcastle wonder-boy Hughie Gallacher was marked out of an FA Cup tie in the year of the General Strike, more hurt piled on the Geordies. A crowd of 31,400 saw Orient that day, perhaps their greatest. And what of Ted Crawford, Orient's gruff but incisive centre-forward? In 1935-36 he scored twenty-three, beating the fallen McFadden's record for a season. Later Crawford revealed he had played for six years with a broken

ankle, sometimes drunk. He was not alone. An Orient legend tells
of the team turning up at Waterloo station for a game at Christmas
time. All were already soused, so when the manager greeted them
with a barrel of beer for the journey things moved from merry to
boisterous. If only they had been on my sleeper train.

During Crawford's spell, Orient moved to Brisbane Road.
Their existence continued to be varied with light patches. It started
off well enough when chairman Harry Zussman, 'a short, plump,
ever-effusive shoe manufacturer, bespectacled under a homburg
hat' according to Brian Glanville, appointed Alec Stock as gaffer.
Stock was player-manager of Yeovil when in 1949 they slayed the
Mackems in the FA Cup, and joined Orient shortly afterwards.
Slow improvement saw FA Cup runs and in 1956 the Division
Three South title, a rare accolade for a team that avoided trophies
as if touching them resulted in gout. Arsenal called for Stock
before that pot was won, though he lasted only fifty-three days as
assistant manager there. On returning to Brisbane Road he came
over all *It's A Wonderful Life*, declaring:

> Hard as I tried, I could never stop thinking of Orient. My mind
> said Arsenal, my heart Os. I realised that friendship to me is
> more important, much more valuable than all the progress and
> prestige I might have had at Highbury.

While Stock was away Orient moved to sign Tommy Johnston, a
pulsating forward who played each game with one arm bandaged,
the spoils of a mining accident. Johnston's goals were rocket fuel
to Orient. Until he reached East London, he had tramped his
battered boots from the coal mining village leagues of
Aberdeenshire to Kilmarnock, Darlington, Oldham, Norwich and
Newport. In Orient he found a home. Johnston's winner snared

that title for the club in 1956, and then he scored twenty-seven the following season and thirty-five in thirty-two games in 1957-58. When Saint Brian of Ayresome brought his Boro boys to Brisbane in October 1959, the Scot shined a light in his eyes. The miner's rock blunted the steelman's scissors. Orient won 5-0. He and Stock had made creaking little Orient a permanent instalment in Division Two. Stock left in 1959 for AS Roma, eternally Orient in the Eternal City. Later, he would light up Luton, such do the clubs of England interlink on their merry ways. Johnston departed in 1961, returning to his vagrant ways before establishing a betting shop beneath bright lights on the Lancashire Riviera. Both had contrived to plant Orient firmly in the minds of their supposed betters. Outside respect meant self-respect, which bred ambition. Somehow, Orient climbed to Division One and played there for a season, 1962-63. While there they cudgelled West Ham, Manchester United and Everton. On the final day Bobby Charlton socked in a special and Orient were relegated. Within four seasons they lingered in Division Three with debts of £100,000.

Buckets for survival were shaken then as they would be again throughout the 1980s. In our touchstone season of 1981-82 Orient slipped back into Division Three after a decade in Two. They soon dropped another tier, and nearly collapsed altogether. 'Os Shocker, Nearly Went Bust!' ran the local news headline in August 1986. Liquidation was indeed perilously close. Saviour came from a combination of copper coins and the cash of board member Tony Wood, a coffee-merchant based in Rwanda. A few years on, conflict once again stalked Orient when the Rwandan civil war left Wood almost penniless. Now chairman he offered to sell *Orient for a Fiver*, as a Channel Four documentary title put it.

I was thirteen when *Orient for a Fiver* was screened. I still have the homemade tape. It was, as far as I was concerned, the greatest bit of television ever screened. Football clubs then seemed more inaccessible and mysterious. Seeing inside a manager's office was as exciting to thirteen-year-old me as finding a black bin bag of porn magazines in the local woods was to fifteen-year-old me. Players were utterly remote. Where did they live, we wondered, what did they talk about? Twitter has since killed that mystery for the younger generation and even killed the memory of what I felt in 1995; if footballers were as inane then as they seem in 140 characters now, I was wasting my wonder.

The star of *Orient for a Fiver* is manager John Sitton, a jug-eared ex-Orient captain who is more Cockney than Harry Redknapp marinated in jellied eels. All of the best scenes take place during his generously expletive, howled team talks. For months after it aired a few of us at school would regularly be caught by teachers acting out scenes. Shakespeare would have approved of our, 'You've had two good games and you think you're fucking Bertie Big Bollocks and you'll play how you like' routine, Pinter our 'You, you little cunt, when I tell you to do something, and you, you fucking big cunt, when I tell you to do something, you do it.' Our teachers did not. Wood, forever in the wings looking like a depressed owl, gets his fiver in the end. Step in Barry Hearn, still Orient chairman today. Grinning my tired grin over thoughts of Sitton scenes, I continue along Leyton High Road towards his club.

I skirt by the end of Wesley Road under a clickety-clack railway bridge. On that street was born Harry Beck, designer of an image that clothes a thousand London walls: the Underground map. Soon I pass a muscular cricket pavilion, which looks like an undisguised Transformer robot, but with Tudor beams and white walls. Essex played games here until the age of punk. Then, typically, they chased the county boundary to Chelmsford. The

High Road winds on and much feeling disappears from my feet. I pause to rest and read a reliably entertaining collection of window adverts. 'Double room to let – £90 a week for 2 Gills'. It seems an expensive way to store fish parts, or is it the desperate work of a man with a fetish for Gillingham fans? Laughter pours from the Mogadishu Restaurant, though not from the Hollywood Smile Dental Lab close by.

At long last I catch sight of red-backed people drifting into bars and nodding at fortnightly friends. The chimney-stacked and bay-windowed houses that lead to Brisbane Road are on the kind of tight terraced streets that should always lead to a football ground. Tannoy tidings are our call to prayer. Despite the horror of the journey, I still feel the clear heaven of a new ground, and I still feel that this, football, is where I should be on a Saturday. It takes more than an existential crisis to stop me needing this game of ours. The outside of Brisbane Road – renamed the Matchroom Stadium after a sponsorship deal, but let's ignore that – is overwhelmingly grey, with red lettering smeared around, lipstick on a pig. The grey is not completely depressing, just functional like a PFI hospital. Bizarrely, there is an NHS chemist's in the main stand. Similarly as strange are the four apartment blocks huddled behind each corner flag. 'Are you a burglar then, mate?' asks a steward as I photograph one of the structures. Fans of Orient and fans of Notts County happily mix outside the supporters' bar. One man has his baby strapped in front of him: a pint in one hand, its bottle in another.

A turnstile takes me behind the goal into the Tommy Johnston Stand. 'Caution. Beware of stray footballs' reads a sign where perhaps a 'welcome' one might be more usual. There is reason for this. As if recreating the quirks and terrible sightlines of an old stand, this relatively new stand has a dry moat at its foot.

Walking at the front of the stand leaves the supporter unsighted. Several times in the first half I think of hiding from the match in there.

To our left is a harebrained concoction of a grandstand too. It is a completed work, unlike Watford's, but I am not sure that is a good thing. Perhaps it is better to look at a classical but rotting canvas than a modern and complete one. A breezeblock wall leads to twenty or so rows of seating, followed in turn by three storeys of office block window slits. At the very top is an open balcony, The Gallery, where today one can watch the game for £40. The ground is saved by its individuality and by the old stand, which remains to my right. From beneath its rickety gable County fans sing in rounds. Some of their number are watching from the balcony of a corner flat, beer cans in hand. Is this the Watford dream, realised?

The goalnets sag perfectly, ridged but not too organised, and the match kicks off at a determined pace. County's No. 6, a midfielder with the figure of the Honeymonster and the brawn of the Hulk, attracts shin-kicks, but is insurmountable. Up front, their No. 40 is masterly on the ball, the best player on the park, though running seems beyond his ken. A strong side-to-side wind quickly stuns cold Orient's tactic of looping passes forward, while County keep things low and brisk. The away side are looking up at the stars while Orient flirt with the gutter, and it shows.

Twenty minutes into the match a bald gentleman in a long coat and a Crystal Palace scarf files into a nearby seat. I am jealous yet again of the nomadic potential of a London football fan. I imagine Saturday mornings studying the endless possibilities of the fixture list and Saturday afternoons in far-flung crannies of Harry Beck's map. A trumpeter seems to be playing the theme tune to *EastEnders*, as if to stomp on my fantasy.

Orient muster a couple of corners and rouse those around me. 'Come on, you Os'. Each corner is pitched high, hung on a coat stand for someone to head. No one does, and the game reclines to familiar County possession. The man in front of me slopes back into his seat, knocking my knees with his back. He turns around. 'Sorry, sir, I am proper pickled.' For a time I appreciate his Dickens the Movie use of English and his advanced state of inebriation. That time ends when he decides I need to hear more from him. 'Where you from? What you doing with that pen? What you writing?' Why is it that people feel it permissible to ask that question? They would never approach someone tapping a text message and say ''ere, who's that you texting? Cor, that's a lot of kisses.' Behind me a couple argue, firstly about the route of a bike ride they once went on and secondly about the definitions of mortgage types. I am the filling in a sandwich of irritating babble.

A through ball dies, but Orient's goalkeeper and centre-back chase it and crash into one another. There follows a top-notch session of fingers in faces, then a calming word from their skipper. 'Russell Slade's red and white army' slowly bays a hoarse voice from the back of the stand. That particular war cry always requires such a throaty, guttural start-up, wherever you are. It needs the spluttering ignition of a dear old car to make it bang. When it fires into action the sound can enmesh the pitch. Here it is stunted dead as Orient, apropos of nothing, forget who they are and play like kings of the earth. There are dropped shoulders, dummies and snapshots. I particularly like their No. 8, a centre-midfielder. He awakens to become the pulse of all this. Best of all, he is wearing ankle strappings, as I imagine lower-division midfielders always do. That such stereotypes hold helps me belong to this game. 'Shirt from Mothercare. You got your shirt from Mothercare' sings the pickled one, but Orient press on like an urgent iron.

Half-time interrupts. An incandescent segment has ended without a goal. Underneath the seats is a bar that bristles with noise. 'No Children Served in This Bar' reads a sign, cannibalism having been a breach of committee rules for some years. I stand with my pint, looking at pictures of old Orient and listening to an American and a Canadian discuss away travel in North America, and the drawn-out half-times of US sport.

I move seat in the second half and sit behind two smiling men in turbans. The temperature falls and the noise rises. Shouting is thermal. A County substitute is called on. Some years ago he spent time in prison for causing death by dangerous driving. 'Murderer' and 'Scum' bay people around me. The County fans worship him as a hero. Morals are both heightened and forgotten at football. He can do little of note as Orient find rhythm once more. Notts become brutish, as if trying to cramp the style that the home side have stolen from them. An elbow flies into a home face. Orient's physio sprints on, a rucksack replacing the traditional bag. As usual, fans start to blame the referee for all ills. And as usual, chiding him is as loud as they get.

There are no just deserts for Orient, in fact justice deserts. With a rare attack County smash a bar and pillage the rebound: 0-1. Their keeper jumps, delighted, fists in air, by an away end in a heavenly frenzy. They can smell promotion while the home fans whiff relegation. Then Orient equalise. I am surprised to find myself jumping, gleeful: 1-1. Except it isn't. The linesman's flag, that sick-bright harbinger of doom, is up.

County attack again and County score again: 0-2. Orient fans begin to shuffle out. One is on crutches, and he battering rams the moat wall as he exits. The turbaned men in front look at one another. 'You?' 'Yeah. You?' 'Yeah', and with that they bounce away into their evening. Punishing those foolish enough to remain, seven minutes of injury time are added. Another goal for County empties the ground almost completely. One man stays and launches into an extraordinarily detailed rant against a County player who is being treated on the goalline, holding up play. It is triumphantly sweary and forensically knowledgeable of the rules. A departing supporter wearing a brown North Face jacket hops up and down to try and be seen over the moat. 'Barry Hearn. BARRY HEARN. FACKING … DO SOMEFINK.'

The final whistle goes and my endless day weighs heavy. Tiredness. Long walks in the wilderness. More loneliness in places I had only ever imagined. In Asda by Leyton station I splash water all over my face and hair. I breathe heavily and attract frightened glances in the mirror. I want to go home. I need to hit the north.

Chapter Seven
Chester

A couple of weeks on and I have calmed down. I have, to quote a
nonsensically sensible Teesside phrase, 'had a word with myself'.
I am glaring too intensely at the magic eye; the image must come
to me. Manchester helps. As we shudder into Oxford Road station
I feel calmed by the cherry bricks and damp archways of this
poised city. I wait for the 11.53 to Llandudno and drawled voices
of Mancunia further soothe me. My train, its signage proficient in
English and Welsh, tiptoes above the city on Victorian stilts and
out past Old Trafford. We work up a speed into the Cheshire
countryside. The move from urban to earth is one from dark to
light, a dimmer switch turned. Wet stone gives way to blanket
fields of yellow rapeseed. Lambs gambol on small hills and snooze
in tiny valleys. They look like white mice climbing ladles in a
cutlery drawer. The north is putting on a show, redeeming me and
my journey.

We stop at Newton-le-Willows, the birthplace of Rick Astley
and once home to Pete Waterman. With such a devastating
heritage it is the musical version of 25 Cromwell Street, Gloucester.
Earlestown comes next. Wilf Mannion, the Boro golden boy
whose feet made the ball dance, the Mozart of football, managed
Earlestown FC in 1960. Prior to that appointment he had worked
on the production line at Vauxhall, Luton. Football, England: all
interlinked, all small.

A toddler stands on the table across from mine, lost in the
world rushing by his window. 'Preston', calls his mum, 'Preston,

we have to get off in a minute, love.' Given that we are in England's
north-west his name could well be sourced in the Brooklyn
Beckham vein. I sincerely hope he has a wee brother named
Skelmersdale. Behind them a slurring man phones home and
promises to give his child 'a love'. This sounds exceedingly sinister
until I remember that my Leeds-based relatives used such
phraseology, at which stage I downgrade it to 'plain weird'.
Outside the train, industry has been tossed on to the countryside
as if from the palm of a giant Spiderman. Above Runcorn is
Rocksavage Power Station, a retired Star Wars space station of
frames and flues, then the metal twists and towers of chemical
plants. There is beauty in land and toil, and beauty in the two
combined. The industry inhales the oxygen from the land. I
thereby twin the area with Teesside and order a ceremonial cup of
tea.

At Frodsham, hometown of Gary Barlow (what is it about this
route?), Chester supporters board in groups of four or five.
Blue-and-white striped shirts hang over the tops of denims like
butcher shop fly-screens. They sit and talk about days gone by
and days to come. This has been a champion season for them, and
the next promises more. Their calmness, their conversational
lulls, fit a stereotype I have long attached to the city of Chester
and its football club, and indeed other places like it. I cannot
imagine groups of men heading to the match in the north-east
being as tranquil as those before me. They don't even have cans.
Chester, I reflect not for the first time, is too posh, too *nice*, for
football.

Being a keeper of the well-worn faith that football was a
working-class release valve, I struggle with teams like Chester.
Ditto, among others, Cambridge, Chelsea, Cheltenham, Exeter
and Lincoln. In my world of simplicity and romance, clubs were

founded to give hatters, railwaymen and knitters a place to breathe and berate when Saturday came. Who went to watch Chester City, and what release did they provide? A break from the strain of manning a tea-room urn? Escape from the pressures of high-octane gift shop commerce?

My scepticism comes not only from the past. The football I watch, whether in Scotland or Middlesbrough, and that I have seen so far on my journey, remains a traditional, largely working-class game, or a low-wage one at least. It is not a bourgeois fad as for some at Arsenal or a middle-management daytrip as at Old Trafford. There is nothing middle-class about Kenilworth Road. In Middlesbrough's case, a compelling, widely applicable one, a fall from grace has stripped the club of floating, disposable-income fans and left those who would sell their child's Christmas to buy a season ticket. They are unlikely to be fund managers. Then in Scotland, a club like Cowdenbeath is the only remaining unifier for an ex-mining community. Of the six months in my season so far, little has hinted at the Sky-ed up to the eyeballs environs of the Premier League.

This is not to say that my football is solely watched by farmhands and call centre workers, but it is closer to being their game than it is to being the preserve of the hobbying middle-class. Sky and the Hornbyfication of football never really happened at their clubs, and if it did it was fleeting. *They* endure. For the crowds at Brammall Lane and Vicarage Road, it remains an escape, a necessity and a vent, even if that spills over into wild anger at referees. There is the question of age too. So many of the supporters I have seen this season, and indeed at Middlesbrough and in Scotland, are retired. They are retired not in a 'place in France, fly home for a game every now and again' way. They are retired as working-class pensioners who have always gone to the match and always will. This is not the overwhelming state of things, but it *is* what I see. It is also the football I prefer and the one which most resembles the early steam-valve game I lose hours dreaming of. I find it impossible to imagine Chester belonging to it.

My prejudice towards Chester is not helped by the station plaque that greets the arriving traveller. It reads: 'Opened by Gyles Brandreth MP'. The station has the particular elegance of an old Sicilian fish-market and opens into a fine wide street pinned at each corner by grand station hotels. A taxi, for I am feeling flush, flows through the veins of the alluring city centre towards my bed and breakfast. Its driver is more like a host, me a welcome guest in his car. He is enormously pleased that I am on my way to watch Chester FC. 'It's so special now. The town realised what we might lose and now it's a community club.' In the rear-view mirror I watch this proud Cestrian's eyes cloud over wistfully as he tells me of recently taking his five-year-old son to a match: 'It's all dads and lads and mams and lasses now.' Inside my stereotypes of Chester, my crass class analysis of football dies a little at this point. I am not all that bothered, as I like the sound of this.

The driver drops me at the B&B, his wheels crackling on its pebbles as he reverses and leaves. My chamber for the evening is situated in a grand Victorian mansion, all climbing ivy and things I dare not touch. I am welcomed cordially but remotely – think a senior funeral director hosting a family fun day. The proprietor is smartly dressed in shirt and tie (and trousers. Plus shoes, and presumably underwear), and wears sleeve garters. I fail to recall if I have ever seen anyone in real life wearing these before. It is like talking to a museum exhibit. He phones another taxi for me, directing that it should take me to 'The Football Match'.

Another sunny driver speeds me over the river and beyond a colossal racecourse towards The Football Match. He tells me about 'Scouse Day' at the races, when Liverpool decamps to Chester and, supposedly, all cabbies receive a message warning them to look out for forged notes. We trawl through an industrial estate that is more of an industrial society and pull up outside one of the units, which turns out to be the Deva Stadium. From this distance it looks more like the warehouse attached to a kitchen wholesaler: corrugated metal, scaffolding spokes and windowless stretches of breeze-blocks. As I approach the Deva I see that it has devolved its beating heart to the thousands who flutter outside its shell.

Excitement, and ownership of that excitement, is tangible as I circle the ground. It is tangible in the perma-grins that seem to be held up by puppet strings and in the way people are slowly moving between each other to have the same conversations over and over. You can hear their ownership in the words they use. There is somehow more 'double-u' when they use the word 'we' to describe Chester FC, more heart in 'us'. Some pause to look at a banner on the side of a stand that reads: 'Your City. Your Community. Your Club.'

The Blues Bar is packed, its low ceiling of plastered squares recycling the hubbub. If the BBC starts releasing sound effects records again, this track is called 'Merry Mediaeval Inn at New Year.' I order a pint of Champions' Ale, a specially produced local brew, and read the banner behind the bar: 'One Club. 2,000 Owners.' This bar is the happiest I have been in for a long time, football or not. When a rickety double-decker bus carrying away supporters chokes by, many wave and cheer by way of welcome. This contented club is a modern club. They have had to go to hell to find heaven. Much has happened, some of it a grotesque cabaret that speaks for football's recent days, days when the likes of Mr John or Elton are seldom seen.

Chester were formed in 1885, an amalgamation of Chester Rovers and Old King's Scholars. When I finally get around to reading about Chester rather than making assumptions, I smugly note the nicey-nice names of their former homes: it is impossible to picture a working-week-weary blacksmith exhaling his stresses at The Old Showground or Whipcord Lane or The Stadium.

What emerges as I read is a club that had currency in its community, and in return welcomed that community warmly. One example sticks in the mind: when Chester installed a public address system in the early 1930s, each game began with the announcement: 'Hello Spion Kop, Hello Albert', the latter a greeting to a long-serving supporter. Clubs like Chester are not the complete antithesis, it seems, of my own romanticising of football as a working-class kettle whistle. Both Chester and that romantic vision are rooted in communalism, the former of the city's people, the latter of the dock-workers or the steelmakers. Together they stress the ingenuity of football in bringing people together.

Chester spent their earliest days ambling around the Lancashire Combination and Cheshire County leagues. In 1931 they joined the Football League and up until the war were renowned for their luxurious passing game as 'the aristocrats of the northern section'. In that period Chester panelled Fulham 5-0 in the FA Cup, gubbed York City 12-0 and twice won the Welsh Cup. The Second World War, though, halted their momentum. Post-war, they strived for mediocrity and even suffered, in the 1960s, the affront of a takeover bid from the Duke of Westminster, who decreed that under his rule they would adopt family heraldic colours of gold and green.

The beguiling screws and kinks of football meant that soon after that indiscretion, Chester City slaughtered one of the greatest sides in Europe. Their 3-0 win against Leeds United came during a run to the semi-final of the League Cup in 1974-75. 'The better team won on the night,' said a humbled Billy Bremner afterwards, 'they were a different class to us.' In the quarter-final, Chester held Newcastle at St James' Park and lanced them back in their amphitheatre, goalkeeper Grenville Millington repelling Malcolm Macdonald at will. Magpie manager Joe Harvey spat his dummy deep into the froth of his schooner of Brown Ale. 'I don't rate them at all, not one bit. They are a kick-and-rush side with no outstanding players.' Before a semi-final slog with Villa, Chester manager Ken Roberts told his public, 'We are not dreaming of Wembley. We are planning for it.' A 2-2 at home, and they continued to plan. A 3-2 defeat at Villa Park, and the London hotel was cancelled. What a run! Over now, but with the consolation of promotion from Division Four, Chester's first ever elevation. That and the Debenhams Cup in 1977. In 1981-82 they fell back down, rock bottom.

Things went quiet for the two decades to follow. Then in 1999, the Grim Reaper called. The devil had a space for a football club in hell. The first man to try and fill that space was an American named Terry Smith. In 1999, Smith purchased Chester and promised her the world: First Division football inside three years, international signings and sell-outs at every home game. At the time, most Chester supporters were glad of the attention, happy to have had someone look their way. That is often a frailty in the relationship football fans have with their teams: if somebody who appears to have money talks up and buys our club, we ask no questions. When boss Kevin Ratcliffe resigned, Smith made himself one-fifth of a management team. They appointed 'zonal captains' – skippers for defence, midfield and forward line. To fiddle in football's Division Four basement Smith acquired players from Serbia, the USA, Canada and Trinidad. They and their bemused teammates were given seven-page game plans before each tussle with Torquay, each car crash with Carlisle. He even had them utter the Lord's Prayer in the dressing room. It would have been the last straw, had that not upped and left long ago.

In the final game of 1999, Smith's Chester played bottom-club Orient at home. Orient had not scored for nine hours. Result: Chester 1 Orient 5. In the final game of the season Chester played Peterborough. They had to win to stay up. Result: Chester 0 Peterborough 1. The Deva loyal went berserk, trying to drag their club from the chewing jaws of Beelzebub. Smith waved the red-horned one on, after the game bleating: 'I have no regrets about my time in charge, in fact I have achieved 10 of the 11 targets I set for the club when I took over.'

When slight success tickled Chester the following term, Smith claimed credit. He ascribed a run to the semi-final of the FA Trophy under new manager Graham Barrow to his scouting reports and 'design' of the quarter-final's winning goal. Towards the season's close, Smith sacked player-of-the-year Paul Beesley (apparently, during training ground set-piece rehearsals 'Beesley stood in the wrong place, ruining it for everybody') and banned the remaining squad from speaking to the press. He followed up by dismissing a long-serving and long-suffering club volunteer who had supported the club for life. Chester were again line dancing on the precipice, moving back and forth towards the underworld. Supporters arranged a funeral march, hauling coffins through town to the stadium, and club stewards resigned en masse. Their picket lines chiselled thousands off the gate, squeezing it to 700.

In sauntered a Scouse saviour named Stephen Vaughan. Smith's club became his. He would save them; he would turn hell to heaven. They should have checked his tenners were real. Vaughan was a boxing promoter whose ownership of Barrow FC had resulted in liquidation. When Chester were drawn against Barrow in the FA Cup, it transpired Vaughan still retained shares. He quickly transferred them to a local painter and decorator friend so that Chester's crashing out of the FA Cup at its qualifying stages for the first time since 1930 came with moral and legal impunity. Early in his reign Chester fell to the bottom of the Conference. England's own Mark Wright, he of straggly ginger mullet-lite, became manager and helped stave off hell. Vaughan cleared the club's debts and gave him money, money, money to splash. He also tried to buy Tranmere Rovers. Principled supporters who had hounded out Smith kept their questions to themselves while the team hopped out of hell and hovered beneath heaven's door – this, after all, is the football fan's way. In 2004, Wright's team made it back into the Football League, 6,000 Chester people attending their final game of the season. A scent of murk saw Wright resign during the summer break. Vaughan employed the tried-and-mistrusted first-person defence: 'The time for fans to worry is when Stephen Vaughan leaves this club.' Ian Rush, once of Chester, later of some others, became manager. In his first game, Rush crossed swords and swapped stories with Paul Gascoigne of Boston United. It rarely got better than Memory Lane, Rush lasting until the following April ('various events have gradually made it impossible for me to carry on').

Rolling up next was Keith Curle whose early mailbag included a winding-up order from the Inland Revenue. Vaughan had, he said, spent £4 million so far, but the taxman needed another £180,000. The owner responded by buying Widnes Vikings rugby league club, sacking Keith Curle and bringing back Mark Wright. The supporters had, by now, grown tired and found their voices. They could sniff hell on Vaughan's breath. When only 269 attended a pre-season friendly, he blocked all transfers and put Chester on the market for £5 million. Wright felt the chop in the traditional sacking month of April, and his successor Bobby Williamson lasted under a year. In the summer of 2007, Vaughan resigned as chairman and director shortly after forcing a pre-kick-off minute's silence for shot Liverpool underworld figure Colin Smith. Simon Davies became manager for a while, before the third return of Mark Wright ... right, this is getting confusing, isn't it. Think of it as being like the first book of the first testament: Ratcliffe begat Smith, and Smith begat Barrow, and Barrow begat Wright, and Wright begat Rush, and Rush begat Curle who begat Wright again, and Wright begat Williamson, and Williamson begat Davies and Davies begat Wright again ... and as for caretaker managers ... look, it was a mess.

In May 2009, ownership of Chester City passed to Stephen Vaughan Jr, their highly paid midfielder. They voluntarily entered administration, owing creditors £7 million. Wearily Cestrians greeted the devil once more. Remarkably, creditors agreed to accept the only bid submitted, one of £290,000 by a Stephen Vaughan company. They were admitted into the Conference with a 25-point deduction attached. In November, protesting fans invaded the pitch and forced a match to be abandoned. Chester entered 2010 at the Conference's foot, their tally of minus three points a horror story to those fans who dared to look at the league table. As a New Year's gift, HMRC submitted another winding-up order for £1 million due to them. On 6 February 2010, 460 people saw Chester City lose 1-2 at home to Ebbsfleet United. It was to be their last stop before hell.

The following week, the team bus driver refused to leave the car park – that car park in which I now watched the happy masses smiling – until his bill was paid. Chester could not pay their fare. Their match at Forest Green was called off. Soon afterwards Conference clubs voted to expel them and on 10 March 2010 in room 76 of the High Courts of Justice in London, Chester City were wound up. Proceedings lasting less than a minute ended 125 years of history. No one from the club was there to hear the death knell clang.

Back in Chester those that cared had said goodbye to their club long before that lonely moment in court. Purgatory had led to despair, but then plotting. Once hell was reached they could turn death into life in the form of a new club, by the fans for the fans. With help and solidarity springing thick and fast from other supporter-owned outfits – FC United, AFC Wimbledon, AFC Telford United – and their own tenacious dreaming, City Fans United formed Chester Football Club on 20 May 2010. Nearly 3,000 people saw the new club's first game, a 6-0 victory. By May 2011 Chester FC were champions of Evo-Stick Division One North; a year on, they are champions again and next season will be one more promotion away from the Conference. Hell is banished and they are knocking on heaven's door. To complete the *Scooby Doo*-meets-*Brookside* denouement, in 2011 Stephen Vaughan was sentenced to fifteen months in prison for assaulting a police officer.

I file out of the bar among elbows holding pints to chests and head towards my terrace for the afternoon. A lady in a cardigan places a leaflet about prostate cancer in my hand with the words, 'Don't worry love, it's free.' I pay a tenner to push the turnstile, then receive a free match programme and find a metal bar to lean on behind the goal. The sun winks above us. This is not just heaven; it is utopia realised. My neighbour, John, is a cheerful soul in his seventies and has the frayed glint of a club circuit comedian. 'Alright, kidda' he greets me, 'this is the life, eh?' He has a thick Chester accent, which is essentially a thin Scouse one.

After pleasantries we both silently watch the pre-match fanfare engulfing the pitch. As Chester are champions there is, obviously, a samba band thudding and chiming their way up and down the halfway line. I wonder when brass bands were usurped from this role and blame Middlesbrough. In 1995, when Boro signed Juninho, the Riverside rattled to the painful rhythms of steel drums and whistles on a fortnightly basis. Around them the players of Chester and Marine warm up. Their drills mostly consist of lashing balls over empty nets. Hurrah. The terrace we share is ten or twelve concrete rows high and speckled with sky-grey barriers. Everyone has their place, routine as ever an ingredient for the sense of belonging football propagates. Ideological and emotional belonging is complemented here by literal ownership; these supporters belong to Chester FC, and Chester FC belongs to these supporters. In an age when provincial philanthropists are beggared compared to overseas bidders, and of byzantine ownership structures and debt payments, it seems like an entirely logical future for my kind of football. It plays on the unique pull of a club on its people and its town, and acknowledges that such an entity never will be 'like any other business' as many submissively claim. By pitching itself at the opposite end to billionaire buy-outs this kind of club shows us that another world is possible. It reminds us of football's genius for leading the way. On a walkway at the foot of the terrace each new arrival stops every few paces to wave at a Saturday pal or idly gossip about 1-0s, 2-0s and 4-0s. 'I tell you what,' John leans across to me and says, 'I am loving this season, but roll on next year. I love what this club is now. Our club.'

On the tropical green turf in front of us the samba band has trudged off to audience indifference. Tough gig. 'We Will Rock You' sparks up, its bish-bosh drumbeat audibly causing irreparable damage to the intestines of the PA speakers. When it finishes the announcer either skips three tracks or plays the world's briefest medley until we reach David Bowie's 'Heroes', welded into 'The Final Countdown' as the players enter the fray. If we can't have the musical silence I crave then at least he has the decency to play such homely and often reassuringly hammy football ground staples. Routine, repetition; he knows the supporter all right. Besides, at one point he says wearily: 'One last time, ladies and gentlemen. I believe we're getting some new music next season.' Those around me awaken from their cosy chats and slowly chorus the anthem of the hour: 'Championies/Championies/are we are we are we.'

Things change from communal buoyancy to shared sadness in the blow of a whistle. We do not need the PA announcer to tell us that there is about to be a minute's silence; we recognise the familiar trudge forward of twenty-two players and the regimental crest formations they form around the centre-circle. John leans across to me again and whispers, 'This is for that babby, isn't it? That poor little 'un who died. Terrible.' Indeed, one of his club's youngest, a boy of seven, has died of heart failure while playing football. Twenty-two players place their arms behind their backs and a further whistle stuns the air numb. The world stops like it always does during the minute's silence of a football ground, and light slides away from the pitch as clouds cloak the sun. It is not often that so many people will be having the same thought. To look around and to watch a normally frantic place turned motionless is like watching the plundering of a killer whale, something that once swarmed with life and presence suddenly idle. We are all grateful when the whistle sounds a third time and it comes back to life.

The blue and white stripes of Chester tip-tap the game to a start. They are up against a Marine side clad in yellow, meaning proceedings resemble a match between Sheffield Wednesday and Brazil, which brings to mind the strange team combinations on the covers of birthday cards my grandma used to give me. Yeovil versus Australia was a favourite. 'Come on Ci-ty' sing those around me – City are dead, long live City. The two No. 6s among two teams in 1 to 11 shirts are dominant in the game's waking moments. Chester's is a centre-midfielder who manages to lord the middle of the pitch despite being as one-footed as a kipping flamingo, Marine's a defender large of chest and intent. The game at this level – effectively Division 7 – takes the same shape as that higher up the pyramid. Similar runs are made, forwards mosey around to shuggle free of their defenders, wingers beat men and fall over, and players that don't quite merit white boots wear them regardless. On the whole, both teams are friends with the ball, though it does not always like them. Difference comes from the pace of play (slower) and the shape of players (bigger-boned). The principle of a move or pass sometimes outweighs the collective or individual ability of its author, so that the most common refrain from the terraces is 'the idea was right, son.'

This is probably an unfair day to make such judgements as neither team has anything to play for. As Chester are up and Marine upper-mid table, it is perhaps like carrying out an Ofsted inspection on the day before summer holidays when everyone brings in a board game. Things have dropped towards the lackadaisical among the crowd too. It feels as though the football is obstructing the festivities. By way of revenge Chester's goalkeeper launches a frenzied attack on the balloons in his penalty area, popping half a dozen with his studs. It seems to stir the crowd. 'Come on!' shrieks a man behind me. 'Get behind the lads. We an't been bloody relegated. This is supposed to be a party. Are all your parties this shit?'

Chester put down the cocktail stick and turn up the music. From here, we cannot see all of the goal at the other end, so shots frequently look better and more likely to hit home than they probably are. This is all down to a pitch camber that feels reassuringly vintage, so rare now are such charming imperfections. It also cuts off the shins of those in the dugout, so that they look like Roman ghosts beneath modern street level, wearing sports gear rather than tunics. John is not looking at the game as he has spotted yet another acquaintance. 'Baz. BAZ. I wanna see you, lad. Did you get rid of that thing?' 'No, John mate, I didn't.' 'Giz £25 back and I'll get rid, mate.' While he and Baz barter over their mysterious product Chester take a 1-0 lead. The goal happens when Marine's keeper decides he is no longer on duty, sauntering as he does into a left-back position. He is beaten to the ball, which is dispatched with ease. As one, the Chester team tear towards the dugout and unveil T-shirts bearing the name of 'that babby'. 'I tell you what, John, he had to score from there' offers someone behind us, the banal co-commentator to John's poetic meanderings on wing-play and objects worth £25.

For the rest of the half a pattern emerges. Chester pass twice, give the ball away, Marine pass back to them, Chester pass three or four times and eventually score. Their second goal today makes it a century for the season and elicits a roar to match the achievement, and their third thuds into the net from thirty yards. They are playing with the brio and largesse of a boxing champ at his career best, the ball stroked around at will and garnished by needlessly fussy outside-of-boot passes. I lose five minutes thinking how odd it is to be at a match that smells of the countryside, and another five realising I have been in Scotland, England and Wales today. The match has become like background music so, before Leyton paranoia or Vicarage Road existentialism can set in, I tune my radar to two men arguing about socks.

'Yeah. But that stripe is *white*. It's a *white* stripe.'

'No, it's *blue*.'

'No, it's *not*.'

'Bloody hell, he's got odd socks on.'

'He bloody hasn't.'

'I'm telling you, he's got odd socks on.'

Their debate is silenced when a third man arrives carrying a can of Coke in one hand and a coffee in the other. 'Double-caffeine. This'll shift the hangover.' Ahh, the football hangover, when you stare at your pre-match pint for an hour and contemplate using a stadium cubicle for the first time ever. At half-time John turns to the hungover sockmen and the four of them plan for next season. His 'I don't think we'll win the league, but we'll definitely go up' meets with approval. Round here, they deserve to lounge in such optimism. As the sun shines down on smiling people, as we watch Chester teams from Under-9 to Under-19 parade the pitch, it feels like the end of a film.

The second period gets under way to the tune of the PA announcer requesting that fans stay off the pitch when the game ends. A teenage girl nearby replies, 'I don't know what "encroach" means, so I'm off on.' The noise gathers as the party approaches. To 'Que Sera' it is, 'Should I be Chester/Should I be Welsh' and 'shoot the Wrexham scum'. To 'Anarchy in the UK' it is, 'I am a Chester fan/I am a Cestrian/Youngy's barmy blue and white army/

Chester FC/top of the league/Cos I'm proud to be, Chester FC.'
The latter, in its craft, in the way it is sung by boys of five and
grannies, in its evidence of the football crowd's creativity, is a
work of art that lifts my heart. Again, football is reminding me
why I fell for her in the first place. 'Oh West Cheshire/Is wonderful/
Oh West Cheshire is wonderful' is less moving.

The Cestrians on the pitch are maintaining a relentless yet slow
kind of pressure – think Leeds United v. Southampton, and Barry
Davies' 'Poor old Southampton … just don't know what day it is.'
Marine cannot get hold of the ball, chase as they might. It is like
watching a beggar fruitlessly approaching people with his palm
upturned. In the stand to our right a teenage bugler plays a slow
lament not far removed from 'The Last Post'. Perhaps he has not
updated his repertoire since the days of hell, a cabaret singer in a
punk world. Things have flat-lined once more on my temporary
terrace home. It is as if we are hidden behind a curtain, waiting for
the star guest at a surprise party to arrive. I begin to admire the
Marine goalkeeper's paunch. He is not overweight, but resembles
how most blokes his, *our*, age should be, and as the proud owner
of a burgeoning spread I like players it is possible to relate to. I am
drifting again. I read the flags strung in the gallows of the main
stand. There is an Irish flag with 'CFC' across the tricolours, one
that says 'Chester FC: Founded 2010' and one that simply reads
'Until the Sky Turns Green,' a line torn from the Stone Roses to
mean, I think, unending support. It is while I am reading these
that Chester score their fourth goal. 'Championies' rings around
the Deva, followed by 'We're going up as fucking champions',
which sounds better than it reads. We pass the 90-minute mark
and reach the final moments of Chester FC's second season.
Today, there are 4,000 people here to see out this seminal minute.
'What you gonna do for the next three months?' queries John of a

friend, a question half a million people in England ask themselves every May. 'At least there's the Euros,' he continues. Then a lone voice bellows: 'Stand up, for the champions/stand up, for the champions' five times over to disinterest and one response: 'You what, mate?' There is a pause and then the singer begins again: 'Sit down, for the champions …' At last, the same whistle that muzzled the crowd into reflection earlier now sends it into rapturous hullabaloo.

A smattering of fans gathers at the front of the stand. Men in fleece coats, jeans and Timberlands bob up and down and use each other's shoulders to balance on tiptoes. They are peeping at a small stage being built in the middle of the pitch over the hoardings, the camber and an oblivious groundsman forking his injured turf. From above is piped essential promotion party classic 'Rockin' All Over the World', before someone called Dame Patricia Bacon is introduced to the crowd. 'Boooo, gedder off, Dame Bacon or not' bawls John. Then, two by two, the players are introduced and treated to applause. The couples emerge in flip-flops to take their acclaim and climb the stage, battered legs on one more surge. Finally, the league trophy is heaved skyward towards the heavens and away from all former hells. The comeback is not complete, but it is at an advanced stage. Behind the players, ticker tape quivers and a smoke machine churns out 1980s disco atmosphere. The squad moves as one, a flock of geese with medals, around each stand and when they reach ours two or three teenagers scale the wall and join them. 'What are they bloody doing?' asks John, and those around me start to boo. It is too late. Fellow teenagers join them in spits then blobs, then the age of invader gets older: teens, twenty-somethings, thirty- or forty-somethings and their children, those children's grandparents. Soon, the terrace has all but emptied. 'Sod it,' says John and, brilliantly, a steward opens a gate on to the pitch for him. Without thinking, I sneak on behind him and join the carnival in the penalty area. To be on the soft turf where dreams are made looking back into the stands is a novel rapture. I watch lads who should know better – some of them are *thirty*, for God's sake – mime crosses, shots, headers and saves in the goalmouths. A heavily ginger man of similar age looks pensively at the length of the pitch before sprinting across it, giant blue and white flag in hand. Whole families dance on the pitch, their pitch. This is football to love, and it has destroyed my Chester prejudice. It is a modern take on a club existing for its community, not as a working-class release valve but as a unifying force. Support is heartfelt and critical, going beyond 3 p.m. and above the bourgeois hobbying of neighbouring clubs. The goosebumps are back and Orient is forgotten. I am among friends.

Dusk is dimming the light by the time I get back into town. Chester's hallowed streets are surprisingly rowdy, manned as they are by numerous Mancunian and Liverpudlian stag nights and hen dos. 'At night, when the tramcars have stopped running and the crowds have gone home,' wrote H. V. Morton in 1927, 'ancient cities like Chester come most vividly to life.' Spanish tourists look up at the heavenly architecture and down on the frothing lads with sombreros dancing around a busker. I stop for a pint in the Old Boot Inn, its abundant beams, golden light and conversational percussion thrilling my senses and evoking an England very sure of itself. The time machine returns me home when I overhear the word banter ('Yeah, there's banter and there's Chantelle. That's not banter.'), newly ubiquitous and permanently baffling. In trying to grab the past back I walk to the Blue Bell, a medieval inn turned Oriental restaurant. Beams abound again – if there's ever a shortage of firewood, Chester's yer man – and an open coal fire turns meat-sweat phizogs crimson. Two couples numbering a gang of four that probably meets up every week and holidays together imbibe and giggle, the familiar motifs of Saturday night England. '*Match of the Day* then bed for me,' says one of the male halves. '*Match of the Day*? You'll be asleep by the news,' replies his wife. 'I watch it sneakily,' he retorts, before his mate adds 'You watch summat else sneakily, Bryan, *Snatch of the Day*.' A couple arrive and are happy not to be left alone. 'Our anniversary today,' the lady offers. 'Seven years. You get less for armed robbery.' Is this 'banter'? Possibly. It amuses me, anyhow, and shortly after my deep-fried something is dispatched I am invited to sit between the two tables for imbibing and giggling.

When I awake to the Sunday morning bells of the B&B's grandfather clock, my mouth feels as though it has spent the night above a Dyson Airblade on full blast. I scuffle to the breakfast room and take my place next to a couple who have clearly had a row. Despite being a Yorkshireman he wears a Manchester United shirt, so mentally I take her side. In their disgruntled silence cutlery seems to clink more loudly and I am glad when the sleeve-gartered host opens a conversation about the contents of his hash browns. I ask for more orange juice (as in most B&Bs, the glasses here are too small for a hungover mouth), and stare at the fuzzy words of leaflets for local attractions.

The breakfast rebalances me; the walk into town eases my head. I cross the River Dee on a grandiose bridge. It has to be large to drape this heavy and glistening river, an expanse of water on which Chester is founded. First the Romans used the Dee as transport, then the Saxons as a defensive weapon, the Normans as a seat of power, the Elizabethans as a trade route and the Victorians as a place of leisure. One river in one city in whose shimmers can be seen the grand strokes of England's history. The bridge leads me towards Chester's city walls, which bear hug her oldest parts. Their turrets and bases are black, their uneven bricks almost ginger in this morning's sunlight. If Watford Junction is a Bourbon biscuit then Chester's walls are the cross-section view of a Crunchie bar. Where the walls reach the city centre they peck the cheek of modern buildings including a multi-storey car park. These are mostly monstrous creations and look like no biscuit I can think of. It is as if the walls are an annoyance and get in the way, a barrier to progress and DSS tower blocks.

After a difficult encounter with a persistent pigeon I continue to The Rows. The Rows are tunnels save for two features: they are open on one side and one storey of a building up. It is as if a long chunk has been mined from several streets of tall mediaeval houses, and some shoe shops inserted. Walking among them imbues a cosy feeling of being cut off from the ebbing throngs in the streets below. I feel like a ghost floating above the future. Not all visitors share my enthusiasm – Daniel Defoe called The Rows 'old and ugly' and Celia Fiennes, who rode through the country on horseback, described them as 'penthouses set on pillars'. There is no living among their galleries today, just shopping. I reach a sofa outlet, which was once called Leche House. Like many of Chester's dignified old houses, graffiti is to be found on its windowpanes. This is not the work of anyone the *Daily Mail* thinks should have an ASBO, but of 'Charming Miss Oldfield, 1736'. Along the street at Bishop Lloyd's Palace each and every window was once cobwebbed with inscriptions like 'Oh that my pencil could the features trace of him I think possessed with every grace', and on from there Jonathan Swift, author of *Gulliver's Travels*, scratched 'Rotten without and mouldering within/This place and its clergy are nearly akin' into the glass of the Yacht Inn. Swift's words were revenge upon the Chester Cathedral worthies who had stood him up when offered an evening meal. It is nice to think that he then blew out the candles and got shitfaced in the dark.

I pull a slightly egg-stained leaflet from my pocket and follow its map to an open-top bus from 1914. This maroon charabanc offers city tours and if I really want to look at and not for England, to *enjoy* it, then there's nothing, says 'casual observer', like failing to hear the history of a place above a howling gale. As the bus slowly fills I read about the cathedral we currently face. Apparently, it contains the shrine of Saint Werburgh, a nun so pure that when she found geese eating her crops she called a meeting with them. Having received Apologies from God and Jesus H. Christ and agreed previous minutes, Werburgh moved to the first item on the agenda: asking the geese to fly away. The geese took off but circled above, claiming one of their number lost. Werburgh found that a servant had cooked the missing goose, and brought it back to life from its bones. The next time someone asks me why I am an atheist, I am going to hand them a laminated copy of the last four sentences.

A Geordie lady of a certain vintage lumbers to the front of the bus. 'It'll probably rain, like' she tells everyone, before unleashing a landslide of doomy predictions ('I cannat see this auld bus lastin' the journey' and 'This'll nee be as good as the one in London, like'). Fortunately, the bus driver and owner is of a more cheerful disposition, but then so is a gnat. A significantly hard-of-hearing man behind me commentates loudly on the driver/owner's well-oiled routine, so that I begin to think he is part of it. 'He's very funny, him. Great sense of humour.' The lauded driver/owner passes the microphone to his wife who sits next to me. At one point I am sure she catches me writing of how the brim of her hat keeps gouging my neck, because she sidles closer and starts work on my cheek too. People wave at us from the street, or perhaps they are trying to tell me that my face is bleeding. We chug through Handbridge, the part of Chester closest to Wales. The Welsh call it 'Treboeth', which translates as 'Burnt Town', so often was it the home of dragon-on-lion violence and retribution. In the 1400s Prince Henry proclaimed that: 'No Welshman of whatsoever state or condition he may be, remain within the walls of the said city, nor enter into the same after sunset, under pain of cutting off his head,' and the Welsh were banned from entering pubs and gathering in groups of three or more. England was either at war or really hated Welsh male voice choirs. It was in Handbridge too, I learn from the hat stabbist, that Mary Jonas, furniture dealer and mother of thirty-three children, lived. Through the nineteenth century she had given birth to fifteen sets of twins, each comprising a boy and a girl. To reward her efforts in contributing the most personally to the British Empire's expansion, *Tit-Bit* magazine awarded her a lifetime's subscription, because she obviously had a lot of spare time to sit around reading trivia.

The tour ends and I repair to a bathroom to check for facial scars. Again one of my journeys is coming to an end and I am in the public conveniences of a foreign town. This time I am content. Chester, and Chester FC, have gone a long way to restoring me and redeeming England. I did not look too hard; I just let it happen to me. Perhaps England demands that kind of distance, like a wild but intelligent primate. When I emerge from the Gents, entire armies of Scouts, Cubs and Beavers are marching in the rain. A brass band starts and I know the north is trying to give me a cuddle. Calm, fetching Cheshire has been kind to me, so it is just as well that I will soon return.

Chapter Eight

Crewe

Twenty-four miles from Chester is Crewe, where the Railwaymen play. While Deva is unarguably northern, its noisy neighbour looks down to Stoke City and Port Vale rather than up to Macclesfield Town and Stockport County. North and south is important in England and there are few greater determinants of which is which and who is who than football. At first glance Crewe's history sits tightly within a narrative of industrialism usually claimed and pocketed by the north. These were the railwaymen. They built trains and they built a town. Day trips for those of us that cars passed by would probably be impossible without them.

Until there were trains there was no Crewe. All of it was fields and scattered farms. 'A mere hamlet of the most uninviting character' said the one guidebook I could find. Then the iron roads spiralled around the ugly hamlet like ivy. They were not even supposed to be there; only when the lobbyists of Nantwich declared 'not in my back field' did the railway re-tune towards the ugly hamlet. From Birmingham to Liverpool ran the Grand Junction Railway, stopping off at Crewe, population: seventy. Further tracks arrived smartly, intersecting like wire wool. The new town of Crewe's geography – accessible from the chimneyed settlements of Lancashire, the Midlands and Yorkshire, and the west coast – was simply too comely to ignore. On this side of England, most trains passed through, their passengers associating Crewe with tea and cakes. On the run following riots in the Potteries, Chartist Thomas

Cooper, a friend of Sheffield no doubt, recorded how 'We had time for breakfast at Crewe, before the Manchester train came up.'

Until that point, Crewe was a service station with frilly tablecloths. Then, its railwaymen decided it should be so much more. Their brave Crewe world would establish the first country of rail's epic workshop and a model town to house those who stoked its flames. At first, they built superior tracks, but soon conjured the locomotives and carriages that slid across them. From the 1860s the people of Crewe made more and better tank engines than anywhere else. Each was created with delicate craft, but built robustly to last. They were doused in bucolic shades of plum and spilt milk, but named after classical heroes from another world. By 1900, Crewe had built 4,000 locomotives; 7,000 households depended on them doing so. Inside thirty years 40,000 people had moved to Crewe. Many of them came from Edgehill in Liverpool, newly usurped as a home of steam. Crewe could do things she never would. England's newest town was an immigrant one, south Lancastrians, Yorkshire folk, Scots and Geordies joining the Scousers so that by 1851 only nineteen per cent of the adult population was from Cheshire.

They found work and they found a mostly pleasant place to live. Crewe was never resplendent, but its heart was fair. Railway company spoils often went straight into civilising their new town. They built libraries, mechanics' institutes, meeting halls, parks and churches. Their housing was of a standard fit for railwaymen, creating a labour aristocracy that lived in clean and comfortable homes unheard of elsewhere. The companies provided baths and street cleaners, policemen and hospitals, water and gas. They dominated lives public and private, visually and mentally.

There were railwaywomen too, working in supporting industries. Some made soap, bricks or artificial limbs. Six-hundred-and-fifty tailoresses sewed the waistcoated uniforms that gave

British trains atmosphere. No one could claim gender equality, but things were pushing in the right direction. A new town meant a generally classless one, according to a *Daily Mail* article of June 1917, and a happy one too:

> There are no ultra-rich and no very poor in Crewe. There is little of what everywhere else passes for public entertainment, but there are clubs of all sorts, social and political, there are musical and debating societies ... all very active and energetic.

Democracy was harder to come by than dancing. With company munificence came company rule. When in 1877 Crewe became an elected Borough, its councils were chiefly populated by railway managers. It could be a stifling atmosphere. There was a puritanism to living in this company town, atmospherically and officially – Sundays of closed shops and no play remained in place until the 1930s. Pint-jar relief and release were difficult, the companies having banned pubs inside their town and shown much deference to Temperance. Railwaymen throats were wet inside boozers built on the edge of town. The recollections of Mike Langley, a Crewe expat and sports journalist supreme, were far from fond:

> The Crewe of those days was a company town dancing to the tune of the works' buzzer, where the sack was every apprentice's 21st birthday present, where the children's swings were chained on Sundays and where licensing justices were a gang of militant teetotallers who, even on VE-night when we won the war, shut the pubs at ten.

Work did not liberate, though there was an awful lot of it going on. During the First World War, the railworks of Crewe employed

10,000 people. Other industries spotted a willing workforce that could whip up a structure faster than most people could open a tin of bully beef. Rolls Royce and Bentley opened factories, the former's supplying the aeroplane engines that bested the Nazis. When England needed fun to forget war, the industrial hangars of Crewe turned out ice cream vans, mobile fish and chip shops and hot dog vending vehicles. Still the locos shunted from Crewe to the world, from the 1960s in colour diesel rather than black-and-white steam.

And then, and then … oh what a familiar tale. By the twenty-first century railwaymen's hands were twiddling thumbs. Dr Beeching hammered the first rusty nail, dividing Crewe into a mere division of British Rail workshops. There were, as we now know, no special cases for such a social butcher and industrial psychopath. Making a department out of a breathing organism made strangulation easy. Closures spread across the Crewe works from east to west, an epidemic that left killing fields of wheel and axle corpses, not to mention pride. If the town existed because of the rails, then how could it go on without trains?

Today there is a retail park where many of Crewe's workshops once were, which is like sinking a sewage works in a graveyard. To reach the Crewe Heritage Centre as I am now attempting to do, you have to walk beneath the stilts of one of those jumbo Tesco barns that will soon have its own Olympic team. On one side of the road signage offers 'Welcome to Tesco Extra', on the other 'The Crewe Heritage Centre'. They are tussling for attention and attendance, one easily winning mine but not many others'. What Tesco can't control as yet is the air, punctuated then saturated by the smell of fire and water on coal. It is a good job such a scent of heaven hangs as the Heritage Centre takes a covert approach to identifying itself, and the main hall is locked. I peer in through its glass door and a figure apparently wearing around her neck the spoils of a raid on a cash-for-gold shop stares back at me from inside.This turns out to be the mayor. I smile half-heartedly – symbolic authority only requires as much – and retreat to a bench. Behind me, Saturday volunteers tinker on a miniature railway. The yard ahead proffers sheeted ghosts – a cornucopia of steam trains and diesels, all awaiting their wake-up calls from beneath covers. Each wears the brass declaration 'Crewe Built'. The Heritage Centre is jackknifed by working mainline railways, a blob at the bottom of a letter 'V'. I enter a building at the far end that contains a cafe, shop, further exhibits and volunteers with intense giggles and gangly hair. I find the general untidiness endearing, an antidote to the new world of Westfield floors.

In a backroom an overhead projector plies the wall full of images. They are not of a smoothly produced documentary on the history of the Crewe works, nor are they BFI images of steam days. The images come from a shaky camcorder film of a diesel train ticking by the platform at Crewe station. The cameraman pans around to show us more of the train, inadvertently flashing up a merry band of enthusiasts as they hum, aaah and smile. It looks to have been shot in the 1990s and captures an England of then celebrating and nurturing another, earlier England. Change and continuity seep over the wobbly edges of the pictures. There is a fondness of times gone by, of what we were that would die without these people and without places like this. I wish we still built things, but at least we remember them. Reminiscence and heritage cannot be bulldozed or made into Carpetrights. All of this is decorated with humour and cheer. There are the three men by the screen fixing some signal parts to a wall. One is up a ladder, talking over his shoulder: 'Off at three, I am. Off to get me toupee done. Then, Cup Final for me.' 'All right, Sean, you've said. You can go at three. I get it,' says the man steadying his climbing frame, looking across at the third, driven to fond distraction. Then upstairs on a viewing platform, a teacher withstands and even heightens the rambunctious and endearing enthusiasms of his charges. One bolts up and down, tracing the progress of each train that passes and shouting its name, besotted. 'Diesel. DIESEL. Virgin. VIRGIN. VIRGIN! OH. MY. GOD!' Another asks 'Can we go in the signal box?' 'Yes, sir,' replies their beloved leader. 'We can do what you want. We have all the time in the world.'

Surfing this tide of awe, I do not even notice Tesco or Wickes as I leave and am quickly in Crewe's neat civic centre. White flagpoles thrice the height of goalposts frame the town hall and market. At the centre of them a statue of Britannia stands tall as if awaiting a penalty. At her feet in modern silver letters are the words of Laurence Binyon: *We will remember them*. Another England with wars gone by impossible to miss. The scent of meat sags in the air inside Crewe Market Hall, a butcher's shop at each end competing. Its aroma reminds me of Watford, as does a leaflet on the noticeboard advertising Knutsford Civic Centre's 'Mind Body and Spirit Event'. The market building, a century-and-a-half old, has the clock-towered dignity of an Andalucian town's railway station. Up close its details are many, like the unexpected number of veins in an autumn leaf. Its inner charms are more predictable and homely. The first stall I see sells knickers the size of cooling towers, fluorescent bibs and Premier League football scarves. Opposite, a woman trades in threads and wool underneath a sign reading Cakes, Biscuits & Pies. There are a number of redeployed or empty spaces like hers, including the Crewe Trouser Bar, here since 1948 but recently departed. An outdoor section of the market flogs dog beds, vegetables, pet gravestones and car boot delights in crates under a cattle market roof. This is the free market in its most inhibited state. Across the car park pensioners are dining al fresco outside the Market Cafe, or sucking cigarettes while they wait. It is brighter inside, owing to its sunny owner and the affectionate airs between old friends. Most people who enter say hello and pay without ordering. 'I just hand over me money, love,' says one woman to me, 'Rachel knows what we want.' Avoiding a daily special of faggots, peas and gravy I order a Full Breakfast priced ridiculously at £2 (videprinter: TWO). I accompany my first-rate feast with a can of Diet Sunkist, a regional speciality deserving of protected status. Rachel bobs and weaves around the room with her dishcloth, wiping and talking. 'Tomorrow you go on holiday, in't it Margaret?' 'Eh, love, I 'ad to take Lottie to the hospital for her needles the other day. She had no lift.' She works hard, this one, surely the granddaughter of railwaymen.

Beneath the gables and bays of the Lyceum Theatre I continue to the shopping streets of Crewe. They are lined with a miscellany of adjoined two-storeyed buildings. All of our friends are here (Poundland, Orange Mobile, Shoe Zone …), so we can never feel too abroad. People scurry busily between street stop-and-chats and shops. There are no pigeon-feeding glamour pusses or mercury-voiced crooners here, but there is a woman playing Cher numbers on a flute and a furious man telling us we are all going to die, which is factually correct if nothing else. He – a bald man in his early forties stood on a ladder stool, angry veins pawing at his neck like claws – is screaming, apparently, on behalf of God. The central theme is death, though there are interesting digressions into metaphors about cheques and parachutes.

It does not really tally with the contented way Crewe seems to be getting on with its Saturday morning business. The only other person I hear carping is a man whose airing cupboard door handle has snapped 'clean off. Bloody thing.' I had been keen not to use this analogy, but there are unavoidably Hornby Town aspects to Crewe. When the tiny models of men that train-set botherers (and I was one once, and probably will be again) place on platforms and pavements talk, I imagine it is about things like door handles. Further, the architecture on streets like Queensway is boxy and cardboard-coloured with small and perfectly rectangular bricks. At one end a clock tower sprouts for the sky and I should not be surprised if it is entirely hollow inside and if there are glue stains on its trickier parts. This town centre is unremarkable and yet charming, surely the very definition of a comforting, unchallenging Hornby world. Later I discover the comments of a lady described in a local history project as Mrs Hodgkinson:

> At one time or another I have been informed of all of Crewe's shortcomings by disgruntled residents. It was drab, it was completely utilitarian and without character. It has no beauty, either structurally or architecturally. It lacked class. It has no culture, and entertainment is non-existent. So what has it? Whatever it was and still is, many of us have come to have an unwilling affection for the lacklustre town that we find hard to explain. We just know it's there.

These are not dissimilar views to those aired in Luton's museum. People in all of these provinces are united by their familial love of their England. It is surprisingly resilient despite dead industry and chain streets, and that is because of one cliché that I am beginning to think of as true: people make places. That platitude works literally too. I realise this as I rest with beer in Hops, a bounteously stocked Belgian bar on a leafy road behind the selling streets of Crewe. It takes a person, not a corporation or government, to decide to establish a Belgian pub on the back streets of a forgotten railway town in Cheshire. In turn, that person creates something unique about a place. All of this comes together in a football club. People in a place build it and then continue to give it its personality by attending matches. This is essentially why matchday experiences at those clubs where sponsors, shareholders and in-comers dominate are charmless and impoverished of character. There is not much belonging and little to belong to. It is Deva Stadium versus Old Trafford, Bury Park versus Westfield centre.

The people that built Crewe Alexandra were railwaymen. They wanted to give their new town a symbol and show their railway children that life could be red, green and dreamy as well as plum, grey and steamy. Depending on whether you asked the yard owners or grafters, 'Alexandra' came from the Prince of Wales' wife or a pub. In 1877 they found a rare spot of land without tracks or sheds and started up the town's club. A decade on, an FA Cup semi-final was reached, and soon afterwards the railwaymen's Railwaymen became members of the Football League's Division Two. They finished one place below those other men of steel, Ironopolis. League football did not return until 1921, and the all-new Division Three North deigned Crewe within its purview. The club mostly bundled along, playtime release for railwaymen and costume makers. There were heroes along the way: before the Second World War, Herbert Swindells scored 137 goals; afterwards, Fredrick Inskip hit a penalty over the Railway End that rested in a coal wagon and travelled to Carlisle. Fast-forward to the cups of the 1960s. The diesel-builders saw Spurs held 2-2 at home (although Tottenham scored 13 in the home tie), and Greavesie's Chelsea beaten at the Bridge. And on to the struggles of the 1970s. Urine oozing from open toilets to the street, goals 'as hard to come by as second-hand coffins' says the local paper. In 1981-82, Alexandra finished at the league's foot, the eighth occasion on which they had done so since 1894 and a record. Around this time, the town that so many passed through had become a halt for footballers. Many stopped here before playing their way onwards. Stan Bowles found Crewe to be a salvage yard for his talents. Bruce Grobbelaar loaned in his steaming-mad ways and flew out a Liverpool player. Under Dario Gradi players such as David Platt, Geoff Thomas, Rob Jones, Neil Lennon, Robbie Savage and Danny Murphy changed trains for bigger times.

Lambton Worms of two-up two-downs once more take me to a home ground, this time Gresty Road. The last brick wall before I turn into the stadium car park sports a heavily political piece of graffiti: 'Use The Bypass'. Ticket office girls, with whom I spend more time on Saturdays than I do my wife, ignore me at first. They have an important matter at hand: one has pinched a bacon Frazzle from the other. 'That's my dinner, ger off.' I manage to buy a ticket for Crewe's Main Stand. This is not just Main by name (actually, it's now called the Air Products Stand), it is the *main* stand. The three others are tiny by comparison. The ground looks like a grand piano surrounded by Tomy xylophones.

Too much dwelling on concourse health and safety posters made by children (we painted castles and goals in my day; one of these, by a seven-year-old, contains the words 'Do Not Play With Matches You Will Die') makes me late to my seat. I file along to tuts and exaggerated glances at watches. I am not only an outsider; I am a late outsider, the worst kind of outsider. My seat is in the hindquarters of this lanky stand, giving gantry views of Crewe and Cheshire. Down to my left are 'homes for heroes' terraces built for returning First World War soldiers and a chippy, the golden light of which must have forced many an early exit on dark winter afternoons. Ahead is a tower block then the flatlands and pimpled interruptions of olive-green Cheshire, to the right spaces and shops where railwaymen once strived.

Crewe quickly make it 1-0. This goal matters. They need only a point to qualify for the play-offs, a towering accomplishment given that earlier in the season they occupied their habitual slot at the bottom of England's fourth division. Where the Chester game meant little more than cakes and ale, its football slowing accordingly, the importance of today instils in the match a hypnotic rhythm. Morning rain has heightened the green of the pitch, and in front of us the reds and whites and blues and whites darting about like painted ants splash yet more paint. Aldershot's manager once plundered goals on the tree's top branches and for a while was a model. Today's Kangol flat cap and waistcoat suggest he kept some of the free gear. The ball flies out of play and he controls it with a suited thigh, cradles it with his foot and lobs it to a thrower. *Still got it*.

In a matchbox stand behind the goal inevitable drums beat and when they die down the people of Crewe sing. 'Should I be Vale?/ Should I be Stoke?' they ask, looking south. Then there is a solemn and blissful rendition of 'Blue Moon', sung to these skies long before it was to those of Manchester. Gresty Road's proportions mean anthems spread from this terrace across to the Main Stand. Soundwaves then make their way across its blocks like a Mexican wave, so that timing is out and it resembles school assembly hymns sung in rounds. When the crowd noise fades it is occasionally replaced by the fleshy sound of shots being blocked by defensive legs. Aldershot are hitting back and hitting efforts from anywhere and everywhere. They hoick a free-kick into the air, a chill wind blows and bamboozles Crewe's backmen. Somehow ball meets goal. Own goal, that comedic hell: 1-1.

Crewe pass and move their way back into the game. Everything they do is prompted by the golden boots of their teenage No. 25. In wristbands and ankle ties he nifts around like a genius alien. Today, comrade Glaswegians from Old Trafford and Goodison hawkeye him. When the summer comes, £6 million pounds will see him swap the Alexandra shuttle for Manchester's express, another Crewe-built departure. 'A Foster's and a Bulmers, in't it lads, I always forget' says the man behind me, not as mesmerised as we the watchers. Aldershot's No. 17 wants some attention too. We are all in the zoo looking at the tiger, so the leopard roars. He wins the ball somewhere around the halfway line, builds a one-two, tips the ball on and then spirals a dancer into the top corner: 1-2 to Aldershot. Look at me! Look at me!

At half-time there is attention-grabbing of a different nature. One, two, three then four people all sidle along to the gangway and slip on a battered haddock, discarded at the game's start as its eater cheered Crewe's goal. There is slapstick in railwayland. The match resumes and the reds and the blues continue in their slick ways. This is zippy, loveable stuff. I need something to concentrate on because I have a new rear-view neighbour. His voice is powerfully nasal. When he shouts he rasps like a foghorn on helium. When he moans, which he does a lot, it has the pace and pitch a newly set house alarm makes until the front door is closed. As the game marches on, both teams indulge in suicide passes, making compelling, kamikaze football. An Aldershot centre-half frequently leaves open wounds by charging forward and then allowing the ball to ham off his chugging tug-boat feet. His forward colleague spurts through, circumnavigates the goalkeeper and must score. He does not. There is no 1-3. 'Pikey!' snarls nasal man at an Aldershot player with long hair. Crewe nerves jangle. A full-back controls the ball and side-foots it to a Timpson shoe repairs advertising hoarding. In the corner, a wrong clock moves meaning it isn't even right twice a day. Crewe need time, proper time to score.

And then, it matters no more. A scoreline somewhere else, in another small town in England, is beyond reproach. Crewe will be in the play-offs come what 12 May. 'Que Sera' spreads like wildfire through the terraces. Moneyed Cheshire types in front of me here to see the big-town team (he waxy jacket and checked flat cap, she gillet and cloche hat) talk of trains to London play-off weekends. Crewe fuel the hubbub by whacking the crossbar, and then cause ecstasy by equalising. It is a send-off goal. The bags are packed for the promotion tilt. 'Que Sera' sing 6,000 railway people, then they medley into an even more striking 'Blue Moon'. They miss the whistle, but know by red arms aloft that they are there, three steps from climbing the ladder again. 'Could each and every one of you remain seated. Do not encroach the pitch area' pleads the Tannoy man. I have seen this film before. On trickle teenagers who spot gaps in the stewards' formations. One breaks through the cordon with a deft drop of the shoulder. If Old Trafford and Goodison are still watching, they may be having words. Another has a profound limp but still outruns his fluorescent pursuant. This time the masses do not join in. Perhaps they are saving it for Wembley. I walk back into town and try to watch the FA Cup final. I can't settle, though. It is being played at teatime and with the season not yet over. How these times at the top repel me.

The next morning I cross the Pennines on a train not made in Crewe. A mum tests her daughter ahead of an exam tomorrow, love and pride hovering in the air. As I stare out of the window I have my own version of the same. This terrain – of canals and old

mills, of Stalybridge Celtic and Huddersfield Town – I consider
my own. It is tangibly the north. Crewe, with its chimneyless
skyline and songs of Vale, I am less sure of. It matters because the
north-south divide apparently matters, to football and the rest.

I first became aware of the north-south divide at Ayresome
Park. Whenever an opponent from a team based anywhere beyond
Sheffield received physio treatment, the song was always 'Soft
southern bastard, you're just a soft southern bastard'. In
retaliation, sparse away ends would bellow about 'Dirty northern
bastards'. Thinking about it, I heard both on that recent winter's
day at the Riverside. There was always a suspicion of southern –
and especially London – teams. Here were our paymasters and
governors from the powerful south. They ran our lives, our
granddads had made the steel that made them money, but we
could show them a thing or two of this northern game. We were
the louder, more loyal and educated fans too. Even gentleman
Ernest Needham of Sheffield United thought so, writing 'the
spectators of the south are not so keen and sporting as they must
be if their teams are to get anything like adequate support.'

However crudely and mythically it did so, football was saying
something about society in England here, reflecting and shaping it
as usual. Our great writers had long been convinced of the north-
south divide's existence and significance. Like many others, Henry
Morton defined the divide by the change in scenery as one travelled
up through England, and in doing so highlighted that there was a
fixed version of 'the north' but less of one for 'the south':

Here was New England: an England of crowded towns, of tall
chimneys, of great mill walls, of canals of slow, black water; an
England of grey, hard-looking little houses in interminable rows;
the England of coal and chemicals; of cotton, glass and iron.

Such themes are discussed at length in George Orwell's *The Road to Wigan Pier*. Orwell also attempts to define 'the south':

> When you go to the industrial North you are conscious, quite apart from the unfamiliar scenery, of entering a strange country... There is nevertheless a real difference between North and South, and there is at least a tinge of truth in that picture of Southern England as one enormous Brighton inhabited by lounge-lizards.

He acknowledged the differences between northerners and southerners, though questioned how useful the typical caricatures were, describing them thus: 'the Northerner has "grit", he is grim, "dour", plucky, warm-hearted and democratic; the Southerner is snobbish, effeminate and lazy.'

From pre-Victorian days to those of granddads at Ayresome losing their steel profits to the south, there was a feeling that northern toil made southern wealth. When the north stopped using its hands there was no work to make that money but the south changed its ways, finding finance, science and service. Between 1979 and 1987, ninety-four per cent of jobs lost were above a line drawn from the Bristol Channel to the Humberside Wash. No wonder we resented them, unfair as that was.

In my thirty years this divide has grown at a pace greater than any time since the Depression. Now, it appears to be at its most profound. I have seen it on my travels, the ghosts and spaces of Teesside and the alive-and-kicking business parks of Bedfordshire. The government is mooting regional pay rates, lowering salaries in the north, and jobs in the north are being lost at four times the rate of anywhere else. Below it, the north has a government rooted in southern support and interests; above it is a Scotland that might well go its own way. It is consistently 'top' of the poverty charts. Always Middlesbrough, Manchester and Liverpool are there. There are, of course, archipelagos: prosperous places in the north (Chester), impoverished places in the south (Leyton). Yet an ostensible, majority divide does exist, though not everyone is sure exactly where it is, just as Crewe goes to show.

Stuart Maconie identified Crewe as 'surely the gateway to the North'. I think it is more the driveway. It lingers between middle and top, delivering the Midlands of Stoke City and Port Vale to the north of Macclesfield Town and Stockport County. To whimsically claim this is to refute an extensive, outstanding piece of research compiled in 2007 by Danny Dorling of Sheffield University, in which Crewe was resolutely in the north. Dorling's line begins at the Bristol Channel and arrows like a plane's take-off to Grimsby. On its way it zigzags between towns and villages, and even fields and houses. It means that somewhere as far south as Worcester is in 'the north', somewhere as far north as Lincoln 'the south'. He concluded that: 'In terms of life chances the only line within another European country that is comparable to the North-South divide is that which used to separate East and West Germany.' Dorling used employment, health, historical and other data to identify a line that:

Separates upland from lowland Britain, the hills from the most fertile farmland, areas invaded by Vikings from those first colonised by Saxons. Numerous facts of life divide the North from the South – there is a missing year of life expectancy north of this line. Children south of the line are much more likely to attend Russell group universities … a house price cliff now runs along much of the line, and, on the voting map, the line still often separates red from blue.

Every bit his academic equal, I used the league tables of Football League Divisions Three North and South, 1921 to 1958. When all else fails, when you can be sure of nothing else: use football reasoning, use football definitions. By mapping the teams that played in those two divisions over their thirty-seven-year lifespans, I was able to draw a line. There are some irritating exceptions that relegated my theory from pseudo-geography to hit-and-hope, not least Crewe's. Coventry City, Mansfield Town, Port Vale, Shrewsbury Town and Walsall played in both, so I defined them by the division in which they most often dwelled. Derby were northern (though that was only for a season), the Nottingham clubs to their north always southern. However, I have my line and I am sticking to it. Otherwise I have scrawled all over a perfectly good wall-chart map for nothing. At its west, my dividing line begins below Wrexham. It cuts right through the centre of Crewe whose stadium is in the south of the town, hence the driveway, borderline status, and safely above Port Vale and Stoke City. It then maroons Nottingham Forest and Notts County in the south, dividing them from Mansfield Town then Lincoln City, also in the north. The line ends below Grimsby Town.

Apart from being rooted in pub-based research (beer is another stain on the wall-chart) and bending Crewe to fit, my north-south divide's weakness is the status of the West Midlands. So many towns there share industrial, cultural, social and political 'northern' characteristics, real or imagined. Moreover, Walsall spent more than ten years in Division Three North. It is in constructing my map that I realise a visit to those parts is needed; a few days in middle England and I might be able to see just who or what she is.

So what does this matter to our story? In one sense it depends whether we consider it a bad thing. I certainly do not mean to sound anti-south, another northerner bashing the Home Counties, but I realise there is bias in my language. In these chapters, too, I have generally preferred places in the north to the south, and found the stereotype of friendlier northerners true. This could, of course, be because I am more comfortable among those I share so much bitterness with. So, negatively the north-south divide matters as a battering ram with which to offend the other half, and positively as offering a place to belong to.

Yet the more I see of England, the less I am convinced the north-south divide matters. There are two reasons for this. Firstly, a man belongs far more to his town and football club than he does to a vague 'north' or 'south'. Secondly, across that divide we are united by a number of things. We are united by our loyalties to our tiny realms on the one hand, but also to this big, cuddly rogue called England on the other. Above that, millions of us are bound by our devotion to football.

Part Three

In the Summer:
Knitters, Clarets and Bantams

Chapter Nine

The Middle of England

I live in Leith, by tradition Edinburgh's port. Until 1920 it was a town in its own right, and there is still something separate about it. Nowhere else in Edinburgh can you drink a £1,200 bottle of wine in a Michelin-starred restaurant on one side of the street and score heroin on the other. Following my exile from England it took time to settle, but I am now happy here, though I have yet to try the wine or the heroin.

In the summer of 2012 Leith certainly felt independent of my home country. From there, so it appeared on television, the English were lapping up the Queen's Jubilee. A plague of patriotic spiders had attacked and webbed England's streets in bunting, and people were even tolerating Nicholas Witchell. In Leith the closest we came was a Union Jack poster in one of our five branches of Greggs. Even the Orange Lodge remained untainted, its unionism outdone by neighbouring Farmfoods' commitment to the Great British Summer Barbecue. Furthermore, in Leith and across Scotland, independence from England sometimes felt inevitable, not least because the idea of the Jubilee seemed so very alien and, well, *English*.

When Euro 2012 began, Scotland seemed less anti-England than usual. During previous tournaments, being English here had been difficult. 'It's not you we hate,' they would say to me, 'It's John Motson and all those guys mentioning 1966 every other sentence.' The logic seemed to be that you hated a nation because of its football pundits, which is a bit like hating Mexico because you once went on holiday there and a weather forecaster's lisp got on your nerves. It helped that those pundits were not so gung-ho this time around; England had a new manager who specialised in playing down expectations, which in themselves were refreshingly low – he basically had the task of convincing the rain it was wet. In addition, heavy patriotism bred apathy among the media and those non-football fans who during major tournaments usually come along for the ride. After a while, any country's arms ache from waving flags.

As happens every two or four years, I was trying my best to support England. On a Monday evening in June I set out to watch England v. France in Leith. I walk by a number of pubs – Leith's are split between traditional (eight or nine men stood by the bar drinking Tennents underneath the tenements) and gentrified (eight or nine web architects sat on sofas drinking German wheat beers in a converted something) – until I am tempted in by the music of one. That music is 'La Marseillaise', sung with surprising melody by a dozen or so Scottish voices. The bar is firmly in the traditional camp, its spirits section a large bottle of Grant's vodka, its menu those nuts that when pulled from their display reveal a naked woman (Scampi Fries are off). I take a seat underneath the television, becoming the only non-standing member of the audience. As the French anthem wilts it gives way to cries of 'Mon the French', 'Ya dirty English bastar'' and a lone 'Mon the English'. I decipher commentator references to Agincourt and Waterloo, and in a moment comprehend many Scots' anti-England stance and wonder once again why the English make themselves such a difficult team to support. Having said that, no nation is worse than Scotland for harking back several hundred years – soon here, there will be state-sponsored celebrations of a skirmish 700 years in the background. Meanwhile, the barman starts to sing 'God Save the Queen'.

It is this song, this soggy, fairy-tale lament for a land of never-never, which helped put me off England. I must have liked the team through childhood and into my early teens. World Cup 1990 was a catalyst that transformed an interest in football into love. In a drawer in my mum's house, I still have the Umbro shell suit to show for it. I can remember the heartbreak of Euro 92: 'Bro-leeeen. Dah-leeeen, Bro-leeeen' and Graham Taylor losing his way. Rarely have I been as upset as I was in 1996, when Gascoigne slid and missed at the far post and Barry Davies wailed 'Oh no!' But then, as I grasped at adulthood, there was Glenn Hoddle dropping my first love, Gazza, and invoking karmic principles on the disabled. Further, as I found myself to be what is known in certain circles as a 'socialist', I struggled with the notion of patriotism, nationhood and national anthems about a monarchy I opposed created by a god I didn't believe in. Surely a nation is a random line in the sand, your birth in it a complete accident? As I moved away from my Socialist Worker early twenties and into my disillusioned late ones, to support England seemed like a hypocrisy: how could I will injury on a Chelsea midfielder in club football one week, only to cheer him in an England shirt the next? Now, at thirty, it is the impossibility of relating to England or an England player that perturbs me most. Theirs is not the football of Sheffield then or Chester now. Wembley was not built by a community and given life by those who belong.

Early in its existence, the England team struggled against the strength of these communities. From most supporters' viewpoint, the club v. country conundrum had an unequivocal answer. England was an extra. It even got in the way, creating dead Saturdays where league fixtures should have been. An advantage England did have was its potential to create national unity between those many communities, yet it squandered this by playing so rarely. There were annual matches with Scotland (from 1872), Wales (1879) and Ireland (1882), but very little else. England did not play a non-British side until 1908 (Austria), nor host one until 1923 (Belgium), meaning there was less to rally around and identify with than there could have been. Neither did football chime with popular cricket imagery of England as a demure, ancient and green land in which hatted couples watched plucky amateurs from behind picnic hampers. Here was an urban, aggressive game that paid its players to entertain and alleviate its industrial working-class viewers.

For many, the World Cup of 1966 (apologies, Scottish family and friends) changed that order, so that England passed from afterthought to jingoistic symbol. Prior to Pickles and Hurst, England were on the wane, their means and methods overtaken across the globe. When in 1953 Hungary won 6-3 at Wembley, the defeat itself was not a shock, merely the extent and nature of it. The two reactions were telling and pertinent: England should acknowledge the growing supremacy of their counterparts and adapt accordingly or, what those other countries had achieved was down to British coaches, and our great nation should steer clear of their filthy foreign ways. In practice, 1966 halted popular support for the former and left us firmly with the latter. A *Soccer Star* piece published a month after England became world champions set the tone: 'Whatever the team lacked in skill it more than made up for it with the type of display that owed more to British character than any special football prowess'.

This victory for conservatism brutalised the popular image of the England team, and allowed tabloid newspapers to define its purpose. As Britain's Empire declined the England team became its Alamo, defending national pride to the last. I well recall the

Daily Mirror's Euro 96 front page message ahead of that Germany game: 'ACHTUNG! SURRENDER. For you Fritz, ze Euro 96 Championship is over'.

Euro 2012 has been another tournament preceded by a style crisis, as in 1953. Should we play to our strengths, invoking the Watford archetype, or begin to breed a generation that can keep the ball and tiki-taka with the best and rest of them? Off the field, it often feels as if we have emerged sheepishly – a caveman coming into the light – from our post-Empire crisis, but then our government invades Iraq or threatens Argentina over the Falklands. My thirty years have changed and stayed the same. To an extent, the England team are helpless victims in this, the spoils of off-field politicking. So, discounting the horrible truth that any of England's midfielders could probably buy Chester FC with a few weeks' wages, I again try to support them, and quietly cheer to myself when they go one-up against France.

When France equalise, the pub roars to life. I try and remain logical, not to feel like an Englishman in Leith, an alien without a kilt. In my time, I have on a thousand occasions cheered the demise of a disliked team. This question, however, remains unanswered: do the Scots dislike them because they are England, or because they are English?

I walk home and realise that I feel a little hurt. Football or xenophobia, humour or malice, it is still not nice to have those of the place you live in dislike something as fundamental as the football team of the place where you were born. Today I feel more English than I have on any of my trips south. I feel the need to be Sassenach, to go to the very heart of my country, the middle bit I have so far neglected, the midriff area that defies north-south categorisation. So I go to watch England in the middle of England.

*   *   *

When I fly to Birmingham in the middle of June, my intention is to travel to a town called Hinckley and watch England from a barstool there. Hinckley United's ground is one of the closest to the geographic centre of England, and I like their nickname, the Knitters. They did not exist in 1981-82, so I am thinking of them as my wild card, only a bit tame (perhaps the three of spades). From Birmingham Airport I take the 900 bus and feel the profound sense of pride that goes with catching a bus in an unfamiliar place. As always, this is followed by the profound sense of fear that the bus is going in the wrong direction. We plough along a stretch of motorway, me unfamiliar with these strange conveyor belts of silent solo travel. At the rear of the bus, a man is explaining to someone on the other end of the phone how to watch a DVD on his new television. 'Get dat big fing, dat's de scartfing, and stick in de grilly, spiky bit. Ye get me?' We are close to Shakespeare territory, and perhaps that great chronicler of slang and street talk himself would enjoy these linguistic ticks. The bus turns from the motorway and is quickly trundling along country roads, becoming an island on axles among a sea of oak trees and furrows. 'Dogging' says a spray-paint stencil message accompanied by an arrow beneath a road sign. Behind a taxi flying the flag of St George we arrive in 'Meriden: The Centre of England', my first calling point of the day.

Meriden, on the road between Birmingham and Coventry, has long been thought of as England's middle. A weather-beaten monument on its village green marks 'THE CENTRE OF ENGLAND', and has done for half a millennium. As I sit on a bench by the maypole and look back on The Centre of England Charity Shop, I feel guilty for thinking this innocent and appealing little place a fraud, and ashamed to question the integrity of the

THE MIDDLE OF ENGLAND

bushy-roofed thatched cottages behind me; the centre of England, geographers recently showed, is a good few miles to the north of here. A wood pigeon looks at me and then has a peck at the old statue. Geographers, visiting writers, birds; everyone seems to have it in for Meriden.

This original centre of England is representative of many other English places, then and now. Behind the green is a neat row of shops – pharmacy, newsagent, butcher, hairdresser, Spar, chip shop. Shiny Union Jack bunting hangs loosely from the guttering of the Barratt Homes opposite, Jubilee remnants in plastic. Salon girls arrive for work, mahogany skins and cheery cherry lips. In drips and drabs, solo men park up to buy a paper, patting strangers' dogs on leads as they go, and old couples pause to gossip. All converse in the same accent, Received Brummie. The main sounds are hedge trimmers and traffic, the smells cut grass and fried eggs. I enter the cafe that produces the latter. It has low ceilings, groaning floorboards and dark oak beams, and wooden panel walls punctuated by oil paintings of fox hunting. Its typical English caff fare should seem incongruous, but works. It is as if the domestic servants have occupied a stately home and turned it into a workers' co-operative. Across separate tables, a woman and two men talk about farming subsidies and barn flooring, stopping only to stare at the dozen workmen that float in when the clock strikes ten. I enjoy the precision and habits of what they order. One asks for 'a veggie breakfast, but with black pudding instead of veggie sausages', another 'a full breakfast, but instead of mushroom, a hash brown' and his mate 'a brunch, but with the fried egg on top of the chips.' As another five workmen arrive, the cafe walls contract and squeeze me out.

In the case displaying Meriden's news and notices, a long list schedules the dates for 'Hoisting Flags in Meriden'. These begin on 9 January with the Duchess of Cambridge's birthday and end on 20 November with Her Majesty's Wedding Day. Flag day highlights along the way include Coronation Day and Birthday of The Prince Harry, when everyone dons a Nazi uniform and shouts 'ya, totally' into an iPhone. Meanwhile a ninety-two-year-old lady is looking for a 'Carer-Companion ... four hours per week. Rates by negotiation.' You would, let's face it, have to be a bit of a shit to play hardball on that one. I call my agent immediately. Items for sale include a glass television unit (there is always an advert for a glass television unit, it's a running joke between English villages), grazing land for two horses, guttering, childcare ('including twins') and a Neostar Desiccant Dehumidifier. If you can tell a lot about a place by its noticeboard, then Meriden is a ritually royalist, lonely rural place with over-estimated moisture issues and free-standing televisions.

I board another bus, this time towards Coventry. Brown signs on the city's forehead mark out the Ricoh Arena and Coventry Cathedral, while another advertises the Godiva Festival. The road into town settles into a rhythm: semi-detached bay-windowed houses followed by parades of shops. The housing far more resembles suburban hideaway homes of the south than accommodation in the north. Along the way Jubilee bunting flickers consistently, silently linking the streets. There tends to be more in apparently affluent areas than in tower block windows. Some of it is sad, such as the tatty leftover Union triangles on a care home wall.

The bus decants me into one of Coventry's lesser areas, where it seems city planners twisted the knife Hitler left poised. Concrete and dark brown glass smothers sightlines. The AXA Insurance building looks like a copper car battery belonging to Gulliver, while the stilted Britannia Hotel looks like something a hungover

Jabba the Hut would emit. J. B. Priestley wrote of the 'extraordinary ugliness' of the 'hobgoblin' locals in Coventry; he would not have noticed them had he visited after the war. I have an hour between buses, so take a walk around town that confirms the people of Coventry as pretty, ugly and normal in the same proportions as everywhere else.

Then, in a blink, Coventry suddenly becomes beautiful. After a Garden of International Peace the twining lanes and secret spaces of Priory Row, Hill Top and Cuckoo Lane lead to the two cathedrals. One is a bombed-out shell, the other its replacement. In the 1960s, both my parents were brought here on school trips from Yorkshire – the old Coventry Cathedral was there to make them remember the war, the new to showcase Jerusalem, their future, now being built. I brush by dozens of French schoolchildren and climb to the original cathedral. To stand in this epic shell is a devastating, unreal experience. Each giant wall is intact; every stained-glass window is gone. The ancient floor remains, the ancient ceiling blistered and collapsed the day Hitler's Luftwaffe sprayed Coventry in bombs. There are monuments to peace now, sculptures of friendship between the bereaved of Hiroshima and Coventry. As you enter, in golden letters a choice and ignored quote from the bible makes eye contact: 'Nation shall not lift up sword against nation neither shall they learn war any more.' Suddenly, the sky cracks in two and rain pelts the floor. It polishes bright the iron statue of two kneeling and weeping bomb victims, and runs down its dedication plaque, which tells how the sculpture:

... reminds us that, in the face of destructive forces, human dignity and love will triumph over disaster and bring the nation together in respect and peace.

It is to be among the most memorable moments of my English journey. Unexpectedly lifted and moved, I walk back towards the bus station. I feel privileged to be in a country where a few rights and lefts take you to something as special as Coventry Cathedral. The middle of England has glitter in its crow's feet.

I change buses again in Nuneaton, where two old men in polo neck T-shirts and smart trousers swap score predictions for tonight's England v. Sweden match. 'Three-nil, no question George.' 'Aye, he's got them hard to beat, Barry.' I am staying in a hamlet outside Hinckley, essentially so I can walk to the other middle of England tomorrow morning, and because all the hotels in Hinckley sounded scary. I enter the village pub, whose denizens would twist as one and gawp at me, were any of them in. It takes some time to get served as the lady behind the bar is reporting a 'car that slowed down and looked right in' to the police. 'I mean, this is the middle of nowhere,' she continues. A regular trots in and she fills him in on the crime spree. 'Well, they use that Google Earth to steal to order these days,' he says. They move on to talk of this eventful year of ours. 'Jubilee. Euros. Olympics. It's a big year, this one. You should be proud to be British,' she offers. 'You should be proud to be British every year,' her customer replies, and I wonder whether they mean 'British' or 'English'. I tune out and concentrate on my copy of today's *Hinckley Times*. There is a competition to 'Spot the Tin Hat and Win £25'. I later learn that, as well as Knitters, the people of Hinckley are known as 'Tin Hats'. This moniker comes from a local shepherd who often boasted he could drink a hat of ale. A blacksmith duly made him a tin hat with which to do so, and this now resides in the town museum.

Today's final bout of public transport takes me to what a welcome sign describes as 'Hinckley: Home of the Hansom Cab'.

I later read that Joseph Aloysius Hansom built the earliest of his vehicles here in 1835, and imagine he still used its first journey to tell passengers: 'Tell you what, you'll never guess who I had in 'ere last week.' The town is most not-famous for its hosiery industry, hence Hinckley United's nickname. It started knitting stockings as the English Civil War raged, its geography leaving it open to regular raids from both sides. No historian has recorded whether Royalists and Parliamentarians indulged in sock-puppet fights, so this amateur one wishes to assert that they did, just because it is a lovely mental image.

There is a vintage about Hinckley that gives its streets an air of supremacy. In England a place can achieve nothing for two centuries, but if Shakespeare mentioned it ('Do you mean to stop any of William's wages, about the sack he lost the other day at Hinckley fair?' *Henry IV, Part 2*) then it retains confidence. Some of that constant air comes from a sense of medieval tradition, not to mention the routine of religion. In living memory here there were Sunday School Union Festivals, a Procession of Christian Witness, Self-Denial Week and the Hinckley Carnival with its Queens and Maids. Where in Luton the factory girls wore the sashes, here glamour was ancient and ritualistic. What is missed by the current generation is sometimes unknowingly passed on by osmosis and manifests itself in behaviour – I realise this when, after the England match, men and women spill on to the streets and go on merry parade, an impromptu carnival. Though Bacardi Breezers have replaced prayers as unifiers and enablers, the Midlands, as far as I read it, feels very old and is happy to be stuck in its ways.

I decide to walk the two miles to the Knitters' top of town home. Hollycroft is as genteel as it sounds, a mild hill with thickset lodges from grander days and a red phone box in somebody's garden. The police station on Upper Bond Street seems unfeasibly large for a town of this size. Further up is another apparently outsized penal building, the magistrates' court. This has a hefty glass portcullis topped by a dome the shape of a sailor's hat, and black cricket-stump pillars. Maybe these places were built with history in mind. Two hundred years ago the Knitters of Hinckley rowdily indulged in some of the first flushes of Luddism. They thwacked hosiery machines with sledgehammers by way of protecting jobs. Many were imprisoned, but across Britain it caught on. Technology won in the end, and this summer evening it shows. Cars whoosh by at speed, a relentless thrashing noise to replace that of disused hosiery factories. On my walk, I see only three people on foot. I am pleased to note that 'Knitters' does not merely mark a past pursuit – the art deco premises of the Nylon Hosiery Company appear to be in fine health. Next door is a larger, disused hosiery factory, windows sore from stones hurled through, redbrick fading to black.

The hill steepens and town turns to suburb. A long stretch of hatted semi-detached houses in the Watford mould takes an age to pass through. Looking at each one of them, so prim and wholesome with their gardens and porches, is like being bored to tears by a perfect cousin. The cemetery brings them to a halt, appropriately, though even that is mild – sparse graves, not enough history or misery for my liking. As I progress the houses become more withdrawn from the road and there is even space for ample public lawns in between them. This suburbia is unmistakeably Anywhere England. I am not convinced there will be a football ground at the end of the rainbow. Which is essentially because there won't be – I have missed my turning.

It takes me twenty minutes to reach Derby Road, each step slightly more flustered than the last. Rows of dainty knitters' cottages cheer me up, as does the bold Mock Tudory of the Weavers' Arms. Its white walls and St George flags glow in the sun. The streets narrow into terraces and old factories. Among the two-up two-downs are daunting factory walls, which squash in the houses so that they resemble a skinny kid in a school photo being jostled out of place by two fat ones. No excuses for being late to work here. The biggest old factory still wears its signage: 'T. Jennings Ltd. For Tights, Stockings and Pop Socks.' On tree-ruled streets something mind-blowing happens: I see another person. He, a middle-aged gentleman walking the dog, seems to feel as I do and in tandem we try to strike up conversation. 'No, you go ...' We talk weather and then the England match ('They'll lose, 'cause I'm watching it') and then move off in opposite directions, which is odd as he was going the same way as me when I overtook him.

Soon after the factories Hinckley once again resembles a rural village. On one side of the road are fields, on the other minor mansions that poke through overgrown conifers like clumsy robot spies. Blossom trees, wheelie bins, greenery, cars: repeat to fade. Again I lose belief that hereabouts rests a football ground. I pass Hansom Road, festooned in '20mph Zone' signs, and soon there are paths only on one side. A while later, a dark green sign, perhaps a mirage, offers: 'Greene King Stadium. Home of Hinckley United FC'.

It could be delirium after an hour's walking, but the first stand I see has a roof which seems to jut into the air and resemble a Black Power fisted salute. There is no discernible entrance so I walk by a long hedge, the Berlin Wall keeping me from my destination with a rotting oak tree as its sentry tower. There is at last a cutting and I enter the car park of Hinckley's home since 2005. The club's main entrance looks like that of a modern GP surgery. Its windows are apparently based on an upside-down Tetris formation, and straddle a doorway with pagoda pretensions. Whatever the team, no matter the architecture, I find a stone-dead stadium an interesting place. Even in a modern home like this there are echoes in the bricks, broken-heart stains on the pillars. I peer into the ground. Though a touch flat-pack, its terraces are cosy and a fine example of what 'safe standing' may look like. The Knitters were formed in 1997, an amalgamation of two local sides, Athletic and Town. There had been football in Hinckley for well over a century, though a life bothering the Leicestershire Senior, Birmingham Combination and Midland Alliance leagues was never going to be glitzy. Athletic were the people's club; Town more recent upstarts. For many years, Athletic's 1923 FA Cup Fifth Qualifying Round defeat to Grimsby Town represented the high-water mark of footballing achievement. At its most popular, football in Hinckley could sustain crowds of 2,000, creeping up to 5,000 for derbies with Nuneaton Borough. Hundreds are more likely now; the Knitters were recently relegated from football's sixth tier. My idea is to watch England play from this stadium in the middle of England. I shall take a table in the adjacent Nobby's Bar and sup ale, admiring its purple carpets and scattergun furniture policy. Or, as it turns out, I shall find the bar closed and head back into town. This is what happens when I try to be spontaneous.

I rush down Castle Street. Bar Vis-à-Vis is heroically badly named and so I enter. Sticky floors try to steal my shoes and I eventually stand underneath a widescreen TV by the bar, unsure if I will be rooted to this spot for evermore, a decaying statue. There are sixty or seventy people here, most adhering to a dress code of brilliant white and St George red. The din – belly laughs and throaty shouts – gives this the feeling of not just another Friday night out, but an event. The small town of Hinckley has come together in support of the mother ship. As the game kicks off, England can hear them from Kiev. The Three Lions begin in a direct, aggressive manner, pinning Sweden against a wall, casting wide balls and crosses for the giant up front. In the battle for style Watford has emphatically defeated Barcelona. It works.

A cross from the right ascends to the perfect height. The big man hangs in the air like a Sea King helicopter, Swedish defenders stranded below. Iron neck muscles thrust his head to the ball. On impact it seems to distort before cannoning into the net. Bar Vis-à-Vis erupts, arms and legs, hugs and kisses, some that last to the restart. 'I told you, I told you,' shouts a beery man into my ear. He didn't – in fact, all I remember him saying is 'Is this stool spare, mate?' – but I don't argue. For the rest of the half, Sweden fail to irk England, and the half-time whistle is met by another heartfelt cheer. People swarm around me, leaning for attention from the bar staff, slightly wary of the outsider and his notebook. Drinks restocked, we move our eyes back to the screens and the second-half in north Ukraine. *Come on, England*. The goal hero cheaply concedes a free-kick. When it is taken the ball pings off the defensive wall and into the path of a Sweden player. His effort hits England limbs and the post but trickles in. One-all. A goal mired in such chaos rattles England. Composure evaporates. When the ball comes close to them the players poke at it then retreat, as if at half-time it has been exchanged for a grenade. Their opponents hurl it in the box, England heads duck, and a Swedish forehead glances a goal. One-nil up, two-one down. The people of Hinckley react by screaming, shaking their heads muttering 'typical' and ordering more booze. Hands rest on heads. There are even smirks at the familiarity of it all: expectation, anticipation, excitement, let down. Same old England.

Except it is not, and all because of a Roy of the Rovers super-sub. This whippet lashes a curvaceous shot into the net with one of his first touches, then steams through flailing Swedish legs to pull back for a teammate to score. Three-two. 'We never beat Sweden,' says the bargirl, 'I can't believe it.' When it matters, everyone is a pundit. The noise is infectious, stirring. The final whistle blows and the Vis-à-Vis stereo cranks up to 11. 'Three lions on a shirt ...' sing the men and women of Hinckley. I mouth along, struck by goosebumps built on recollections of being fourteen and heartbroken when that ball flew by Gazza at the far post, and on the sheer collective glee of being part of something as big as England. Watching and finding I care has told me something: my exile and my travels have swelled my Englishness. Each new England feels like something worth hanging on to. The team and the community, the belonging it occasionally breeds is another of those Englands. Tonight, I *am* an England supporter, and we *are* a community, even if we have other priorities and our players are overpaid dickheads.

The morning after I have paid a taxi driver £18 to take me the three miles home ('It's 'cause I crossed county boundaries, mate.' 'Into where, Mexico?'), I set out for the other middle of England. I am pathetically clad and shod for a walk involving the countryside and an Ordnance Survey map, but if I can survive the night train to London I can survive anything. Precision orienteering (using my fingers to translate the scale) suggests my walk should be just under four miles. The thunderstorm starts during the second. From underneath my hood I chart the repetitious country roadside as I go: nettles, ditch, bush, McDonald's cup, nettles, ditch, bush, McDonald's cup. When the skies clear I look up to find fields of comfort and barley. They eddy in the gathering wind. I can do this. I shall not rest until I find the middle of England or one of these tractors gores me. I look at some sheep whose returning glances make me realise I am singing from the soundtrack of *Stand by Me*. I hope there is no dead body at the end of this hike. If there is, it is probably mine.

Each corner brings another long stretch. I do not mind the length; I mind being able to see it. Luckily, there are plenty of stones to dribble and gates to shoot at. When I turn off the road into woods, contentment washes over me like the thick and muddy spray of a truck splashing in a ditch, which shortly afterwards also washes over me. If my map reading is correct, if the path my frozen finger rests on is this one, then I am just about here, a field near Lindley Hall Farm, a field that is geographically the centre of England. As I approach what I take to be the spot, a figure emerges from the farmhouse ahead. It seems to be a lady, and she seems to be asking what I am doing on her land. When I apologise and explain, she replies in a friendly if flustered manner. 'Oh,' she begins, 'we don't publicise that. It was a shame, a real shame, taking it from Meriden like that. They will always be the centre.' Ritual over science yet again in this corner of the Midlands, this centre of England? Possibly. Or a farmer's wife who does not like sodding men in sodden jeans on her driveway. Before her intervention, I did feel something bordering on excitement to be in England's middle. It may only be an accident of geography, but so too is supporting England, and this morning I feel like that matters.

I walk on towards the spires of Fenny Drayton. It is almost lunchtime, and this English idyll looks like it must house a stonking pub with a roaring fire. I turn another corner in England and find another piece of history. Fenny Drayton is the home of Quakerism, the teetotal home of Quakerism. I do not like all of the corners I turn. The next bus to civilisation and/or Nuneaton is in two hours. Onwards I walk, until I reach the neverland between signs denoting 'Leicestershire' and 'Warwickshire', which I am close to declaring my own republic if only so I can open a pub to drink in.

The Midlands I have seen are different and separate, neither north nor south. They are traditional, but in traditions they made themselves. There is order, ritual and mythology, a sense of continuation with ye olde, medieval England. This permanence breeds a self-assurance that can come across as unfriendly. They are of an England that is very sure of itself and does not worry about which half it is in or which side it is on, unlike a north in permanent flux and a south turning through trends as a fork churns soil. Such a mood of assurance has enabled me to say that, yes, I am an England fan, only quietly, and possibly not in a pub near my house. Now for the uncertainty of the new football season.

Chapter Ten

Burnley

First day of the season. Five words that mean the world. Five words that let us breathe again. Five words that represent hope and radiate optimism; the sun is out, our shirts are new and anything can happen. We say we would be happy with mid-table, but secretly we think promotion is probable. It matters not that our best players have left since relegation – we like the look of youth. This is August, our month, one whose dictionary definition in our minds reads '*noun:* start of new football season.' Even just rolling the word around our mouths conjures first days gone by and the fiery glow of chance.

Our Saturdays are back. If we are not at the match, we can listen and watch; 5 p.m. is the day's pinnacle again, not just another time on another long day. Even if the football man or woman still has things to do, chores to complete, he or she can do them with the commentary on. From now until May he or she will be a happier and a sadder person, exultant like a baby with a balloon one week, inconsolable when it bursts the next.

This particular August I feel defensive of us football people. After Hinckley and all that, England were ritually ejected at the quarter-final stage on penalties, which was comfortingly familiar if nothing else. Then came the Olympics. People were allowed to enter that mesh hamlet I saw before the Orient game. Gold, silver and bronze made its grey heart blaze, a thawed mammoth. British achievement captivated. The Games as a whole hypnotised a nation. Watching handball at midnight suddenly seemed like a rational activity. In itself, that was fine. Delightful, in fact. Then they went for our sport.

The people and the press gassed lyrical about the evil of football and footballers compared with the Olympics and Olympians. Here were Corinthian titans running, throwing and rowing for the love of the sport, spurred by joyous and positive congregations of wholesome families in Union Jack hats. Set against them were voracious footballers, injury-feigning and philandering, berated by boozy hoards with bellies seeping from nylon. All athletes were smiling gorgeous role models like Jessica Ennis, all footballers brag-traders and fist-wavers like Joey Barton. In the *Guardian*, Geoffrey Wheatcroft wrote of the 'incurable social disease known as Association Football', which 'sometimes looks like a game owned by crooks and despots and played by racists and rapists.' Today, as I travel to Burnley I read the same newspaper's letters page. It contains the following:

Geoffrey Wheatcroft reminds us that football is back. So is 'wife bashing'. Our women's refuge had no requests for space during the Olympics. We had six by Tuesday.

If I believed that football was a game played by rapists and watched by wife-beaters, it might dampen my August enthusiasm somewhat. But when Wheatcroft *et al* write of 'Association Football', they are writing of top-end Premier League, of multi-millionaire players. That is not my game. That is a faraway outpost of the sport, one bruised fingertip. It is not the football that unites post-industrial towns when so much else is lost to them, and it is not Chester FC running themselves. Neither is it the football that acts as a social lubricant when I am at a wedding or in the workplace, straining for common ground. I could go anywhere in the world, a dusty African village or Sydney, and find a game or a barroom debate to join. Rowing and equestrian, incidentally, are none of these things. Yes, I can do class prejudice too.

These thoughts are jangling as my train passes through the Lake District, its speed smudging Wordsworth's England. Luckily August conquers all. Burnley v. Bolton Wanderers at Turf Moor on 18 August, a compelling, history-scented proposal. I change at Preston where tribes of lads await their carriages to the new season, sampling the poetic delights of the timetable boards: Corkickle, Dove Holes, Flimby, Langwathby, Poulton-le-Flyde, Ramsgreave & Wilpshire. My route to Burnley fares well in the romantic stakes too, encompassing Pleasington, Cherry Tree, Oswaldtwistle and Rose Grove.

On the train, the heating blares and the windows are glued shut, which at least keeps the gossip in. Behind me two ladies in their sixties are nattering in heroically foggy Lancastrian accents: ''e smokes too much, 'e smoked on 'oliday, 'e smokes at 'ome, in that liddle room upsturz. Mind, 'e never smoked in Australia. Smoked when 'e got back, mind. It's no life.' 'You're not wrong, luv. I sez to 'im last time I was thuir, I sez: "Kenneth, you have got to stop," but 'e teks no notice.' We skirt Irongate, the neat wee home of Bamber Bridge FC tucked between tracks and houses. 'I sez you'll get nowt at car booter for that. Give it charity shop.' The land is lush, peaks and troughs, up to Accrington. We curve towards Blackburn's red bricks and towers of old, churches, mills then minarets, a visual history. 'I sez to Roy, I sez, "There's a sale on." 'e sez to me, "You never buy owt anyway. Let's spare t'bother and stay at 'ome. You can watch shopping channel if you like," he sez.' After they leave the train at Hapton, I miss the rattle and hum of their conversation and hope Roy has put the kettle on. The train jolts into Burnley, above us the motorway, below us the canal, further topographic context. Burnley Central station is a bungalow with an added aura of 1960s asbestos and more recent moss on gravel. I take in its facilities – a fence and a bin – and leave. Ahead is the abandoned wreck of the Adelphi Hotel, a grand old haunted house with its eyes patched by chipboard.

In Burnley's 1950s heyday, fans would splurge from the train and into the Adelphi. Wearing their claret and blue scarves over Saturday corduroy, they would gather here after steaming in from Colne, Nelson and even Skipton, over the border in Yorkshire. Ale necked, those supporters would walk downhill into town, sweeping hills above and beyond, choking chimneys in the middle distance. As they crossed an iron bridge their clogs and boots would clop and clank; many had come straight from the morning shift in mill or mine. On Yorkshire Street they passed under the nobbly bolts of the Leeds-Liverpool Canal viaduct and filed to their 2 p.m. destinations. Some went for a pint in the Miners' Club, some into Fitzpatrick's herbalists for red sarsaparilla, some into the butcher's for strips of tripe, eaten from a greaseproof bag in the street. If they did not live in the town they probably worked in it or at least knew its every nook and cranny, past and present.

During the Industrial Revolution Burnley grew from a market town backwater to the earth's largest producer of cotton cloth, and from 10,000 people to 110,000. Pitted in the dungeon of a valley its damp air provided perfect conditions for making cloth, and the Empire's growing markets invited exploitation. There was innate artisanship among Burnley's people, cultivated by centuries of spinning wool from the sheep that loitered on the hills above the town. Before breakfast, mills supplied the home market and for the rest of the day the world, went the legend. In their hundreds chimneys speckled the skyline like giant stone trees. Those who did not work in mills mined the rich carbon beneath their clogs – a number of Burnley's mines were in the town centre. The Leeds-Liverpool Canal with its wondrous Straight Mile, shunted supplies in and exports out.

The work of the spinners, weavers and miners should not be glorified from distance, though its effects deserve to be lionised. The harm they put themselves in the way of helped make Britain rich, contributing the revenues with which Teesside steel built the Empire's infrastructure. Their lives were hard. While the sun was still up in some other part of that Empire, the workers of Burnley would be awoken by a 'knocker-up' man. His job was to rat-ta-tat-tat with a cane on bedroom windows and stir the dirty-nailed sleepers within. Mines we know were dangerous, but mills too. Thunderous machinery bred a staff of lip-readers and turned many deaf. Oily machinery, air clouded with dust and wooden floors meant fire spread wildly and tragically. Burnley was predictably filthy on land and water, with bronchitis in children as common as nits. The same damp air that made it a boom-town withheld smoke and sulphur, concocting a gritty smog that reduced visibility to five yards.

When the First World War finished boom times turned to hard times in Burnley. During the 1920s Depression, unemployment hit fifty per cent and unrest bubbled. Cheaper foreign markets had taken jobs away. The Second World War saved Burnley by driving employment upwards and, when it finished, mill modernisation and pit nationalisation continued the trend. When Burnley won the league in 1959-60 though, decline had again begun to claw at the town. There was still the kind of work that merited those clogs on the way to the match – over a dozen working chimneys remained – and coal was still being wrought from the earth, but Burnley knew it must change or die. That same 1959, the one in which Luton lost the FA Cup final as Reginald Dwight looked on, the town pinned its hopes on familiar redevelopment plans based around a shopping centre, bus station and ring road.

Four days before the 1959-60 season kicked off – a faraway August with identical hopes and themes – the closure of the Benjamin Thornber and Son Mill was announced. Thornber's had been in Burnley for a century, but was now to become another statistic among the 6,000 looms scrapped in Lancashire by the Conservative government's Concentration Plan. Burnley's players will have known about this grumbling malaise – most lived in the town and travelled by service bus to games. Over the next nine months they produced football that made the entire town suspend its woes. That town backed them in force. The average Turf Moor crowd of 27,000 meant that a third of the town's population attended matches. The First Division average was twelve per cent.

Burnley had long cherished its team, residents of homely old Turf Moor since 1883. The club had a significant early role as leaders in the charge for pay and professionalism – they signed waged Scots and threatened to break away. In a town like Burnley, all labour had to mean a wage. The link between work and club was strong. Most Burnley players were miners or millworkers through the week, and when they won the FA Cup in 1914, thousands of workers went on strike to join the victory parade. Seven years on Burnley won their first league championship, going thirty games unbeaten along the way. Then as the town slid so too did the team. The pair have often mirrored one another. Burnley's population declined dramatically, falling to 80,000 when the league was won again in 1960. That year seemed to mark the last of 'old Burnley' with mill and coal work still sprinkled around by the magic dust of the post-war boom, as such representing a final pinnacle for town and team.

The latter went out in style, renowned as they were for their princely play. Jimmy Greaves referred to Burnley's game as 'poetry' and 'smooth, skilled soccer that was a warming advertisement for all that was best about British football.' Indeed, only Greaves' Spurs matched Burnley in their swift passing, possession-oriented game, modelled on the methods of Italy, Spain and those Hungarians who destroyed isolationist England and instigated our identity crisis. It was a Burnley man, Jimmy Hogan, who instilled 'push and run' football in Hungary, the nation dedicating its 6-3 victory to him. The Claret and Blues were best friends with the ball, happy in possession and fluidly exploiting space when not. Burnley football's pivot was Jimmy McIlroy, a sumptuous and languid centre-midfielder who seemed to stop all the clocks and find a pass. When no player was ready to receive, the ball was his hostage; as the opposition stormed the kidnapper, he released it into the captivity of pitch room. The Wolves manager Billy Wright admired the Burnley way, 'every man searching for space.' Theirs was an early version of Total Football with rigid roles melted away into a loose arrangement of barnstorming full-backs and centre-halves who could play a bit. Freedom was injected into their DNA. This team and their style left an indelible mark on those who saw and read of it while young. My own dad, then a young Leeds United fan, can still recite Burnley's line-up of Blacklaw, Angus, Elder, Seith, Miller, Adamson, Connelly, McIlroy, Pointer, Robson and Pilkington. What a shame that for today's young fans huge squads and high player turnover will kill the future joy of recalling notorious XIs, lounging over every syllable.

Each tier of Burnley team played in the same way, youth to reserve, training and matches. It was part of a progressive approach to training encapsulated in the club's belting training ground, dug from nothing by players in search of a summer wage. Then manager Alan Brown recalled in Arthur Hopcraft's classic *The Football Man* how, 'The players got down to it – famous ones, like McIlroy and Adamson – and dug ditches with me.' These, of course, were Maximum Wage days, days of scarcity for some players, and days when Davids like Burnley could compete with the Goliaths of wider Lancashire, Merseyside and London. Training was intense but pioneering, coaching advanced but clear. It fostered fiddle-fit players with speedy minds and super quick feet, whizz-kids from the Moors. Squad additions needed raw qualities that could be built upon, and they needed to be good lads; this was a close-knit team, which won and drank together. Their wives were a collective force to be reckoned with, influential and well known across town.

Two key figures built this Burnley, a club from an unfashionable Victorian town playing advanced football, the scarecrow in a spacesuit. Harry Potts had arrived at Turf Moor in 1937, a sixteen-year-old centre-forward who soon became his club's No. 10. He became manager in 1958, quickly building on footballing principles laid down by his predecessor Brown. A fatherly tracksuited tutor through the week and a firebrand when Saturday came, Potts was loved by his players. The manager, who moulded his team on the training ground and quietly encouraged each player in turn at a quarter to three, was transformed by the whistle. On the touchline he headed and kicked everything, a bonkers street mime act. This could overspill: during a European Cup tie in Rheims, Potts became incensed at the home side advancing free-kick positions. He ran on to the pitch and retreated the ball himself.

Potts' chairman was Bob Lord, according to Kenneth Wolstenholme a 'fair man' who worked 'the sort of day that would make younger men wince' and to Danny Blanchflower 'a self-made man who worships his creator.' Lord was elected in 1955, a lifelong fan and successful butcher, the paternalist Victorian town chairman after his time. Despite the time warp, many of his ideas for Burnley and football were undoubtedly progressive, or at least they foretold much of what was to come. It was his idea to upgrade the training ground and put emphasis on a youth programme. He supported the professionalisation of referees and abolition of the Maximum Wage, a rare trait in a chairman, and presided over the gradual upgrade of Turf Moor. He even flew his team to some away games. Yet Lord also resented supporter input ('We don't recognise any supporters' associations … My ambition is for the club to function completely without any money coming through the turnstiles at all. That is the road to Utopia'). His labelled 'bluntness' was in reality often plain offensive ('we have to stand up against a move to get soccer on the cheap by the Jews who run television'). Lord's humourless demeanour and habit of banning journalists for criticising his club meant he was, wrote Hopcraft, 'labelled in print as "the Khrushchev of Burnley", and insulting as that description was it had a certain physical aptness.' He even sold Jimmy McIlroy, and that behind Potts' back. McIlroy's sale was the first of many. Lord's stands, with their heated floors, were subsidised by the departure of talent.

If Lord's means and words were often, in modern political parlance, regrettable, his and Potts' results were wonderful. In the red-hot summer of 1959 they pokered Leeds 3-2 and scorched Everton 5-2. 'Stand in with us for all you are worth' wrote Harry Potts. Champions Wolves were destroyed 4-1 at Turf Moor. 'The ball was on our side,' said McIlroy afterwards. Only because he made it so. The FA Cup holders Forest were given an 8-0 seeing to, Bolton just the four. At Highbury, aristocratic Highbury, the mill boys beat the posh boys 4-2. Soon, top of the league Spurs visited Turf Moor. The pass-masters were turned past-masters. Two nowt to the Burnley boys. Still, Potts' men were not perfect. Flexible football was open football. Gaps at Molineux meant a 1-6 defeat, and the Clarets faced a must-win at Manchester City on the final day. Win they did, 2-1, on fierce Moss Side. Back home in Burnley, Potts danced on the town hall steps and the hordes cheered Lord. Their men had lifted a town that knew it was on the precipice of decline. Potts and McIlroy had set out to see the people smile again. Mission accomplished.

The Adelphi's old wooden sign swings in the breeze today, its faint pastels of two Fauntleroys ghostly. Behind this dead inn is Sainsbury's where men wearing claret and blue shirts push trolleys, shopping first then the match. I walk downhill into town, my modern office-boy shoes registering no noise. Old mill chimneys still mark the sky like disused parentheses and beyond them are motionless wind turbines. The turbines are set on gentle hills, the kind of which surround Burnley on all sides, giving a secluded feel as if inhabitants are the inmates of an organic prison. Though placed similarly, it feels more isolated and secretive than Sheffield, as if it could not care less whether you knew it was there or not. I arrive at St James' Street and the first buildings I see are humbly pleasant and intact Victorian shopping blocks with flats above. Their shops have kindly wooden fronts whose names swither between museum piece (Empire News) and modernity (Bibi's Kebab and Pizza House). Behind the main row and about 100 metres apart are more mill chimneys, emphasising just how physically central industry was here. The last town centre mine only closed in 1971, the final steam-powered mill in 1982. All of these buildings are in chunky stone the colour of dirty straw. This quiet grandeur masks high unemployment and poverty levels. Burnley has finished mourning, but is still suffering. Its population level remains in decline and those who stay often work elsewhere. Rather than the refined and refurbished mainstays of lower St James' Street, an abundance of dirt-cheap shops at its highest end tells Burnley's truths. As I walk around I see children holding yellow and blue balloons pronouncing the opening of a new 99p shop. Its competitors will include Poundland, the Original Mega Pound Superstore and Wacky Pound, among others. Just as the penny stores of Victorian times are back, so too are the pawnbrokers. Today's proffer DVDs, games consoles and furniture for rent. *Furniture for rent* in the world's seventh richest country.

I sit on a bench, surrounded by hanging baskets, last night's hardened kebab onions crunching under my feet. There is calmness here and a soft happiness that will always triumph over rented furniture. That, a thousand times more than the Union Jacks that line St James' Street, makes me feel patriotic. These people have had everything hurled at them, but still stop in the street to laugh together about last night's telly. Not that much has changed. Burnley is a perfectly decent place because of these people.

There are shirts of claret and blue everywhere in Burnley today. The club still belongs to the town, as it did in 1959, and to support anyone else is an act of treason. New shirts in August, bare arms before winter; all part of the gleeful first day ritual. When I see a child in full-kit (including shinpads) I know everything is grand in the world. In the Charter Walk shopping centre one such shirted man tells a flock of old ladies of his NHS woes: 'There's going to be a helluva a lot of suing going on, I tell you.' Hereabouts occurred one of Burnley's rebellious episodes. In 1842, the Plug

Riots – a General Strike across Britain inspired by Chartism – reached Burnley. One report recalled how:

> All the shops in the neighbourhood were demanded of their contents. The crowd made a special design upon Horatio Hartley's butcher shop. Being well-stocked with meat, he and his brother armed themselves with knives and kept back the plunderers. The mob deemed it prudent to leave his shop alone.

Today in the market hall the butchers shops are being demanded of their contents again, albeit politely and from queues of nattering locals. One's window stickers offer 'Black pudding, hot or cold,' another boasts 'Tripe sold here. Honeycombe seam. Dark and Roll.' Burnley Market contains the usual bright menagerie of sweet stalls, grocers and poster/print/flag stands, and a lively fancy dress emporium. It is busy, most units are occupied and the packed booth-like side cafes leave the air heady with gossip and chip fat. In a side hall an old boy artist paints the Burnley he remembers and 60p VHS videos linger unloved on a table.

Back on St James' Street my nostrils guide me to Oddie's Bakery, my ears towards the bandstand. Whoever is in charge of my *Truman Show* life is doing it again: a brass band. I sit, look and listen. They are a bit cheerier than a Yorkshire brass band, knocking out sing-alongs for the blue rinse crowd. A band member shuffles among us offering lyric sheets, and the conductor tells stories of each song. One involves an extended anecdote about 'Ben', a Michael Jackson record. An old man in a Disneyworld T-shirt heckles something derogatory about 'that oddball Jackson'. Beyond the bandstand, more claret and blues swarm into twin corner pubs, nodded in by Robocop bouncers. I potter down backstreets and eventually reach the lapping waters of the Peace Garden, complete with Princess Diana plaque. Every time I read or hear her name, I think not of tragedy and the People's Princess, but of football being postponed. In 1981 (that year again), as dewy eyes watched her royal wedding, Burnley responded to a Conservative government edict asking councils to spend money on civil defence by declaring itself a Nuclear-Free Council. The Peace Garden is a monument to their defiance. It is surrounded by serious Victorian buildings, built to enable the working class and keep secure its streets. The library, building society and police station assert civic order in a reassuringly deep northern voice. As I stand and admire them I catch the bass of Bolton fans arriving from Burnley Manchester Road railway station. 'White army' they bellow. On Manchester Road stand the pillars, porticos and frills of the Mechanics' Institute and the town hall, further glorious stone elegies to Burnley's buzz town years. At the Weavers' Triangle the worm-brown canal shimmers briefly before turning still again. More claret and blues stare at their reflections in it and sup pints.

I walk from the peak of Manchester Road, hundreds of clarets and blues, peppered with whites, lumbering towards the match in front of me. It feels as if this town exists today for the football and the football only. Everything else is a side matter. It is a football town in which every road leads to 3 o'clock. Me and the August shirts reach Yorkshire Street and cross under the bolted viaduct like millions before us. On this road of yellow bricks Turf Moor comes into view, a hazy Emerald City. There is no eating of tripe today; just burgers snaffled quickly in-between swift ales at the Brickmakers' Arms and the Turf Hotel. Off the main drag I walk through the guests' door of the Miners' Club and pay my 20p entrance fee. Twenty pence – take that, Luton. By the pool table is a monument to 'Those who worked and died in the darkness, still loved the light' – nineteen miners who lost their lives in the Hapton Colliery Disaster of 1962.

I order a pint of bitter and a 'Bene 'n' 'ot'. 'It'll give you strong stomach that, flower' says the barwoman. A Bene 'n' 'ot is a Benedictine liqueur with hot water. More Benedictine is sold in Burnley Miners' Club than anywhere else on earth. It was a taste cultivated by the East Lancashire Regiment in the trenches of Normandy during the bitter winter of 1918. Today, their great grandsons and daughters lap it up. A proud barfly reels off the story for me, and tells me how 'We've had them all here. Sky. BBC. Even a Canadian film crew the other week. That's one of only two gallon Bene bottles in't world. Other's in't monastery.' The Bene 'n' 'ot smells ever so slightly antiseptic and is the colour of a 'sample'. Despite these unpromising medical beginnings it tastes marvellous – sweet menthol meets a brew made by Nana. Here's to the Burnley boys in the trenches making their best of a bad lot.

The first day sun beams invincibly as I cross from Yorkshire Street on to Harry Potts Way. Both sets of fans are mixing easily despite the presence of police horses, which always seems to heighten tension. Many supporters stroke the gee-gees fondly as they pass. 'I've got a tenner at 5/1 on you, cock,' smiles a tubby Boltonian. The noises of matchday stoke up once more, a routine soundtrack blown on and dusted down like a photo from a loft. 'Programmes. PROGRAMMES. Get yer programmes,' then something intelligible from a half-time draw salesman in a bib, and solo male voices growling away the frustrations of Pools-free Saturdays. 'Yooooouuuuu Whites.' 'Come on the Burnley.' Those who have not seen one another since May shake hands and sometimes embrace in the street. Names are not always known, but once you have had a season ticket next to someone for a decade it is too late to ask.

I walk around the outside of Turf Moor, the ground that Bob Lord built. Only two of his stands remain, one named after him. Lord died a week before I was born, not living to see Burnley go up as Division Three champions in 1981-82. That was a temporary reprieve – far had they fallen since those halcyon days. In 1987, only the last ditch defeat of Orient preserved league status. Although the enclosures and food kiosks are named after Burnley greats, there is a strange lack of football's former world for such an old ground, save for the painted scars of a disused turnstile wall at the far end of the David Fishwick Stand. That, though, is by design; Lord was, remember, a modernist. The innards of the Jimmy McIlroy Stand host 'UCFB,' which offers, apparently, 'university degrees and executive education in football business.' It is probably what our Lord would have wanted.

I turn a corner and spot a queue. Hundreds are waiting patiently for beer from the canteen hut of Burnley Cricket Club, whose ground neighbours Turf Moor. The far boundary brushes against the stand behind one of the goals; these Siamese venues were a Victorian entertainment complex. The whites of Bolton have commandeered the sizeable pavilion and a youths' game played to parents this morning is now cheered riotously by the visiting hundreds. The roar that goes up when a wicket is taken inspires jubilant scenes in the slips, a glimpse of the big time long to be cherished.

Passing new stewards meeting for the first time I heave a turnstile into the Bob Lord Stand. At the John Connelly Bar I wait for my pint of Thwaites to settle and note that they too stock Benedictine, which beats even Mr John's Portman Road brandy as a football ground catering surprise. Youth team players hover in official tracksuits, their first-team fantasies intact for now at least. I perch on a wall while two bulky Burnley fans who were born with plastic forks in their mouths pick at chips and talk about holidays. 'You've been to that Sharm el Sheikh, haven't you Steve? She fancies it but I'm not going over there while it's like it is.' 'They wouldn't leave our lass alone over there. Blond-haired, in't she.'

From the dark of the concourse I climb into the wide-open light of the new season and am transfixed by the varnished wooden seats that pack the stand. These are working antiques, with their ornate brass joints as close to arts and crafts as stadium seats get. The brimming Bolton end has them too, though most in there stand up and glare distractedly on to the lush pitch.

The lull before the players enter the pitch is filled with songs from both sets of fans. This is all too perfect until the man in charge of the PA responds by blasting everybody with some unwelcome Foo Fighters. Thankfully, when the claret and blues and the whites stroll on even he turns things down. The players' tunnel is located behind a goal, so the bench battalions must cross the pitch to reach their dugouts, situated in front of our wooden wonders. This allows cacophonous barracking of the away manager, once of this parish. 'Jooooooooooodas, Jooooooooooodas,' sing the boys and girls and the men and women of Burnley. Loyalty remains prized among supporters. To move to another Lancashire club is like shacking up with the tarty girl next door.

The sun climbs higher, visor arms move to foreheads and the season kicks off. From home and away the noise rises, amplified by the end of non-season boredom and the swagger of new season hope. The Wanderers fans in particular are strident, which they never seem to be at the Reebok. It recalls for me early 1990s trips to intimidating Burnden Park, and highlights that the best noise now is often made by away fans, and often the best place to watch your team is somewhere else. The racket transfers straight to the hearts of the players who begin frantically, passing quickly, tackling sharply and shooting wildly. It is all very English and very enjoyable. Wanderers, newly demoted from the big time, try to slow things and engage in the artful. A delicately chipped free-kick intended to be ornate backfires momentously, trickling out of play. The Burnley mobs jeer as one. Welcome back.

The treacherous away manager moves to his touchline, causing those around me to rise and bellow biblically. Not one of them looks harmful or readily violent and I reflect how, if they saw him in the street, they would probably engage in polite conversation. This kind of hostility seems more traditional and theatrical than the needless vitriol I have seen elsewhere, though perhaps the hands of my moral compass are looser following a summer far from the madding crowds.

Wanderers have an implacable mountain up front. Born in Sheffield, he is built for the days of shove the keeper and Ernest Needham. For nigh on a decade he has been the peak at which teammates have cast long passes and crosses like picks on ropes thrown into the snow. If he had played for Graham Taylor's Watford he would have been a superstar. He was born after his time, but simply by refusing to change has earned opposition respect. It is not a deferential respect (this is football), but one detectable in the jubilant celebrations that greet the floppy-blond Burnley left-back who clatters him. Footballing respect is grudging, perverse and will never be admitted. Though his team do initially try to pass the ball on the ground, when no joy is found they seek his head. Burnley, with two narky ferrets up front, keep things concise. This is in contrast to their supporters, who in song manage to wring three syllables from the word 'Burnley'.

Things become niggly as players wheeze in heat, which reminds them that the beach is only a few weeks behind them. Fitness does not yet match intention, making for late tackles and one or two circus moves. Two opposing midfielders try to outmuscle one another and end up resembling a pantomime horse without its costume. Short-hit passes are seized on ('well read, lad') and possession veers quickly between the sides, ending usually in a fit of pinball rebounds that serve to keep the crowd cooing and being unfeasibly grateful that football is back. In the neon frenzies of August's first day, there is nowhere else to be. This is heartfelt football in which ability does not always meet idea and ball is not always taken before man.

Burnley begin to find their range, firing in a succession of long-range shots. One swerves and reminds me of the heat you see on continental airport tarmac. Somehow the Wanderers goalkeeper gets both wrists to it and bats it over for a corner. One of Burnley's ferrets irks Wanderers' lanky centre-half, snipping at his ankles and sniffing for crumbs. The home side are tenacious. When they shoot they follow after the ball and sometimes seem to overtake it. Such forcing and hunting brings them a 1-0 lead. 'Jooooodas, what's the score, Judas Judas what's the score?' sing those around me.

Wanderers kick-off, but Burnley again set about them. Away shoulders drop and most in white become guilty of propelling missiles in the direction of their big man. I look at their loyal army behind the goal. To a man and woman they are stood, many with arms folded. Last year's tepid relegation stretches out behind them, the long season ahead in front. The half-time whistle goes and they are not sure whether to boo or laugh, so in the main keep silent. The man in front of me rises revealing on his seat an ancient remnant of floral carpet. I imagine he has had this since Burnley were champions. He reaches for his flask because it is never too hot for tea. Ahead of us substitutes thrash footballs at one another and on a pitch within the pitch school kids play the game of their young lives. In the gents, half-time analysis is curt. 'They are utter shite,' says one man. 'I think we might go up,' another.

The second-half begins with two free-kicks each in the opening thirty seconds and a purple butterfly hovering around us. 'Even that bugger is Burnley,' says carpet remnant man. Burnley force the pace again, though Wanderers strive to remind us they are alive with thudding challenges. The home keeper indulges in a short spot of keep-ups before floating a pass straight to an opposition midfielder. He has a clear run on goal and is bawled on by those behind the goal whose noise rises as he reaches the penalty area. Their sound crescendos like that of the paddock as an outside bet nears the finishing line. Wanderers will equalise, go on to win it and probably be top from now until May. He falls over the ball. A few minutes later Burnley make it 2-0.

The second comes when a cross is hoiked in and Bolton's centre-halves and goalkeeper stare at the ball as if it is a difficult Japanese puzzle. A Burnley player nods it in to the gaping net. The new season is an hour old and the claret and blues have promotion in their nostrils. To the tune of *Wild Rover* they chorus: 'No nay never no more/Will we play Bastard Rovers.' Across from us in the stand-edge nearest the away supporters, hundreds are turned towards their Lancastrian brethren, jigging and jibing. A few twirl their shirts over their heads revealing expansive stomachs. Jooooodas creeps forward from the bench to be met with cries of 'sacked in the morning/you're getting sacked in the morning.' His instructions make no difference as Burnley continue to probe when on the ball and harry when not. Wanderers have lost their map to the penalty area and instead shoot implausibly. When anything looks like it might be on target, a Burnley leg, chest or head blocks it. It makes the away side lose heart, and even when they keep the ball their forays seem more like contractual obligations than investigative experiments.

Burnley inhale the pressure and strike Bolton on the break. Full-backs and wingers overlap and swap roles, the living ghosts of 1960. Their left-winger runs with one shoulder lower than the other as if pressed to the mill. As he labours three stepovers and lands another cross on top of the net, those behind the goal ponder the defeated away fan's dilemma: stay to boo and see who claps us; leave and make the earlier train? Today's Man of the Match is awarded to Burnley's No. 8 who celebrates with a crunching centre-circle tackle that puts hairs on the chest of his opponent. By the referee's third and final peep an almighty roar fills the air. Happy Clarets drift off into the evening sun and before long I am left alone in the wooden seats.

Litter blows across the players' car park and the wind carries a scent of ageing burgers and police horse manure. Just after Yorkshire Street I cross high above a small stream and waterfall, church bells chiming a street or two away. I begin an uphill walk to my hotel for the night, passing the Duke of York pub, centrepiece of riots here in 2001. What were initially reported as race riots turned out, according to an official inquest, to be drug gang turf wars exploited by racist groups external to Burnley. Scapegoating and mythology allowed the British National Party to crowbar a divide. In 2002 they made their first breakthrough into UK politics in Burnley, winning three council seats. They were able to paint a town flooded by foreign invasion and bursting at the seams. In fact, this is an emigrant town whose population decreases every year. In council elections three months before my visit, the BNP lost their token remaining seat.

Along Colne Road Asians and whites inhabit the same space without mixing. Sharing social class and geography, they are silently bonded by having nowt. Some rows of terraces remain, some are boarded up and four of five streets have been bulldozed, rendering a crater of a community. Any sadness I feel is tempered by the sight of young kids of every colour hammering a ball about in the rubble.

The main drag is a mix of Burnleys – and Englands – old and new, both still breathing. On one side of the road are Byerden House Socialist Club and then Paradise WMC, on the other sari shops, halal butchers and a Polski Sklep. I imagine there is still tension, but there is also a pact of silence that is hopefully a welcome stepping stone to future integration rather than simmering resentment. Ten minutes uphill, I cross a road and things change. The houses are gradually larger and farther from the path. Eventually I reach mill-owner mansions now inhabited by tanned Lancastrians and multi-Mercedes Asians, both of whom have left their people down the hill behind. If one road on my travels is an exhibition of England's narrative, then this is it. At this end, no one ignores his neighbours because of race, but because isolation is what middle-class people do. In this strange way does becoming bourgeois unwittingly fight racism.

In the hotel bar dregs of a wedding party slur their disapproval of the modern world. A Lancastrian businessman of sixty-three sits with his Mauritian wife of thirty-seven (I am not guessing this. He tells most who enter the room). 'There will never be another generation like ours,' he says to a Cockney man of similar age who looks and sounds as if he once managed Status Quo. 'We pulled ourselves up by the bootstraps. Worked our backsides off. Not like this lot today.' Quo replies: 'I have this saying – "You get out what you put in."' I am not sure that is strictly his idiom, but

I let it go. The conversation turns to which cars they 'let' their wives drive (Quo: 'Don't let her near the Bentley now; 35k of damage the bitch did') and which nationalities they will not allow to rent their properties (Sixty-three: 'No Poles. They are dirty people'). I leave hoping that indeed my generation is not like theirs and reflecting how, despite 1981 and all that, we not are Thatcher's Children: they are.

The bus into town redeems my mood. First, we pass a horse and cart, then, a man in a flat cap gets on and tells the driver jokes that we can all hear. I walk by the Keirby Hotel, a dreadful concrete hive and the showpiece of that 1959 ring road renewal plan. It resembles a decrepit block of flats wearing a conservatory as a tutu. Outside the Bier Huis Claret sleeves raise toasts to 2-0. I seem to have arrived during clientele shift changeover, as all-day drinking husbands swap with dolled-up gangs of wives. They complete their substitutions, a peck on the cheek instead of a high-five. Ales are abundant in the Bier Huis, but even hops and oats do not fill my stomach. For some time I walk the streets of Burnley in search of food. The polished cobbles and thudding chain bars of Hammerton Street are empty of people. A small mill at the road's end has been smartly converted into nightclubs called Lava and Ignite. Next to the canal, a rat runs over the shining night-out shoes of a man smoking outside a bar. I remember a conversation I recently had with my mum. 'You've been to Burnley before, love.' 'Have I? When?' 'On that canal holiday. There was a dead sheep in the water. Or a cat. I forget.' I end up eating my first McDonald's in well over a decade. In my lifetime McDonald's went from the height of exoticism (everyone my age remembers their first – mine was in Milton Keynes) to a hated symptom of all that was wrong with the world. It is now somewhere in-between apparently because it sells salads and tells you how pleasantly its cows are killed. It is bright, just as I remember it, and the servers still smile even though they would rather be anywhere else. I pity the young girl that serves me: the end of the drinking shift has brought hunter-gatherers in nylon Claret. After chips that taste exactly how I remember – a not unpleasant sensation – I return to the hotel feeling a bit grubby.

The next morning I cleanse my soul with a walk high above Burnley. I pass through an estate where children kick a flat ball in the road and one two-up and two-down has a St George's cross painted across its entire front. As I glance down on this unique little place of bold stone, foreground chimneys and background hills, I see that Turf Moor is almost at the centre of the landscape ahead of me, which feels like its natural place. The club matters today as much as it did when it was founded. It matters even more than it did in 1959; it, and football, are things worth belonging to and believing in.

Chapter Eleven

Bradford

Spent raindrops race one another down a carriage window as the train pulls out of Newcastle. Saturday has come again, and so I am travelling south. The rain shatters against the Angel of the North. From this angle she seems to be turning sideways to stop the front of her face getting wet, lest her slap runs. Passengers loiter in gangways and by the toilets whose system of buttons a German lady is struggling with. When the conductor arrives she requests 'information on the relevant complaints procedure.' Teesside skies and the Cleveland Hills mark our passing into Yorkshire, home sweet home.

The first sporting crowd I will be among today has congregated at York station. From beneath fascinators and bright dresses, or clad in finest suits and ties, Geordies, Mackems, Mancs, Scousers, Teessiders and Loiners merge on their way to the racecourse. There are thousands of them, their accents colliding into white noise. The sport of kings appears incredibly democratic on days like this, not least because the bookies will beat them all.

The train to Bradford careers by the village I grew up in, and I feel a little bad about the furore caused by a recent sarcastic article of mine about the place. 'Mrs Denton has photocopied it and distributed it,' said my mum on the phone, 'and the Church Table Tennis Club are livid. Everyone went silent when I went in the Co-op.' Still, these lands are my heritage, my family on both sides being miners-turned-bus drivers from Leeds. We curve out of their city and away from Elland Road, that intimidating house of prestige. Across from me a pair of teenagers absent-mindedly pursue different conversations. 'It's called a capo. It helps you play higher notes' and 'I keep forgetting words. I forgot "skirting board" the other day. And "oven glove."'

The dark reds of outer Leeds brick turn to the striking yellows of inner Bradford. Even underneath a sky the colour of whale flesh these sandstone temples to Bradford's glory days are cheerful. The city was built on civic confidence, its choice of stone reflecting optimism and a sunny alternative to dour satanic Leeds.

The sky gives way and makes drowning rats of us all. This is epic rain. Rain to stand in doorways and watch. It pingpongs on the roads and kerbs. Waiting on high for the weather to pass allows me to take in Bradford's terrain. Whereas Burnley sits in the flat foot of a valley, Bradford seems to be a series of brows surrounded by larger hills. Everything is a climb and yet you never seem to reach the top. Miles of terraces file up hillsides, solid infantry regiments. Old mills and newer minarets are scattered among them, as is Valley Parade stadium, almost comically large for a fourth division home. 'Bradford's role in life is to make every place else in the world look better in comparison, and it does this well', Bill Bryson wrote in *Notes From a Small Island*. He must have had his eyes closed.

Even if Bradford were unspeakably ugly, the history behind its look makes it an attractive proposition. They were weaving wool here even before they were in Burnley. John Leland wrote in 1536 how Bradford 'standith much by clothing.' In the English Civil War the city defended itself from Royalist invasion by hanging cumulus bales of wool from its towers to muffle cannon fire. The Royalists returned, 10,000 of them. When finally they took Bradford, there was no genocide as was the norm – a ghost had apparently told their commander, the Earl of Carlisle, to 'pity poor Bradford'.

Modern Bradford began in the eighteenth century when production switched from wool to worsted, giving it the clumsy nickname 'Worstedopolis'. Mass industry means organised labour or, in the eyes of government, rebellious notions to be quashed. Bradfordians reacted to parliament's 1726 Act forbidding combinations of weavers by forming a National Union of Hand Woolcombers. Mechanisation led to further agitation – those smashers and meshers of the Luddite movement familiar to the knitters of Hinckley. Nothing and no one could stop the Industrial Revolution, of course; Bradford people instead strived to make it work for them, first through graft, then through crusading for political reform.

Bradford linked to the same Leeds-Liverpool Canal that soups through Burnley, making Worstedopolis a world player via ports on the Mersey and Humber. Steam powered mills sprang up and squeezed out millions of cloth yards. Human toil paid for the mill-owner mansions that still straddle the city's outskirts. Thirteen-hour days, teen labour, sooty air, no sewage, water or lighting – the charge sheet is familiar. Bradfordians did not just let things happen to them, however. They rebelled, gradually forcing the changes they knew governments or industrialists would not willingly enact. Strikes and strong support for Chartism helped shift the sands. After the mid-nineteenth century Bradford's slums were pulled down and an infrastructure built. In the late Victorian years prosperity and consensus were threatened by deathly industrial decline. When working conditions were strangled and jobs made scarce, Bradfordians knew how to rebel. Troops were sent in to quell their more radical waverings, such as the Silk Street riots of 1891. Means of effecting change calmed, but desire for it did not.

The advances of homely English socialism thrived in Bradford's Edwardian days. It was a place and a time that J. B. Priestley knew well. His words make him a vivacious guide to the city, past and present. Priestley crops up among mills, in the surrounding countryside or at the match. His is a Bradford of wonder in simple and golden days before world war changed it forever:

> Consider what Bradford had to offer us – three daily papers and a weekly, the Subscription concerts on Fridays, the Bradford Permanent series on Saturdays and superb choral singing almost any night, two theatres, two music halls, two or three professional concert parties, an Arts Club, a Playgoers Society, one football club that had won the FA Cup not so long before, several fine old pubs from the George in Market Street to the Spotted House, easily reached from the band concerts in Lister Park.

It was, he said, 'considered the most progressive place in the United Kingdom …' Exotic in-comers with their wool samples from the Andes, a rampant arts scene, radical politics and ideas – Bradford was doused in possibility. Campaigning won shorter working hours that could be spent enjoying it all. Outside the arts, first came the rugby clubs that would later be the backbone of the League game, then their football brothers. Cycling and rambling groups took Bradfordians into their beloved, surrounding moors. As Priestley wrote of the thinly veiled 'Bruddersford' in his *Bright Day*, no 'man could be exiled from the uplands and the blue air; he always had one foot on the heather.' The groups who helped locals 'to hear the larks and curlews, to feel the old rocks warming in the sun' were often run by the Independent Labour Party (ILP). Formed by the Bradford Labour Union in 1893, the ILP existed separately to the Labour Party for three decades, finding particular success in Scotland. The young Priestley's family were first Bradford Labour Union members and then ILPers. Their contemporary socialists won high positions and oversaw changes with implications far beyond Bradford. School Board leader Margaret McMillan founded eight elementary schools that gave 24,000 children free meals, milk and health inspections. The pupils that made cloth did not have much of it to their name – when they arrived for lessons it was found that more than a hundred of them had not changed clothes for over six months. Their garments were burned, the children fumigated. Poverty was never far from the eye even if it lurked at 'back o't mill' Other Bradford socialists pushed for and won a clean water supply, and influenced a progressive civic state that became the first town in England to supply electricity. In 1904 the city demonstrated its pooled wealth at the Bradford Exhibition, an extravaganza of stalls, rides and fireworks. Sadness sometimes grasps the coat-tails of glory in this town: most of the Africans imported to take part in the exhibition's 'Somali Village' contracted influenza and died.

When the rain gods go on a tea break I make for Valley Parade. The terraced houses that descend towards it contain mostly Bangladeshi and Pakistani Bradfordians, ranging from those who came here to man the mills in the 1960s, to their great grandchildren. The stadium skulks among their streets, a castle over the village. Despite such ostentation it feels logical and as if this is exactly where a football ground should be. In the club shop a thirty-something son tries to buy his mother an Official Bradford City raincoat. 'But it's yer birthday, Mam. Come on. Let me buy it yer.' 'You're not spending twenty quid on me.' 'Mam, I've got money now. Let me.' He wins and she fondly watches him go and pay, her moneyed boy done good.

Outside my smile fades at the sight of golden names on black marble. I have reached a memorial plaque whose dedication is appropriately stark: 'In memory of the 56 people who lost their lives as a result of the fire at this stadium on 11 May 1985'. I spend a couple of minutes reading their names. The youngest victims were eleven years old, four of them. Samuel Firth was the eldest at eighty-six, and a former chairman. He was born before Bradford City even existed. Eleven of the victims were women. The thing that sends me from quivering to crying is realising just how many dads and lads, and other family, died together. There went Jack and Leo Coxon, seventy-six and forty-four; there went Howard and Sarah Turner, forty-one and sixteen; there went three generations of the Fletchers (Andrew, Edmond, John and Peter, eleven, sixty-three, thirty-four and thirty-two); there went Felix, Peter and Rupert Greenwood, thirteen, forty-six, eleven; there went Gerald, Richard and Robert Ormondroyd, forty, twelve and twelve; there went Craig, Jane and Trevor Stockman, fourteen, sixteen and thirty-eight. Of course, the names of those that died alone strike hard too: did Herbert Bamford's wife wait and wait at home? Did Edith and Fred Hindle, seventy-nine and seventy-six, have kids who survived or were elsewhere? Did Nellie Foster attend alone and die alone?

That May day, infamously, started as a day of celebration. Bradford had that season earned promotion to Division Two. Their upward trajectory began in 1981-82 when they finished as Division Four runners-up to Sheffield United. That season, player-boss Roy McFarland, a man schooled by Saint Brian of Ayresome, led the Bantams to nine early wins in a row. Things stalled and an arctic winter robbed a month of games. Come the end of March, 25,000 saw them fill their senses with a draw at Bramall Lane. Promotion was solidly back in the reckoning, and soon achieved. Bradford were spurred on by their dependably inspirational captain Ces Podd. Podd, a right-back, is something of a lost pioneer: he was one of the first black players to enjoy a long

Football League career, and the earliest to receive a testimonial. Podd's name brings smiles to Bradfordian faces: after retirement he coached deprived youths and even acted the lead in a Leeds Playhouse production.

After facing sudden liquidation in 1983, Bradford began their 1984-85 promotion season with a Don Revie man, Trevor Cherry, in charge. Their win at Burnden Park on 6 May ensured that five days later Valley Parade would be fuller than normal for the match with Lincoln City. It had been fifty-six years since sun had reflected off silverware at the old ground. Thousands that day saw steel girders in the car park as they arrived. These were the frame of the new main stand on which work would begin after the game. The extant one had been in use since 1911. That day the wind blew in a different direction to usual, away from the Kop. When ancient rubbish under the wooden stand caught fire, that bluster carried the flames across the old main stand like a cavalry charge. Inside four minutes it had engulfed the entire structure and taken most of its victims. Survivors poured on to the pitch. Television pictures should have been cut, but rolled on. Few who witnessed them can lose the image of a supporter running across the pitch, engulfed by flames.

The rain drops on to metal vases and pots at the memorial's foot. It sounds like the ticking of a grandfather clock. They remember quietly here. Perhaps it is the Yorkshire way; a song and a dance are summat for Saturday night. Once a year Bradford gathers and Fletchers, Greenwoods and Ormondroyds stand in peace. They are joined by that generation's City players, still scarred and silent.

I walk towards the modern Kop, where the glassy front, corrugated silver walls and amber ribcage of the main stand are a far cry from tradition and should be. Even for a stadium traditionalist like me there is no room for sentimentality here. Opposite the turnstiles is Bradford's former superstore, built in times of Premier League expansionism. Little over a decade ago the Sky wagon was in town. Two top-flight seasons left a souvenir of two periods in administration. But what memories: from the jaws of 1985 to the clouds of 1999. There is a supporters' cafe within the superstore's blocky greys now, and a 'Free School' is due to be opened here soon. As such, the state will be buying the Bradford City Superstore.

I watch the people of Bradford float towards their turnstiles, the bottoms of their trousers sodden, and think of Priestley's unsurpassable evocation of 'Bruddersford' and watching football:

> It turned you into a member of a new community, all brothers together for an hour and a half, for not only had you escaped from the clanking machinery of this lesser life, from work, wages, rent, doles, sick pay, insurance cards, nagging wives, ailing children, bad bosses, idle workmen, but you had escaped with most of your neighbours, with half the town, and there you were cheering together, thumping one another on the shoulders, swopping judgements like lords of the earth, having pushed your way through a turnstile into another and altogether more splendid kind of life.

Today, and indeed often through my journey, it has been hard to believe that much has changed. The detail is different, the themes identical. All of us are still escaping when we push for that more splendid kind of life, and the pressures that make us want to do so are markedly similar. At the levels and places I have watched football, we are often working-class and very rarely of the corporate spectator middle-class. We are escaping from credit card debts, some of which have been generated following football. We shop in Sainsbury's at the start of the month and Iceland by the end. Not dirt poor, not comfortable. We still feel part of a community even if we can't quite define it, and in fuzzy days it is best embodied by our local football team. I cannot speak of those who do not go to football and answer whether they have been excluded by the price of the game, but this is what I see of those who do attend. Then when we are inside the ground and the green has lit our faces we are still Priestley's characters. Nowhere else do we soberly hug strangers in ecstasy and cry out in agony. We feel more together with humanity here than in our own families. Admit it. On no other subject are we such seasoned experts; there are very few entertainments you can go and see where the audience is convinced, as one, that it knows more than the professionals on stage.

Underneath a sign that reads 'No Ball Games in This Area' I enter the Kop. Bradfordians talk and laugh in groups, hot or cold plastic liquids to hand. Gangs of friends and families, who know each other from home, work or here display Christmas levels of cheer. It is intriguing to watch such bonhomie in such sparse and dank surrounds, the faint balm of processed meat tickling the air. Under a sign declaring that 'Bradford City Have the Following Vacancies' someone has scrawled 'Fans.'

It takes a good five minutes for me to reach my seat at the top of the Kop. I face the back wall panting and turn slowly around. This gigantic stand, this expansionist white elephant, may be a reason for Bradford's financial demise, but the view is spectacular. The stadium feels like an opulent Tudor castle built from the spoils of war. Disregarding that the stadium is now owned by a pension fund (rent: £370,000 p.a.), I marvel at its otherworldly scale. The Kop is adjoined to a main stand that can hold 9,000 people, and itself has capacity for 7,500. To my right I watch each ruler-straight row of the main stand's lower half become more than three quarters full with Lego-sized people. The Kop's lower half is also the busier one – up here, my next-door neighbour is ten seats away. I am isolated and looking down on things, a human CCTV camera. Along the left touchline is a decent-sized stand rendered into Subbuteo scale by comparison. The end behind the goal is realistically tiny, which feels disappointing.

When the matchstick men beneath have finished their warm-ups and disappeared into mousehole doorways, the pitch waits empty save for one or two plodding mascot figures. Across the stadium people stand and stare at the dear green place ahead of them. Occasionally they share their thoughts but as the small hand grasps at '3' they are either alone in their heads or together in song. As ever the choir must overcome the Tannoy, now belting out The Skids' 'Into the Valley', a paean to the waste of war. The music relents. 'Aye oh City, City Aye oh' they peal like hoarse church bells. Then in the far corner the matchstick men stroll on to the pitch and a lone trumpet blasts from the speakers. Even if a fan is not speaking to their team after a recent humiliation, he or she loves them in this moment. We all know that on some days, 2.59 p.m. will be as good as it gets.

Led by three men in black the players stop on the halfway line. Claret and ambers shake the hands of blue and yellows then dart off to drink the rising praises of their crowds. The trumpet intro has ripened into a wholeheartedly performed local anthem ('Proud to be a Bradford man, City through and through/Blessed to be a Yorkshireman, God's Country that is true'), but most have stopped noticing as they attempt to work out the line-up and formation. Once the captains gather for their centre-circle photocall, singing is left to the experts. 'Come on City, Come on City,' shout the Kopites in quivering voices desperate to win, their fists pumping the air with each line. 'We love you City, we do.' As full-backs star-jump and forwards shake their legs, the clouds part and the pitch is suddenly lit from above. Even God needs escapism.

My isolation ends when two teenage girls arrive and sit in the row in front of me. An awful lot of young people have found Valley Parade the place to be this Saturday afternoon, which delights me. I am still thinking about my game's rosy future when Bradford score. One-nil happens when a Wimbledon defender ducks under a vague punt from a home centre-half. City's winger nips in from the cold, intercepts the ball like a squirrel snatching a falling acorn and swiftly makes the net swell. The glee of an early goal provokes a different noise to the normal one. There is a hint of shock in there, laughter even, like the noise of receiving a surprise present. 'One nil, to the Bradford boys' sing the teenage girls, eyes fixed on texting screens ('1-0, Dad. Gr8 gl', perhaps). I pause and look around: these colours, noises and smells, the communality of strangers, toiling players making five-yard slide tackles on the sopping green ... football, you'll do for me.

As if proof were needed that this was the original and best Wimbledon, the visiting blues insistently hoist long-balls towards no one in particular. Perhaps they are waiting for the ghost of Fashanu to flick them on. Bradford, by contrast, push the ball around snappily and shoot whenever the goal is in view. They are not immune to an intense rally or two of head tennis, re-started each time by a centre-half's chest, thigh then satellite volley. This brutal manoeuvring seems painfully slow from up here. Distance has altered time and given me the slowed-down vision of a fly. City eventually bring things down to turf. The ball is spun out wide, thundered across the six-yard box and rerouted into the net by a thrusting Wimbledon leg. Own-goal, 2-0. The og receives a cheer different to the early goal and also to a regular one; there is strong comedy to its tone. The rag-tag travelling ensemble from south London try to rouse their team. Even the flicker of an eyelid will do. 'Should I be Bradford? Should I be Leeds? Here's what he said to me ...' sings the Kop.

Eventually Wimbledon stop trying to find God and embrace earthly football. Their twisty winger stretches Bradford, but baffles himself into losing the ball, a dog chasing its tail. City's No. 10, a centre-midfielder, is intolerant of sharing possession with the opposition. For a period he repeatedly collects the ball from his back four and spreads it among them, one-two by one-two. His distribution is equalled and measured, a parent making sure every toddler wins at pass the parcel. When the back row has had its turn, he unleashes Bradford's pair of scurrying wingers. They jab away at Wimbledon's full-backs, who poke desperately at their twinkling feet. Corner follows corner, each time greeted by clapping hands on the scoreboard. The hands are clad in white gloves and their slowly pixelated motions give the impression of a sarcastic croupier. One of the City wingers provokes a foul, forty yards from goal. As several players stare at the ball and the crowd sing 'Oh West Yorkshire, is wonderful' a City centre-half lobs the kick into the area. It parachutes from the sky, swaying downwards. The keeper paws at air and the ball lands in the net. Three-nil, and no one quite knows how. There is disbelief in this round of hailing. Three goals in the first half-hour. Wimbledon agree that this is too good to be true and pull one back. A free-kick is curled in lusciously and their No. 9 kisses it with his forehead, the net rippling artfully. Two minutes later Bradford's big man/little man front two tease a corner from Wimbledon. They bob and weave as it is winched into the box, rattling their opponents. One blue swipes for the ball and volleys only the wind while another slips over. With ease a Bradford player sweeps home. Four-one before half-time.

I relish the way Wimbledon and Bradford react after what is the away side's fifth tip-tap on the centre-spot. The former charge gung-ho; the latter defend valiantly. The Dons' pressure play musters two must-score moments, which invoke full-blooded Bantam blocks. Both teams seem to be imagining themselves in a cup final, 119 minutes on the clock. The Kop bellows its approval of every chest, thigh and head thrown in the line of bullets, and the teenage girls go teenage giddy. Passes, errors, wayward goalkeeper punches, slide tackles, crosses and headers – this match is relentless. 'We want five', everyone sings, and today they can always get what they want. The fifth is a showreel of this side's best features. Their defence wins and distributes, their central midfield threads it on, their winger bolts to the ball and centres it, their taller centre-forward cushions it into the net.

'Five-one at 'alf-time,' says a pensioner in the pie queue. 'When wa' the last time that bloody 'appened?' 'Five different scorers an' all,' replies his mate. 'I reckon they're all gonna get one today.' Before the second-half begins I find a spare seat halfway down the stand. The loneliness of the long-distance watcher was interesting, but football viewed alone is an incomplete experience. Besides, there is no roof here to block my view of life beyond Valley Parade. To the left I see terraces and fluffy hills. A large mosque rests among the sandy houses, its golden minaret pincers stretching high. Ahead, beyond skinny Dalek floodlights, are old mills and their chimneys, tower blocks and 1960s horror-show offices. After them can be seen open countryside. Happily, in times of dullness or defeat the Kop also acts as a gantry from which to view the layout of this absorbing city.

Bradford re-start the game and are taken aback, offended almost, when Wimbledon charge them down. For a long period, the away side play as if they have mistaken this not for a new half, but a new match. Several around me are hypnotised into the same disposition: when their heroic winger gives the ball away, they rise as one and barrack him. 'Slack as owt,' says the man I have moved in next to. In front of me sits a woman in her sixties, an old Umbro boot-bag containing a flask and biscuits by her side. With 1985 on my mind, I can't help but wonder if there was someone she once went to the match with.

City foolishly retort by switching to a long-ball game of their own. I ponder how difficult half-time must have been for their manager. His task is akin to motivating an office worker to populate a spreadsheet on the last Friday afternoon of a hated job. They eventually settle back into a rhythm where wingers left and right stretch Wimbledon gaunt. Both incessantly twist, drop shoulders, cut in and curl, cross and shoot. Reprieve is a mixed blessing, coming only when a Dons centre-half is sprawled motionless across the floor, goalkeeper towering over him semaphoring to the bench with two whirling hands, the international sign for 'substitution'. The player's treatment goes through the usual stages. At first the home fans boo and one squat physiotherapist jogs on to the pitch. Then three more medical staff join him, followed by five people in fluorescent greens, the last of whom brings a stretcher. An age of careful rolling and strapping later and the soldier is stretchered off. When we see his neck brace we stand and applaud. His withdrawal makes a quietened crowd silent. There are no amusing remarks to fill the space. That is the trouble with an outcome already settled like this one – it kills sarcasm.

One of Bradford's wing wizards beats three men and finds himself alone with ball and keeper. The church atmosphere helps us hear the noise his scuffed shot makes, that of a butcher hacking squelchy steaks. The game slumbers towards full-time in five-minute periods of good football and then chest smack head, chest smack head, repeat to fade. At one point, a lumped clearance dawns on Bradford's crafty centre-half. He has space all around him, space to use his ample ability to bring down the ball and run or pass. He watches the ball descend and lands a thwacking header on it, his spammer vibrating as if a recovering bell. Bradford should really score again, but treat trying to do so as a heavy duty and not a prize honour. Besides, the Wimbledon keeper has been transformed from one who could not catch a cold to one who could catch the moon.

The game is dead; it has been since half-time. Talk turns to plans for tonight and television schedules ('There's fuck all on on a Saturday night nowadays. That's why I just sit and get pissed'), and games to come. The stretcher incident means ten minutes of added time. The referee should put down the match, assisted suicide for Wimbledon, blessed heaven for Bradford. In the Kop, we need to get home and place our damp garments on radiators. 'Let's blow, ref, let's finish it,' says my neighbour. On rumbles the match, a dying dog with trembling paws, until at 5.01 the referee calls halt on the 5-1.

The rain is falling again as I approach my hotel for the night, The Midland. Outside its opulent front a wedding party of Bradford Asians squashes in for photos. The women wear bright turquoise and purple dresses that force a glare out of the waxy pavement. Typically cheerful sandstone makes a perfect background as they whoop and jig.

Just over a century ago Bradford City celebrated here too, at an official reception for their capturing of the 1911 FA Cup. They were founded only in 1903, built upon the assets and Valley Parade ground of Manningham rugby league club. Incredibly, 'The Paraders' were voted into the Football League having never played a game. Perhaps the Football Association sensed the city of Bradford's sporting zest: it was a cradle of what became rugby league, and, with the creation of Bradford Park Avenue in 1907, would soon support two professional soccer teams. Five times over the years were mergers with Park Avenue suggested and rejected, extinguished by the strength of identity Bradfordians placed upon their teams.

City reached the First Division in 1908 and remained there for a decade. They would not climb so high again until those Premier League days, days whose debts may mean it takes another eighty years to rise again. Their FA Cup-winning season of 1911 brought fifth place in the league too, and was their greatest. The psyche of early days of glory and then sweet nothing forevermore does pervade at Bradford. There are no delusions of grandeur about them, just a keen sense of what was. They are like a great grandson of the Russian monarchy, proud to show his photos and medals and tell a colourful story. Their FA Cup win *is* a story worth telling, though, and its timing thickens the golden hue of Bradford's, Priestley's and England's Edwardian and pre-war eras.

When City won the Cup, it was the modern version's first outing. Coincidentally, a Bradford jeweller, Fattorini's, designed and constructed the trophy, a piece whose silhouette is engraved into the imaginations of a million people like me. To reach the final, City beat New Brompton, Norwich City, Grimsby Town, Burnley (40,000 at Valley Parade) and Blackburn Rovers, the favourites. At Crystal Palace in the final they drew 0-0 with Newcastle United. They were weakened that day by the absence of outside-right Dickie Bond, suspended for using 'improper language' to the crowd at Woolwich Arsenal. Bond had courted trouble earlier in the season after misbehaving on a night out in Otley with fellow Scots Jimmy McDonald and Robert Campbell. Footballer misdemeanours are not new, only now they create moral panics. A crowd of 67,000 watched the replay at Old Trafford. After a quarter of an hour, the wind caught hold of right-half George Robinson's punt at goal. A Frank Thompson and Jimmy Speirs tag-team headed it onwards, and Frank O'Rourke charged towards goal. It was enough to bamboozle Newcastle goalkeeper Jimmy Lawrence. The ball crept through the mud and over the line – 1-0 to the Bradford boys. The Magpies pecked away at the Bantams but could rob nothing, and so it finished that way. Bradford's victory had a tartan tint – eight of the first XI were Caledonian, including the Otley revellers.

Back over the Pennines the *Bradford Daily Telegraph* had printed special editions with updates as the game progressed. At 5.10 p.m. a newsboy announced the score from his pitch at Mildred Court prompting an uproarious throng to gather outside the town hall. Soon the crowd stretched through the city centre. When the team's train arrived at 9 p.m. the Idle and Thackley Brass Band could barely be heard above the din. Bradford supporters marked the day by presenting the club with a flag and mast known as 'Peter's Stick' and donating a commemorative cot to the hospital.

Though City had peaked, football's capacity to help the toilers of Bradford escape never waned. Valley Parade always offered entertainment, intrigue, interest: Harold Walden, in 1912 a key player for City and an Olympian with Great Britain but within a decade a comedy star and foil to Hylda Baker; Louis Bookman, an outside-left and the only Jew to be capped by one of the Home

Countries; Willie Watson who, when caught on enclosed premises at the start of his stalwart career, pleaded that he had been 'ghost hunting'; inside-forward Abe Rosenthal, a prominent member of Bradford's Jewish community who in the 1940s and 50s played semi-professionally so as to keep his hand in at lollipop making. Once upon a time these Bantam fairy tales helped people escape. Now they add to a romantic nostalgia that cloaks the club. I need only read the names of former players to feel it: Irvine Boocock, Charlie Rackstraw, Watty Shirlaw, Aubrey Scriven. Even the name of Bobby Ham evokes his era, the 1960s, and the way they never quite swung in West Yorkshire. Ham played for both City and Park Avenue, and was with the former when the latter ceased to be in May 1974. Liquidation of Park Avenue robbed football of one of its great derbies, indeed the only provincial city clash to be played in all four divisions. Park Avenue were wound-up in a conference suite of the Midland Hotel, above which I now stand in my room for the night.

I switch on Radio Five Live to try and catch up with the scores. Instead, I hear a man from Hampshire who wasn't at the Manchester United game talk about the Manchester United game to an ex-footballer who wasn't there either. I switch off again and move to the ample bay window. Immediately below is a huge fenced-off muddy crater. There was supposed to be a Westfield shopping centre here, but the recession saw its developers withdraw. They may well still get their shiny way, but it seems to me like a benefit of the global financial meltdown. Admittedly, I am scarred as Westfield was a plot feature in my Leyton hell, but I also like The Hole as it allows an unencumbered view. Besides, the council are about to turn it into a temporary garden, picking up capitalism's pieces. I stand and watch this space, listening to cars and buses hiss along the wet road. The night is falling, eclipsing the grey sky with its own black one. Couples share umbrellas and well-dressed Sikhs talk on corners. Mums race pushchairs along; each flagstone crossed one towards somewhere dry. To the right is the last man standing, a Victorian corner bank attached to nothing since the bulldozers dug The Hole. It is defiant, its chest puffed out while all else around is modern folly and nothingness. Behind the bank is an office block with its skeleton on the outside, a thousand rectangular windows framed by matchstick bone. Directly opposite, 100 yards away, are the white and grey towers of Premier Inn, a hotel chain unlikely to bookend the footballing history of a place as the Midland has. To the left is a high and handsome row of old mill buildings and warehouses, each seemingly coloured in with a gold felt-tip featuring a slightly blackened nib. This is the outer edge of Little Germany and it is enticingly beautiful, which is why I find myself back in the rain five minutes later.

'This area, known as Little Germany, was the centre of textile warehousing in late 19th century Bradford' reads an iron plaque. (It doesn't actually. It reads 'This area, known as Little Germany was the centre of textile warehousing in late 19th century, Bradford', but I'm presuming the sign-maker was having an off day with his commas.) As I enter Little Germany I look left and see Valley Parade, murky in the distance, but pluckily raised. I imagine textile workers finishing the Saturday half-shift and beginning the slow uphill walk, pint on the way, the world theirs until Monday. They would leave the low town smog behind for songs and goals up yonder. Sanded, polished, cleaned-up and given prettily typefaced iron street names, Little Germany, I find, is striking. It consists of a main thoroughfare built on the kind of hill that makes handbrakes take early retirement. Long lanes of high buildings run from it. Each has ornate stone carvings and frills on edges where there is no need for edges, never mind frills. There seem to be windows as far as the eye can see, all dizzyingly symmetrical. On each corner they fan out, New York flatirons broadened by Yorkshire brute. The area was built upon the money of German-Jews drawn to Worstedopolis. Their arrival turned Bradford into an unlikely cosmopolitan hub. Hearteningly, Little Germany now is a living, working museum of warehouse apartments and web-design companies.

I bypass The Hole and head for the centre of town. After Little Germany's lavishness some of Bradford's shabbier streets are a shock. Looking so far back and indeed up has allowed me to forget the poverty that undermines and underlines this city. It can be seen, as in Burnley, in the pound shops and the shut down shops, the tatty and the derelict houses. Perhaps I also forget because so many buildings are the reassuring, richly comforting colour of Werther's Original packets.

Outside the Kirkgate Centre two merry Wimbledon fans stop and stare at its malevolent concrete walls. Built in the 1970s when Bradford tore up much Victoriana and planned a future, it resembles an industrial oven with which the devil warms up hell. As I pass the two drunk Dons they are, perhaps surprisingly, deep in conversation about schools of architecture. 'This kind of Brutalism will become sainted. You mark my words, Paul.' 'No chance, Dave. It hardly matches the Neo-Classic and Gothic Revival stuff down the hill, and we're realising that now.' I suppose it beats re-living the five leaked goals. I head towards their Neo-Classic and Gothic stuff. I have no idea what style the Wool Exchange is, but it is mightily impressive, as are most of the tarted-up old buildings on Hustlergate and Market Street. I cross the road underneath lights suspended from one building to another wishing Bradford a Happy Eid. A shop worker locks up at The In Plaice just as a man in his forties reaches her. 'Oh love. You're not shut, are yer?' ''Fraid so, flower. It's gone 8.' 'But I want haddock 'n' chips, love.' 'Sorry flower. There's Nando's over there if you like that?' His look suggests not.

Nando's is part of the Centenary Square development, a gaping, gorgeous space recently restored to its best. Opposite it lounges City Hall, Bradford's huge and haunting civic centre, a Gothic *Titanic*. Its tower rockets for the sky, symbolic of old money used to breed pride and forge ambitious citizens. A big screen pipes the Last Night of the Proms across the square, Union Jack colours reflecting on to the vast new pond and fountains. 'Excuse me, Sir' a man asks me, 'can I borrow 67p?' As I appreciate the precision of his request I give him a pound. I leave the square and cross the road by the Media Museum, filing by the cloudy light bulbs of the Alhambra Theatre. Beside the Alhambra is Bradford's war memorial. The First World War ended Priestley's golden England, slaying a generation of Bradfordians in harrowing numbers and changing the make-up of the city. 'The men who were boys when I was a boy are dead,' he wrote of a war he too fought in. Outside regular regiments, 2,000 local men joined the 'Bradford Pals' – 1,770 were killed.

I walk uphill, passing the German Evangelical Church with its plaque to Dietrich Bonhoeffer, a pastor killed by the Nazis for plotting to assassinate Hitler. Bonhoeffer visited this church and made his 'Bradford Declaration,' denouncing in 1933 the rise of Nazism. Guided by the neon lights of pizza and chicken outlets, I find Bradford's main curry district, or at least the place with the highest concentration of recommended restaurants on the map my wife has lovingly created. The first has a tremendous scent, but veers too far towards soup kitchen for a Saturday night. The second is bright and buzzing, but as I enter I am pretty sure I have gatecrashed a family party, so I leave. The hill steepens, the street lights become sparser and the rain begins its night shift. I think about turning back, but am lured towards the promising bright lights of the World Famous Mumtaz. Inside the Mumtaz is a factory-scale restaurant with in-built delicatessen, as well as a display devoted to the Queen's recent visit. It is a loud, happy place, both in its marbled bling decor and its atmosphere. With alcohol banned I wolf down my sublime curry with a soft drink, an alien but endearing experience. Ninety per cent of the people here are of Asian descent, and the lack of white people could have something to do with the lack of alcohol. Happily, the ten per cent 'others' are not sat among themselves, but mixed as individuals and couples in large family gangs of gassing and giggling Asians. A decade ago riots here saw Bradford labelled a 'racial tinderbox'. Across the city segregation remains, but after the low of Luton, I am beginning to think things are heading in the right direction.

I leave the Mumtaz and walk back downhill into town, past Desmond Tutu House and the Peace Garden. Two sights that stay with me end my night. One is a man in a Mr Bean mask trying to fight a fellow drunk. Both have girlfriends pulling them apart. The other is a carefree lass of seventeen or eighteen, dancing in the Centenary Square pond, her shoes in her hands, her face turned to the moon. Her boyfriend sits on the edge, looking on. Eleven cathedral bells ring and I feel so glad of Bradford, of England.

Part Four

In the Autumn:
Blues and Peppermints

Chapter Twelve

Carlisle

Four months after I started attending football matches, the English game sunk into a man-made hell. Hillsborough became one of those names like Hungerford, Lockerbie and later Dunblane. When we thought of it, we thought not of a location, but of a terrible event. Saying 'Hillsborough' conjured images not of grand old blue and white stripes, but of tearfully desperate Liverpudlians searching the pitch for their own. It prompted thoughts of that often repeated concept whose impact seems, if anything, to become harsher as the years pass and make it more remote and impossible: going to the match and never coming home.

On 10 December 1988 I went to Ayresome Park for the first time. I was six and, true to cliché, my dad lifted me over the turnstile for free. The selective recollections are all there. We climbed uneven steps cut among a grass mound towards a doorway in what appeared to be a barn. At that doorway my dad lifted me up again and I saw it for the first time: the felt-tip green, stretching in front like an interesting version of the farmers' fields that surrounded our village. The pitch was partitioned from the stand by a red mesh fence, the central part of which had a topping of brass spikes. We took a place near the back of the Holgate End, me sitting on the crush barrier, dad holding me there and watching the game over my shoulder. From up there I could see the bobbing heads of a thousand men. Several times during the match, the heads swapped places, some landing a good distance away from where they started. They reminded me of the way baked beans splodge from the pan on to a plate.

When Boro scored, which they did three times, I was both frightened and exhilarated. The roar was deafening but thrilling, and the way everyone bumped into each other like dodgems I found disturbing but funny. The game finished and everyone moved quickly towards two or three exits. I could only see the backsides of the people in front so I remember looking at the feet of those around me. They seemed to shuffle and scuff along as quickly as was possible given the heavy swarm of bodies. Looking upwards I saw many hands urging on the person in front by a quick nudge of the waist. A new rush of other supporters joined from behind, boisterously geeing on the pack. Space tightened and my dad just managed to hoist me on to his shoulders. Behind his unalarmed expression was both paternal stoicism and the experienced mental shrug of a football fan in the 1980s – this was just how things were. When Ayresome Park spat us on to the streets, almost immediately I forgot about how scared I had been and pestered my dad to take me again soon.

A month after the horrors of Hillsborough, Middlesbrough played there. Tarpaulin was draped across the closed Leppings Lane End fence, but if supporters craned their necks they could see buckled crush barriers. In front of the haunted terrace the players trampled over grass that had seen all the sadness of a Flanders field. Boro lost 1-0 and were relegated. It should not have mattered, it should not have even been played, but still thousands of Teessiders travelled to the game. Though buoyed on my journey by football's resolve, this is an episode I find hard to fathom. Surely the rest of the season should have been cancelled?

On the train to Carlisle, I telephone my dad. Three days ago, the Hillsborough Independent Panel published its findings. Even the unshakable are shocked. Those who cited cover-up and conspiracy and were labelled attention seekers or cranks are vindicated, though their victory is pyrrhic. Those within and without football are gripped and emotional, save for the man across the aisle from me who this morning is reading the *Sun*. I ask my dad how football could have continued. 'We just expected something like this to happen, really. It was how you were treated at football. So we were devastated, but not surprised.' We discuss South Yorkshire at that time and we can't help but talk of the police force that altered 116 of its statements and took blood samples from dead children in search of alcohol. As any left-leaning Yorkshireman will tell you, this was the same force that perpetrated class war against its own at Orgreave and elsewhere.

From the comfortable position of 2012, Hillsborough looks like the consequence of class war too. Even though it must have contained thousands of Thatcher's valued working-class voters, the public that went to football matches was an enemy of her government. To them it was a single group of hoodlums and Labour voters that tore up cities when it was not tearing itself up. The casual hooligan movement spoke for all fans. It behaved like animals, and so it should be put in pens and fenced in. In that government's eyes, the football public had transformed from the mixed crowds of the 1970s and before, to the violent creatures of the 1980s that needed fences to stop them running riot. That grounds being fence-free had prevented disasters in the past was lost on them. The football public was deigned faceless and treated to authoritarian rule. That is why Hillsborough was not a surprise.

Ninety-six deaths were the culmination of this and football's tipping point. We know that the partially implemented Taylor Report gave us all-seated stadiums. Though I long for the architecture and atmosphere of old, I am inherently grateful that most of my football watching has been safe and that there will never be another Hillsborough. However, big football missed an opportunity in the early 1990s. It could have been re-built with the fans at its core. Instead, the faceless masses were hastily bought by television and their game marketed out of its hole. It should have been slowly and soundly constructed by those fans according to their wishes. We would have liked safe standing, involvement in the running of our clubs and affordable ticket prices.

Thankfully the spirit of old imbued with the safety of new exists, as I have seen time and again this season. Outside Carlisle's Brunton Park home I watch two Swindon fans joke with a police officer, unthinkable until Hillsborough. 'We got the train up, actually mate. It's better, innit? You can walk around a bit, have a wee.' At ten to three I rest upon a silver terrace barrier and look across at the hulking modern stand opposite. Very few people have elected to sit in its eight or nine personality free blocks. Here once stood the Scratching Shed, a pitch-long terrace liked so much that its official name became the Popular Side. Its replacement, built upon delusion and absurd promises, is a breathing metaphor for a very modern broken dream. It is also longer than the pitch, overlapping the butt of Carlisle's now-closed traditional away end terrace, the Waterworks End. Behind the other goal is Brunton Park's beating, baying heart, the Warwick Road End. With its mossy zigzag roof and orange lighting, 'The Warwick' remains recognisable and unique. It conjures nostalgia now but once did the same with fear. In the 1970s, Peter Bonetti of Chelsea was stoned from the Warwick and Pat Jennings of Spurs heard a dart whistle by his ear.

My own artful terrace runs to the correct dimensions. Behind it is a small but refined tier of seating that constitutes the main stand. This replaced the original in the early 1950s following a fire with chilling similarities to Valley Parade's. Mercifully, full-time had long gone when it caught fire following a 1953 friendly with Falkirk, as had the supporters. Discarded cigarette stubs ignited years of litter beneath the stand and a prevailing wind carried the flames across its wooden floors and seats. If only football had learned its lessons like it did following Hillsborough. Not many mourned the stand's loss. Manager Ivor Broadis had once described it as 'reeling drunkenly under the weight of its years,' while his successor Bill Shankly plumped for 'a glorified chicken coop.'

Brunton Park's appearance and historical name-checks like Broadis and Shankly whisper of a fine vintage here. The club was founded in 1904 in a Temperance hotel. For a time they had fierce rivals in their battle for local affections in the guise of Carlisle Red Rose. United tugged most at the city's heartstrings, roared to success in the Cumberland League by early crowds of 5,000 people. They joined the Lancashire League and soon won its second division before finishing as runners-up to Everton in its first. In 1910 the northern upstarts went to West Ham in the FA Cup and dominated. They could muster only a draw. West Ham paid them £160 and half the gate not to play the replay in Cumbria and won it 5-0 in East London. It was just as well: that year, United nearly went bust and were saved only by supporter fundraising and a donation from Newcastle United. The frontier club, not quite sure where it belonged, soon joined the North-Eastern League and by the 1920s was prospering. They finished second in 1927-28, which allowed them to stand for election to the Football League. Few thought they would get enough votes with clubs repelled by the cost and distance of playing in England's extreme north. Football knew better than that, and perhaps even fancied the novelty. Carlisle United were voted in.

United won their first ever league fixture 3-2 at Accrington Stanley. Their first goal was scored by Jimmy McConnell, a new signing. A newspaper report described how he:

> ... suddenly, without warning, unleashed a terrific shot which flew into the top corner of the goal, causing those gathered behind the Stanley keeper to stoop down in fear of the ball bursting through the net and taking off their heads.

Born in Ayr, McConnell had reached Carlisle via a nomadic phase in the United States. There he played for Springfield Babes, Providence Clamdiggers and Bethlehem Steel. The lure of Cumbria was greater than that of romantic team names, and in any case McConnell's goals ensured love was in the Brunton air. 'The goals he scored,' said teammate George 'Ginger' Harrison, 'illuminated his life and that of thousands of others.' McConnell scored forty-two goals that season, and in total 126 in 150 Carlisle games, including fourteen hat-tricks. His reward for becoming the first United player to 100 was a three-piece Chesterfield suite. Emotional bonuses came from his peers within the game, particularly the great Dixie Dean of Everton. Following an unlucky 4-2 FA Cup reverse for Carlisle at Goodison, Dean described McConnell as 'a phenomenal goalscorer with more pace and ability than I ever had.' As always at Carlisle, a city without industrial takings to sate the coffers, money was short in McConnell's time. He was sold to Crewe in 1932, his strike partners Davie Hutchison and Sammy Armes to Luton and Chester, all three of them teams we know well.

The 1930s were grim for Carlisle. In 1934-35 their captain Bob Bradley died suddenly at home, and his club finished bottom of the whole league. Two years later, defender Jack Round passed away during a routine appendix operation. Football's suspension at the start of the Second World War stopped the rot at Carlisle United. At conflict's end they regrouped under Ivor Broadis, a twenty-three-year-old player-manager who would go on to play fourteen times for England. Broadis had wider ambitions and sold himself to Sunderland. His replacement was a former United player and serving director's nephew, Bill Shankly. Nepotism has its positives.

In Shankly's first job as a manager the charisma and erudition that would mark him out at Liverpool stirred. He immediately set about changing the culture of the club and ensuring Carlisle had only players and staff with the attitude and ethics that marked his kind of socialism, 'everyone working for each other'. Involving himself immediately, Shankly moved into a house next to the ground and jogged its neighbouring streets every morning. He persuaded the club to buy properties in the same area for new and young players to rent, and to build a clubhouse in which they could socialise. The Scot prowled the streets of the city centre canvassing views and opinions on his club from residents. Fifteen minutes before each game he would take control of the Brunton Park public address system and explain his team selections to fans, updating them too on club news. On the pitch, average players were made to feel anything but. He cajoled them into earning a 0-0 draw at Highbury in the FA Cup, a game they might even have won. Five thousand away supporters saw United winger Billy Hogan tear strips from Arsenal that day, provoking them to select him for special treatment in the replay. After that match, a 4-1 defeat, Shankly reflected how:

It was a great shame they felt the need to kick Billy Hogan into the terracing. I felt we could have given them a good game up here ... I'm very disappointed, not at losing, but at the way Arsenal resorted to acts of thuggery.

Shanks' work was noticed. Grimsby Town fluttered a player budget that Carlisle never could, and he took the next steps on a road marked 'Greatness'. He died in, you guessed it, 1981.

Shankly's last season as Liverpool manager, 1973-74, was one of Carlisle's greatest. Under another former player, Alan Ashman, they were promoted to Division One. They even met Shankly's side in the FA Cup, achieving a 0-0 draw at Anfield before the Scot came to memory lane for the replay and won 2-0 in front of 21,000 Cumbrians. Ashman was a magician and another man to find himself deeply affected by Carlisle, place and team. While a player, the club had tried to sell him. Unable to think of a life elsewhere, Ashman took a job on a chicken farm instead. His Carlisle was a team built on long periods of possession and killer-punch goals. They finished third behind Middlesbrough and Luton, pipping Orient to their place in the sun.

If the game of football had ended at 5 p.m. on 24 August 1974, the people of Carlisle may not have minded too much. At that point they were top of England's highest division. On the season's first day United won 2-0 at Stamford Bridge (before the match, Chelsea chairman Brian Mears had boasted how his club's giant new stand 'cost three, maybe four, times as much as the Carlisle side'). They followed up with a midweek win at Ayresome Park and, on that glorious 24th, a 1-0 home defeat of Spurs. Carlisle United had touched the sky, but only with their fingertips: they finished bottom of the division.

By 1981-82 Bob Stokoe's trilby and raincoat hung on the manager's peg at Brunton Park. Carlisle had fallen further from the clouds, to Division Three. In the second of his three spells, Stokoe led the side to promotion behind Burnley. After a storming start, inspired by the hunched genius of a soon-to-depart Peter Beardsley, Stokoe's side faltered. They stumbled over the line with a final-day win at bottom club Chester. Promotion was a temporary reprieve. By 1988, Carlisle were back in Division Four, and by 1992 in the ownership of Michael Knighton, to a generation the bloke with the moustache who did kick-ups at Old Trafford.

The Champions League notions on which the stand opposite me today was built were Knighton's. His megalomania tarnished a club already suffering the reputational difficulties of distance and separation. Outsiders who presumed Carlisle an oddity in the middle of no man's land nodded knowingly when Knighton made himself head coach, declaring: 'I have more qualifications than most managers and coaches at this level put together.' Knighton is long gone and the club has clawed back the respect its support and tradition deserves, sinking to the Conference, but now in English football's third tier, probably its rightful place.

When the blue and whites of Carlisle emerge with Swindon Town's all-reds, the king-size stand is less than half full. Three hundred of its occupants are from Swindon, one per mile for the distance between the two places. It is functional and cold, a hangar with plastic seats. No wonder most head for the terraces. The dormant Waterworks End looks sadly on to the pitch. By way of grabbing attention from the populated areas, Eddie Stobart haulage videos flash from its big screen. The homely smell of frying onions coats me in nostalgia. I look around and recognise feet and legs that recall Ayresome. Most have on trainers and jeans. The side view returns several beer guts, their frequency a more modern development (if you have to watch those images of Hillsborough again, note how skinny by comparison fans back then were). Most people lean on barriers with their hands clasped in front of them as if praying. Those without anything to lean on keep their arms crossed until a player's endeavour merits un-crossing. The supporters have gathered, mostly in gangs of two or three, though some are larger and many are alone. Very few of the gangs arrived together and I imagine met through their liking for a similar spot, possibly because Carlisle won handsomely the Saturday they first stood there. A high number of the lone fans have satchels and plastic carriers at their feet holding flasks. Because the autumn sun is so lofty, everyone has a stretched shadow that seems to populate the gaps and make the stand feel full. Looking at the shadows alone it is possible to imagine yourself at any point over the last century.

For the first half-hour vuvuzelas whine along like emasculated foghorns until the children parping them lose interest and begin instead to sing 'wanker, wanker, wanker' at Swindon's Italian manager. They have been provoked by his rampant gesticulations.

In prime footballing conditions upon a perfect pitch, Carlisle and Swindon spend the opening ten minutes acting like two gentlemen who will not enter a doorway first for fear of offending one another. Neither holds on to the ball. When possession is achieved it is quickly surrendered as if from embarrassment. Then a Carlisle defender barges through the nonsense and punts a long ball forward, towards the vacant Waterworks End. It bashes off a counterpart and into the orbit of a home striker. He too cuts the niceties and ploughs the ball into the net. One-nil. Celebrations comprise applause more than wild bounces of joy, perhaps because a goal among such timidity has come as a shock. On the dusky cinder track between stand and pitch, the away manager turns to his bench staff and delivers a combustible soliloquy. Swindon respond well to the back of his head. They begin a tentative friendship with the ball that graduates to infatuation. Soon their ten outfield players are all in the Carlisle half, possession semi-permanent. The shots they aim on goal are full of effort rather than guile, though United's keeper darts around his box like cotton wool in the wind. Sensing the opportunity to snap him in motion or the coming of a Swindon goal, a photographer swaps ends. His bright bib gives the away side's Irn Bru-topped striker a marker at which to aim. When the ball bounces outside the penalty area he guides it with precision into the photographer's corner of the net. It is such a good goal and they are so far away that it takes Swindon cheers a while to surface and travel. I'm sure I hear the net ripple before they do, which is attributable either to heightened senses on such a vigorous day or a brain frazzled by nigh on a year's travelling football.

The hails are immediate and hearty when Carlisle go ahead again a minute later. Their squat striker, whose ten-to-two feet move surprisingly fast, chests the ball towards his lanky partner. He choreographs his body as if mocking up a coaching textbook and riots in a half-volley the Swindon keeper can only wave at. The goal is a shock, hence the wild roar. Swindon's dominance and then equaliser had cynical home minds dreading a gubbing. 'You watch,' said a man behind me, 'they'll dick us 4-1 here.' The carnival quickly leaves town as Swindon make it two-all 120 seconds later. The fourth goal in eighteen minutes comes when a hopeful pass that bobsleighs down the gulley strikes a Carlisle defender's heel, setting clear Swindon's second forward. He motors goalwards with the freedom of Cumbria, lures the keeper and bulges the net. After barely half an hour, the game's scoring is over. Another week; another flash flood then thirsty drought. As if to torture us with the prospect of more goals there is a pinball scramble just before half-time. Carlisle should score, but a header thuds against an Eddie Stobart hoarding, prompting the familiar agony of a 'Yeeeeaaaah' turning into an 'haaaawwww'.

The half-time whistle peeps and Morrissey's 'Every Day is Like Sunday' soon strikes up. Both managers walk from the touchline over the cinder and stop and consult quickly with their coaches. Mozza sings of walking on damp beaches towards wooden benches. I could quite imagine him here; Carlisle and Brunton Park has that melancholy about it, forever longing for and smiling over a time gone by. Beneath upright toilet brush floodlights a pretty couple kiss, her reaching upwards from the terrace step below him. There *is* a certain romance here, appealing even if its nostalgia is more 1970s sideburns than succulent sepia. I drink a swift half beneath the main stand in a box room with strip lights known as the George McVitie Bar. McVitie, I learn from frames charting his career, was a flying right-winger who, like so many here, left for pastures new but soon came back. It strikes me again what a hold Carlisle United seem to have had on players and managers. No one, it feels, can keep away from this peculiar northern temptress.

At the second-half's start I find a spot alongside the halfway line. It proves to be a wise choice as the ball spends most of its time in the central third of the pitch. Both sides will it forward manfully, but attacks repeatedly end with pass-backs rolled for goalkeepers to batter into the deepening sky. In particular, I like the Carlisle keeper's kicking method. He seems to scoop his foot into the earth and dig the ball out, a nine-iron for a right foot. His whole style is entertaining, his bravery vintage. Where there is doubt he asserts his fists or charges forward with scant regard for his personal safety. It is noisier here. To my left are a disparate group of four or five, a Saturday family. One, a lady in her seventies sporting a perm and purple fleece, is no fan of Swindon's touchline griper. 'Oh shurrup will yer. Moaning on like that. You'd think we'd shot their right-back.' Her neighbour, folded T-shirt arms and creased forehead, grows quickly tired of the referee's frequent whistle. 'Don't get involved, man. Let the game bloody flow. He thinks he's a bloody shepherd, this fella.'

Providing consistent rhythm behind their sporadic outbursts is a man with the unfortunate hair of Noel Edmunds. Every minute or so he implores his team to 'waken up, for Christ's sake.' On top of natural passive aggression, there is something about the Carlisle accent that makes many sentences sound sceptical or scathing. It crescendos high from calm beginnings like applying helium to a mid-sentence Geordie. Strangely, it isn't a million miles from the Teesside accent, a fact that has long confused me.

After Swindon sustain an attacking period more reluctant than relentless but fail to score, their manager fizzes. He frequently rips his hands from the pockets of his jacket, sending it flapping behind him. 'Oh Mama bloody Mia' says the old girl, then, strangely: 'pizza or pasta?' Carlisle revive towards the end, speeding forward on the break. A fine cross dangles and is picked from the air by a silky header. Hands un-cup and rise to ear-height, and mouths open. It grenades past a Warwick End post and a settlement of two-all is reached. The away governor runs across the pitch to take Wiltshire accolades. 'He thinks he's Frank Sinatra, that bloke,' says someone as we shuffle through the gates. Behind the familiar-looking Swindon Town team bus a young boy in full Carlisle kit swings on the statue of Hugh McIlmoyle, an adored centre-forward with three spells here among his vital statistics. Another captivated by the strange magic of Brunton Park, where the clocks move faster than time.

I walk back into the city centre along wide, tree-lined pavements. There can be few more pleasant routes to and from a football ground. The long stretch from Brunton Park is padded by terraced villas with musty orange and dirty-tooth white bricks that together achieve an attractive crocheted effect. On one of them is a blue plaque commending the former home of Thomas Woodrow,

'Grandfather of Woodrow Wilson, 28th President of United States of America.' To make such a leap is difficult after a Carlisle United versus Swindon Town game, but it again reaffirms the many small parts that helped the provinces alter history.

I pass the Lonsdale Cinema whose sad show list reads 'Closed', then a headline board in the *News & Star* office proclaiming 'Callous Carer Jailed'. There are some stunning buildings here, as you would expect in a place of such maturity. 'The City is strong, but small, the buildings old, but the streets fair, the great church is a venerable old pile,' wrote Daniel Defoe in 1724. Opposite omnipotent Nando's is an erect cannon, used to defend Carlisle against Scottish invasion in 1745 and afterwards according to its plaque, 'as morning and evening gun whilst Carlisle remained a fortified town.' This split-shift weapon tells you much about this city and the defensive mentality that long pervaded, and perhaps still does. John Crofts, a merchant from Bristol, wrote in 1759 how Carlisle was 'a small deserted dirty city, poorly built and poorly inhabited … the cathedral is miserably ragged and dirty inside and out.'

Regular invasion meant that there was little point in making Carlisle beautiful and scant attraction in living behind the fortified walls of a military target. Once the Romans left what they called Luguvalium, a fort town at the extreme north-west of their Empire, it became fair game in the eyes of all who wished to rule these isles, or merely fancied a brawl. Where now proximity to Hadrian's Wall makes Carlisle somewhere for American tourists to stop for a cream horn, for 1,500 years it meant a town worth possessing. It fluctuated between English and Celtic rule, with occasional Viking and other interludes. The only constant was brutality. In 1322, Harcla, put in charge of Carlisle by King Edward, attempted to make a pact with Robert the Bruce and bring peace to Carlisle. Edward's men arrested him for treason and sentenced him to be:

... hanged and afterwards beheaded; to be disembowelled and his entrails burnt; his head to be taken and suspended on the Tower of London; his body to be divided into four parts, one part to be suspended on the tower of Carlisle, another at Newcastle-on-Tyne, a third at Bristol and the fourth at Dover.

Three months after his death, the English signed a peace treaty with Bruce. At least Harcla got to see Dover. The Bishop of Carlisle responded to peacetime in the only way he knew how: he requested a tax rebate from the Pope, on the grounds that the Scots had 'slain men and women ... and destroyed the whole county.' Peace did not last long, which probably meant another set of forms for the bishop to complete. As if armies sacking Carlisle were not enough, Border clans from either side of Hadrian's Wall turned their areas into bandit territories. These 'Reivers' regularly nipped into their neighbouring country to steal cattle and violently extort money. Their dalliances ended only with a peace won by the cannons of 1745, and the development of Carlisle's weaving industry as a provider of income that did not involve robbery or kidnap.

What the people of Carlisle were able to earn as weavers still left them skint. A visitor in 1846 despairingly described the way of life typical to them:

On what do these people live? Oatmeal gruel forms their breakfast; potatoes with dripping or the liquid fat from a little morsel of bacon, their dinner; and either a drink of beer (so small that it is sold at a penny a gallon!) or a mere drink called 'tea' is taken with bread as the evening meal ... a man saunters in the lanes or into the fields, rather than show his tatters and threadbare habit in church or chapel.

The poor here would not have recognised such a hopeless profile. Frequently they rebelled and rioted against their lot, the spirit of their fighting forefathers employed for more positive use than defending a monarch's outpost or a despot's target. A Conservative parliamentary candidate, Sir Philip Musgrave, came here to court popularity in 1826. His views on the Corn Laws sparked a piece of direct action in which he was placed on a loom and taught to weave. The rest of his party were ducked in a mill-dam. Sir Robert Peel, Home Secretary, responded by creating a police force for Carlisle. When the city's weavers found out its leader had assisted in the Peterloo Massacre, they rioted again. As lords of a former citadel, the authorities were in the fortunate position of having troops on tap to quell disorder. Their public relations record was not great: during the same 1826 riot they fired shots in the air and killed a woman watching from an upstairs window.

In these generally quiet and complicit times of ours, it is always hard to imagine such boisterousness and refusal to accept the order of things. I feel this keenly in Carlisle, which though busy this early evening, is sleepily calm. The buildings are low, trees and greenery abundant, the streets wide and the traffic sparse. People are neither chat-on-corners merry nor scowling and unapproachable. It is a middle-of-the-road kind of place, which probably has much to do with its location and historically confused identity.

Where the main pedestrianised shopping street unfolds into a large square with outdoor cafe seating included, I survey the city noticeboard. There are adverts for a recent gig by The Temperance Seven, beardy jazzists judging by the accompanying photograph, a coffee morning and, of course, An Evening of Clairvoyance at the deaf centre. I get the feeling that Carlisle is a small town masquerading as a city, its long history tiresome and a burden. It has too much to live up to; it just wants to be a market town. I walk by the erratically beautiful, old town hall and arrive at the cathedral, a sharp upright building. It too feels uneasy, crammed on to a bit of grass behind a shopping centre.

A frontier city so far from others, of varied ancestry and uneasy in itself, Carlisle can seem as if it is hell-bent upon avoiding eye contact with the rest of England. It must feel difficult to belong to a country run from afar. Historically, governance brought only invasion, then control through the nationalisation of pubs to curb rowdy bomb factory workers, reversed only in 1971. More recently Foot and Mouth disease, then flooding, must have made Carlisle wonder what England had ever done for it. Attitudes to the football club have helped shaped a narrative I am guilty of swallowing – football's final frontier. Witness this from Brian James's 1977 book, *Journey to Wembley*:

> Nothing moves out there. It is a football frontier post guarded by sheep; the notion that a ball kicked over the fence would go on bouncing until it dropped off the end of the world is hard to shake off … Carlisle, the Alice Springs of league soccer, is a place that demands gradual acclimatisation if a team is not to suffer from football's equivalent of the bends.

Perhaps, though, the point of Carlisle and Carlisle United is to offer a true definition of that quality England claims to hold so dear: eccentricity. City and team are, in some ways, an implausibility, out on an edge, difficult to find reason to visit or move to. Yet they are England as much as anywhere else and fought harder than most to be so. Besides, wee Brunton Park on a Saturday afternoon is a marvellous place to be.

The End

Newquay

At Edinburgh Airport three teenage boys discuss the periodic table. I feel like dashing into WHSmith and buying them a copy of *90 Minutes* magazine, except it no longer exists and we are about to board an aeroplane.

We climb over the River Forth into a crisp September sky, the peaks and tenements of Scotland's capital below us. I will feel sad if this country decides to elope from England. They say we will stay friends, but after a while the calls will dry up and only chance meetings will maintain our acquaintance. One effect of my English journey has been a change in my attitude to Scottish independence. Where before I felt ambivalent towards 'the union', its history too tied up with that of Empire, now I feel modern England is above all that and a place worth hanging on to. This, of course, is selfish and a matter for the electorate to decide, but I will find it hard to live in a country that chooses to split from my own. On the one hand I will be in an ever-opening world that may, eventually, broaden horizons enough to end segregation in Luton or Burnley, and on the other I will be in a country that has just re-built an ancient border with its neighbour. The people of Carlisle must be rolling their eyes and saying 'oh not this again.'

Thankfully, there is no need for further, Orient-style destructive thought as the flight experience distracts me. First of all, a stewardess uses the word 'de-door'. Then I pick up the in-flight magazine, suitably dog-eared as they always are, and flick through its pages ticking off tired modern language. Much is 'iconic', hotels are 'boutique' and many living people are 'legends'. The catering trolley arrives and, as ever, has no change – it must refuse to carry coins just as a celebrity carries only Amex. It is followed by a trolley sporting watches and aftershave, among other things, and as usual no one makes a purchase. The half-page dedicated to my destination, Newquay, has been ripped from the magazine with precision, so I look out of the window.

I am travelling to the south-west because I have so far missed a hefty and splendid chunk of England. Liverpool are the twelfth team I should be visiting, but little fresh can be written about team and town. Besides, ending with a Premier League game would be like finishing a wholesome, happy marriage with a cocaine-fuelled orgy. The result is a visit to Cornwall and Newquay AFC, in 1981-82 South Western League champions. As much as anything else, the end of England feels like a perfect place to finish.

We surf the cotton wool-dab clouds over Carlisle and the Lake District. By now I should not be surprised at the greenness of England and its wonky fields panelled shapeless by ancient tithes, at its silver streams and snaking rivers. I should not be so naively enthralled at the way towns and cities suddenly appear and are then quickly lost to countryside. I am, though, and I feel glum that my travels will soon be over, all those places and lives and accents and teams below left behind. We trace the coast's outline. The wheelie bin-green Irish Sea laps and pounces north of Blackpool and I catch sight of Bloomfield Road stadium, a stretched beige oval filled by a pitch waiting for people. To pass a town by train and spot floodlights thrills me, to fly over a stadium overheats me. As we approach Liverpool I fear for my health. The plane seems to turn off at the Mersey and scud along its centre. After thirty seconds or so, I spot them: Goodison, then Anfield, crowded in by terrace roofs and separated by Stanley Park. Only last night Blues showed their solidarity with Reds by wearing shirts and waving banners in honour of the Hillsborough dead. I awoke today feeling proud of football. Even at the top its soul occasionally peeps through. The final stadium I spy on this brief re-cap sweep over England is Chester's. Oh to have enjoyed the gradual pitch invasion from up here.

The plane slides the length of Wales and falls gently towards Cornwall, verdant as everywhere else, but with sea poking out of it. We swoop over quarries with the concentric lines of Ordnance Survey maps and pools that seem to be filled with chocolate lime juice, ignored by snacking sheep. The wheels lower, bash the tarmac and make the plane shudder. I leave the terminal – more of a village hall that serves lattes – and am greeted by an advert for clotted cream, bucolic aromas and a field of cows. As the only passenger to board the number 556 Western Greyhound bus at the airport I feel the heat of nosy eyes when I take my upstairs seat. Perhaps my fellow travellers, none a day under sixty-five, think me exotic or impossibly young given rural Cornwall's demographics. I decide against telling them how dope I am or treating them to some banging tunes and instead stare from the window. Hills sheep sea, hills sheep sea, hills sheep sea: the spluttering bus seems to repeat a mantra inspired by its surroundings. From all four sides the view resembles a dreamy idyll as depicted on a butter label. This beauty is so exquisite that it seems like a construct. Or, as I say to the old man across from me, 'dis is sick, innit.' We crawl through Watergate Bay where surfers and septuagenarians glide around behind studied suntans. It makes the pallor of Carlisle feel appropriately distant.

Most dwellings on the main road into Newquay are bed and breakfasts or hotels. Some look pleasant, most are tatty and one has two bay windows dedicated to a busy collection of porcelain dogs. From the bus's right can be seen cliffs, beaches and the sea, from its left swathes of charmless and unkempt buildings and establishments. This part of Newquay is unarguably ragged. I think back to Brunton Park and Morrissey's dishevelled Sunday resort town. Surf shops abound, bringing with them a dripping army of long-haired men with an aversion to shoes. By my early reckoning Newquay is the most alien place I have been to. I only vaguely recognise it because I have holidayed in Benidorm and used to watch *Home and Away*.

I buy a postcard and queue in the post office for a stamp. Ahead of me, a Cockney lady pays her electricity bill and behind me a Brummie yabs into his phone about Aston Villa. Back in the street I hear Yorkshire, Lancashire and East Midlands accents. Presumably most of these people are tourists, but many others have moved or retired here, fleeing for an olde England and turning their backs on the real, breathing one. The pavement is made mazy by the number of mobility scooters that clog it up. Some, like many of the buildings here, have black and white Cornish flags attached to them. These serve to remind me that Cornish people are often as stringent in their regional identities as Yorkshiremen, and even Scots, and that again I should not be looking for a part of England that necessarily connects with the rest. As I have seen, they rarely do. I manage to make it into a bakery and order a pasty. 'You want a cake for dessert, my love?' asks the gleaming old girl behind the counter. There's nothing 'in-comer' about her.

I find a bench on which to eat my pasty next to a group of young Londoners who are all searching their iPhones for somewhere to eat. 'There was a Pizza Express back there', one says. The paper bag containing my lunch tells the story of how Cornish Pasties were invented by tin miners in the seventeenth century. When I bite into its contents they are so hot I suspect it has been cooking ever since. I look up and am sure I see one of the Lucky Buddhas in the furniture shop opposite me holding his nose to avoid the stench of fresh 'Ocean Pinks' from the fishmonger next door. I throw my historical packaging in a bin advertising the Coast of Dreams and move over the road to enjoy a newsagent advertisements board. 'Exchange Wanted,' reads one, 'Our property is in Burnage in South Manchester ... We are desperate to move to Cornwall, coast preferred but will go anywhere in Cornwall really!!' I happen to think Manchester one of the greatest cities on earth, but that does seem a tad ambitious.

Clouds surrender and the sun begins to beat down. At the same time I turn a corner and Newquay improves immeasurably. Away from the scruffy areas are kindly streets of tea-rooms and tiny shops. A sharp hill leads down to the harbour, but before descending it I nip for an outdoor pint, that cherished pastime. The pub's patio garden sits high above the harbour and beach offering a view that makes my jar of Tribute Ale taste even better. The beach is no dainty sandpit, but an expanse that curves in a vast semi-circle. At a time four or five ripples of sea gang up and invade its face. Families brave its exposed situation to chase footballs in the wind, brush sand from their sandwiches and loiter in rock pools. Ahead of them, people in wetsuits do things with boards and sails I fail to comprehend. Noises come together and become pleasant background sound effects: the Welshman at the next picnic table talking about an over-priced sandwich; a surf teacher's whistle; the life guard censuring with his megaphone; seagulls; the sea, a constant snare drum.

Newquay's cliff-top streets exhibit buildings that planning regulation forgot. These are not the planned grotesqueness of

Watford or Bradford, but the shabby spoils of quick-buck thinking. If it brings in a clammy pound or two, any development will do. It makes for a confusing place, in one direction tacky, in the other godly. Man has messed up where nature got it right in Newquay. My hotel for the night is in a less tarnished street of long Victorian villas. It sinks budget travel to a new level, with luxuries such as towels available only for a small hire fee. The room is clean and the clawing damp smell soon becomes like an invisible friend. My view offers both Newquays – the beach and Towan Island, a beach-bound hill of rock containing a dull house that could have been pulled from the suburbs of Reading and plonked there.

By posters for a foam party and an Australian theme bar, I walk down to the harbour. With the fall of evening it has filled up with turquoise water. Fishing boats bobble and the sun powers down. Perfection. 'Is this where the seals wait for me?' asks a slightly disturbing man. Why must they always pick their fellow loner? Soon I will burn these notebooks, bury my pen and melt back in with the rest of you. I try and re-engage with the serene perfection of everything but can only concentrate on a Scouse family's yammering. 'Mam, if we get fish and chips can I get sausages?' 'Oh no, not more water, I need a pee even more now.'

Down Fore Street I pass men in flip-flops, surf shops and cafes with 'chill-out rooms' emerging into blustery open space. I walk over grass and reach pebbles surrounding Newquay's war memorial, a rock cross on a plinth of boulders. The memorial's innate drama is heightened by the setting; its only background is miles of ocean. There are over 150 names chiselled into two plaques, one for each world war. Next to it a third plaque bears the solitary name of a local man killed in Afghanistan. That is wretched; the empty space beneath it is chilling.

The wind cajoles me onward, on to a rocky outcrop that stretches at the sea like a sleeping arm reaching for a pillow. I walk by signs advising me that 'A person jumped from here and was seriously injured' and around a corner into a flat area strangely buzzing with people. It is only when I say hello to a glamorous old lady and she ignores me that I realise I have walked on to a German film company's set. A kindly runner ushers me on. Whatever they are filming, their location manager deserves a bonus. The sun is lowering on to a gluey sea that smashes the cliffs with the last of its daily life. Behind us Newquay, Cornwall and England. Ahead of us ... Canada? At the peak of the outcrop is a wooden pagoda with benches on its outside. I sit with my back to England and my eyes on a sun sneaking towards the sea. The clouds ghost towards the land, and the sea simmers ready to accept the sun. I have seen no more perfect sight in the best parts of a year. 'You want a crisp, son?' says a man with binoculars who appears from within the pagoda. I jolt and nearly fall off England then turn down his Quavers and head towards the football ground.

The walk to Mount Wise Stadium involves tackling an incline on to which clings another accommodation district. First there is Reef Surf Lodge, then The Escape, an '18-40s Surf Lodge' and further up Mor surf-lodge-bar. Some venues did not adapt quickly enough to Newquay's newfound Summer Bay leanings – the closed down Pendennis Hotel is the type of place Norman Bates would have run screaming from before repenting and becoming general manager of a Travelodge. Across the road, two men carry surfboards beneath their arms. This did not happen on the way to Portman Road.

Like most bars tonight, the Top of the Town Freehouse is about to show a Champions League fixture between Real Madrid and Manchester City. This will be viewed by far more people in the pubs of Newquay than will be at Mount Wise. If they love football enough to sit and stare at a screen as two nauseatingly wealthy teams they don't care about play out a match that will be dead to them in a week, then surely they love it enough to walk up the road and pay £4 to be part of something. Despite the rising cold, they are the foolish ones.

On Playingfield Lane a proud red Newquay FC sign advertises tonight's fixture with Ivybridge Town, as well as Thursday night bingo and Friday night karaoke in the bar. Between gaps in a closed turnstile gate and the fence I see players warming-up, flip-book imagery accompanied by the sound of walloped footballs and jeered wayward shots. I enter Peppermints Bar, the social club carrying the team's nickname. Newquay earned their moniker in the early 1900s when it was pointed out that their red and white striped shirts resembled the wrappers of boiled sweets. In the entranceway on the left are varnished teak honours boards, first for the men's team, then the women's. A noticeboard advertises fixtures and points out that pin badges are available at the bar. Through double doors I step into a 1970s world of maroon suites, red carpets and orange curtains. The bar is draped in other clubs' pennants, the walls filled with pictures of Newquay teams gone by and a long display cabinet hangs in the air proffering medals, shields, an international cap, handbooks, letters and shirts.

Peppermints Bar is a social club and a social history museum. Half a dozen regulars lean against the bar, burring in deep Cornish accents. All are engaged in a long debate about industrial weedkiller. A sprightly older gent with wellies over smart trousers and a flowery sunhat above his suit jacket walks in purposefully. He reads the team line-ups to the drinkers who groan at a couple of selections and walks out again. A few minutes later he returns and asks whether anyone has a spare light bulb for the referee's room. The barman looks in the back but finds none and returns scratching his head. 'We bought a ten pack last week as well,' he says. Picking up a universal theme there are nods when the only woman present moans about the fixture list. 'Poor Ivybridge, all this way on a Tuesday. I don't know who dreams them up.' The lights go out and the barman ushers his customers towards the match. I have half a pint left but hand it in for collection. 'Oh don't leave all that, sir,' says the barman. 'Here, I'll stick it in the fridge and you can have it at 'alf-time, how's that?' He shoves aside a bottle of WKD and carefully stores my drink. At Middlesbrough, they take the tops from bottles of Coke.

The red gates are now open so I pay my £4 and shove a turnstile for the final time. Four quid. My first ever paid ticket at Ayresome cost that. A white iron bar runs around the perimeter of the pitch and behind it on the opposite side is a roofed stand the length of the centre circle at its longest. There on backless benches sit a dozen away supporters. If they crane their necks they can see miles of Cornish countryside and the waving arms of a wind farm. Behind me is a stand that runs from the halfway line to the corner flag, at which point it adjoins the tea bar and the buildings containing Peppermints and the changing rooms behind the goal. Assertive mural lettering on their outside wall denotes that this is Newquay FC, though to me it is more like heaven. I am besotted.

As they await the arrival of their teams, most of Newquay's seventy fans chat on the three steps of terrace beneath the stand, the garden benches with plaques to fondly missed supporters at its rear or outside the tea bar, cradling a hotchpotch of homely mugs. The referee emerges with the two teams behind him. He makes them gather before reaching the pitch in full sight of all. It reminds me of a cruise ship cabaret singer introducing himself in the first person from the side of the stage. At the same time, on a long-cabled microphone Sunhat Man reads the team line-ups from a clipboard and updates us on this Saturday's cup fixture with Sticker FC: 'It'll be an earlier kick-off. I can't remember what time, off the top of my head.' Floodlights stir, the three officials then make a signal to the captains and our twenty-five entertainers for the night walk on. At the toss-up Ivybridge elect to swap halves despite there being no hill or wind and no one at either end, though the sky is prettier above their chosen half to the one Newquay are left with, pink to its blue. When irritated Newquay heads have been shook and every man is in his place, there is just time for motivational speak from the home keeper. 'Do the right thing or don't do anything,' he barks. At 7.30 p.m. the referee wishes everybody 'an enjoyable evening' and starts the game.

The pace is frenetic meaning much wheezing during the relief of set-piece breaks. The football on offer is the very definition of 'honest endeavour'; mistakes are plentiful but only made with good intention and never due to effort dropping. These are the kind of players who concentrate so hard their tongues stick out. Although I have the advantage of actually being able to hear them, I'm sure they shout more than their colleagues further up the pyramid, a symptom of increased passion and ideas outweighing ability. 'Gamble! Somebody bloody gamble,' the away keeper repeatedly hollers. There are shouted exchanges between players, too. 'High fucking foot!' shouts a centre-back; 'low fucking head' replies his fellow No. 5 up the pitch. Ivybridge's version is a tall bald man whose forehead gives the ball a happy slap whenever the two collide. His side are much the better in the first-half. They use the springy turf to their advantage, passing crisply to feet and thus avoiding too much wading through its weight. It is so peaty that a group of two players chasing an errant pass sound like a heard of trampling wildebeests. Two blokes walk around from the away end and stand on the highest terrace step behind me. One is telling the other about his new medication. 'Oh they're great them, Mick. Just don't have one with a whisky,' his mate replies.

Newquay drag themselves up the pitch and hit a post. 'Stop fucking panicking!' bawls an Ivybridge centre-half. Inspired, his team pass their way up the pitch. Their No. 9, a wiry skinhead with low socks and the paciest player on the park, finds himself one-on-one with the goalkeeper and cracks in a shot. It passes underneath the keeper, but he reaches backwards beneath himself in a move I last saw performed by Dick van Dyke during the 'Me Old Bamboo' dance on *Chitty Chitty Bang Bang* and captures the ball. 'Unlucky, Mikey son,' shouts the Ivybridge manager, a sonorous north-easterner. His team continues to pressurise. They win and waste a free-kick on the edge of the area when Mikey is fouled and does his very best to stay upright like a drunk, an anti-dive. The only Newquay man who can match Ivybridge is No. 4, another baldy and a crafty centre-midfielder. Though his legs seem aged, it suits his languid, tired but wily, style. He is also enjoying himself. It is there when he commits an obvious foul, sarcastically questions his booking and reacts to being told to 'shut up' by laughing, and there when he wins the ball, drops a shoulder, finds a yard and spins a pass out wide. There is similar glee in the eyes of the Ivybridge baldy when he remembers how good he was at school and dribbles by three flailing challenges before passing the ball out of play. The game is theirs to love and they make a grand job of it. 'They're a smashing team, Ivybridge', says the linesman to the three of us behind him, 'I can't believe they're second bottom.'

'Here 'e is!' The barman welcomes me at half-time, my half in his hand. 'We've only had a little sip each!' The other drinkers settle to their pints while I allow the walls to teach me about a club once known as Newquay One and All. The black and white pictures are rich and plentiful, here a bustling crowd falling on to the pitch in the 1950s, there a dozen players riding a Hinckley-invented Hansom Cab to the 1907 Easter Monday final with Wadebridge. A large golden frame is reserved for the champions of 1981-82, a skinny crew grinning behind much facial hair. Only a couple of their faces look serious, one of whom is Chris Morris. Morris is Newquay FC's most famous son; he has an entire cabinet to himself on the far wall to prove it. He went from here to play for Sheffield Wednesday, Celtic and Middlesbrough. I remember him for two things: hearing the Ayresome cheers from outside when he scored a rare Boro goal while my dad and I ran back to the car because he'd left his wallet on the dashboard, and taking out Newcastle's Keith Gillespie with a judo kick to the groin.

A country black sky has set when the teams re-emerge for the second-half. I move to the away side, on my way enjoying an amusing dispute between the home manager and referee. When the latter marches over to warn the former, something falls from his mouth. 'I've lost a bit of bloody gum for you,' blasts the referee while gesturing at Newquay's boss. It is behind the other dugout that I settle, however. I am intrigued by Ivybridge's booming boss, whose volume is rendered homely by a soft Northumbrian accent and the manner in which he encourages his players, whom he collectively calls 'sons'. 'Oh that's tremendous, sons,' he excitedly shouts as Mikey breaks clear, 'go on, Mikey son ... Yessssssss!' One-nil to Ivybridge; as deserved in this young half as in the first one. The manager balances his words by being critical in the mode of a disappointed father to the officials, 'Oh liner, man, you're not even looking!' and 'dee-aaah meee', each vowel stretched like pizza dough. He wears shiny shoes, smart dark trousers and a winter sports jacket, suggesting a manager who has come straight from work. He totters around his tiny technical area gesticulating, somehow made more charismatic by the confined space, and coaxes his sons' every move. Most general things are repeated two or three times in a row. 'Stay on yer feet, stay on yer feet.' 'Close him, close him, close him.' When players are singled out they do not look over, but you know it must be satisfying. 'Great cross, Westy.' 'Well done, Ben.' 'Brilliant, Mikey son.' I become hypnotised and can hear no one else. 'Get up. And again, Westy. Man coming, man coming. Great ball. Well done, Westy. That's the way. Have a look. Shape shape. To a man, to a man. Always be aware of this man here.' When later my head hits the pillow and I close my eyes, he is there – 'go on, son. Off to sleep, off to sleep. Sweet dreams. STAY ON YER FEET.'

With twenty minutes to go, a thumping diving header signals 2-0, then Mikey saunters free and bags another. In front of me the manager calmly strolls on to the pitch and yowls uproariously. He talks his sons through the cold dark night, stopping only to occasionally chide the linesman. 'Where's the advantage? WHERE'S THE ADVANTAGE?' The Ivybridge coach implores the referee to end the match: 'How long to go, Ref? I'm up for work at five.' The man in black comes back with: 'Well, I'm enjoying myself listening to you so much, I could go on all night.' After four minutes of injury time he ends the joke. The Ivybridge manager looks to the stars in joy. The whistle has blown on my year.

The next morning at the end of England I catch a bus to Padstow. A lady on the seat behind me commentates on the entire route, her husband offering expert analysis in the form of 'Yep.

Yep. Yep.' 'Oh, a Wendy house there. Has seen better days. Pub there, meals 12 till 2 and 5 till 9, all day Sundays. And a dog, male by the look of things.' I tune out but only along the dial to an elderly lady from Leeds who informs us, 'When I get up for a wee in the middle of the night, I can go straight back to the same dream afterwards.' We arrive at the harbour and I walk through town and sit on a bench at the top of a hill. Beneath me is elegant Padstow and the ocean sparkling in the sun. It isn't a bad place, this country of mine.

The dozen or so places I have visited do not matter to many people from elsewhere. As a miscellaneous whole, though, they tell the story of where England came from, who she is today and which direction she is heading in. These provinces were the Industrial Revolution, are now charmingly flawed mini-Englands and will develop into world places with layers of identity. The process has already begun. Where I expected to see a society still hung up on its role as a world leader, I saw Little England, a place increasingly comfortable in its own skin and not hankering to police anywhere else. Our problems are many, but in their typical wit and resolve the people of these small towns will show England the qualities needed to overcome them. The post-industrial towns in particular brim with pluck and resolve. Middlesbrough and Burnley are, in parts, dirt poor but still they are there, still their people gather and laugh. In the USA they would be gold rush ghost towns, but something here makes people want to remain, bound to the soil, tied to history and often their football club. Their towns are each unique – do not listen when you are told that everywhere now is the same. Blinded by consumerism, those who make that judgement are talking only of high street chains. They do not account for the individual histories, accents, smells, colours, senses of humour that make these places and, in turn, England. Their diversity contrives not to make one England, but contributes to the glorious and messy, multiple state it is in. I started out wishing for England a uniform identity like Scotland's and thinking our uncertainty a bad thing. That is not so: it is our greatest attribute.

I was sad to see how racially segregated Luton, Burnley and Bradford were, yet in each there was a binding unspoken tolerance and evidence of change. When the current young are adults, they will not see colour. Football can take the lead, it is at its best when it does; let us see all kinds of faces in the stands and on our pitches. In Bradford I saw youthful mixed-race couples and rejoiced to hear how locals of every creed united to overwhelm an English Defence League demonstration. It should not be left to the EDL to define England. It is what we, the majority, make of it and how we see it in a thousand different ways. We should not be afraid of finding pride in our Englands. I am a reluctant patriot, surprised to find myself so content with my country. Perhaps it is because I don't live there. I do not think it a better country than any other and can think of few sentiments dafter than 'my country, right or wrong.' It is just an idiosyncratic place in which I can't go longer than fifteen minutes without smiling. That must mean something.

What of football? At the top, it is clear player wages will not fall, television will not go away and ticket prices will remain extortionate (plus booking fee). While capitalism has had nigh on a decade of crisis in the wider economy, the Premier League has become even more profoundly free market. It won't change. There are two things we can do. One, we can chip away at it where possible. We can protest until supporter places in boardrooms are the norm, or demand small things that make a difference and give us back the game we knew, like a return to home-away-home-away fixture orders or safe standing areas. Secondly, we as supporters can abandon the highest level, and leave it to become the closed shop, perhaps pan-European, league desired by chequebook men and watched by wealthy tourists. This will not be for everyone, and tribalism is hard to shake off and harder still to accrue. But if we two-time we can start anew, become involved in our smaller provincial clubs, embrace football at its most flawed and loveable, rawest and rewarding. More of us should get out there; team adultery is not a sin. The jaded modern fan can feel what he or she first felt about football, and fall in love again. A whole new sense of belonging is possible. 'Originality is returning to the origin,' as Gaudi put it.

Overall, the game I saw – *my football* – was in rude health. Away from the jaded cynicism of its highest reaches it remains a social movement I am honoured to be part of. Down in the provinces, it *is* affordable and accessible. Contrary to my fears, young people are still catching the bug. No computer game can beat the thrill of getting your favourite player's autograph or being an active part in a bustling community of interest. The experience of going to the match remains vivid and life affirming, the action itself an eccentric art form. In an England of flux, where no job is certain, families break up or live far apart, community or church is loose or weak, football is more important than ever. It breeds belonging in an uncertain world. For ninety minutes no one is alone, everyone is united by a shared purpose and sense of identity – brothers and sisters of the terrace lost in the match. In my thirty years England and the game have changed cosmetically. Their underlying genius has not. At 3 o'clock on a Saturday, I know where I belong.

Acknowledgements

In goal for Hatters, Railwaymen and Knitters FC, my agent, Stan at Jenny Brown Associates, for his tenacity and faith.

In defence, local and football club historians, for their solid work and concentration.

In midfield, Charlotte Atyeo and Nick Humphrey at Bloomsbury, for their tireless running and sparks of genius.

Up front, Marisa and Kaitlyn Gray, for being the superstars that make me tick.

Also, above-the-head applause to the loyal supporters of HRKFC: my Mum, Dad, sisters and their families; the Maw-in-Law; Pikeys FC, Gez and Seats; Trout (for kind words and our days gone by); Paddy Dillon; D.B.; Kilsby and Williams; Fleming types; Dave Scott; Gary Sutherland; Gavin MacDougall; Rob Nichols at *Fly Me to the Moon* fanzine; Billy Gould at *The Leither*.

I am indebted to the Bard of Barnsley Ian McMillan (www. ian-mcmillan.co.uk) for permission to quote from his ace mural poem outside Sheffield Station, and to Lemn Sissay (www. lemnsissay.com) for the excerpt from his spellbinding 'Spark Catchers'. Special mentions, too, for the marvellous copy editing of Julian Flanders, the proofreading of Eugenie Woodhouse, and the inspiring works of Stuart Roy Clarke.

A final thanks to the many nameless walk-on characters whose words and actions colour this book, to its towns for making me smile and to its football clubs for being the flawed and wonderful institutions they are.

www.danielgraywriter.com
@d_gray_writer

Index

geographic centre of 198
middle of 208–10
nostalgia for 1–6, 13
original centre of 198–200,
    209
England (team) 193–7, 211
    Sweden match 202, 206–8
English Civil War 203, 235
English Defence League 75, 77,
    290
English Journey (Priestley) 16,
    201, 236–8, 241
Englishness 1, 41
Ennis, Jessica 212
Essex American Hall, Braintree
    93–4
Euro 92 195
Euro 96 197
Euro 2012 193–4, 197, 202,
    206–8, 211
European Cup 4
Euston Station, London 130
Evans, David 74
expletives 33, 123

FA Amateur Cup 21
FA Cup
    1911 248, 249–50
    1914 216
    1959 73–4, 215–16
    1974 266
    1978 91
    Sheffield United wins 40, 43–4
Falkland Islands 3
Fenny Drayton 209–10

Fiennes, Celia 169
first day of the season 211
First World War 24, 37, 44,
    137–8, 174–5, 215, 224,
    254
    peace riots 65–7, 138
Firth, Samuel 239
flag days, Meriden 199–200
Fletcher family 239
floodlit match, first 39
Foot and Mouth disease 275
Football Association, origins 39
football clubs, world's oldest 40
Football League, 1981-82 season
    3–4
Football Man, The (Hopcraft) 218
Football Manager computer game
    47
footballers, evil of 212
Foster, Nellie 239
Foulke, William 43
France (team) 194, 197
Frodsham 150

Gainsborough, Thomas 95
Gallacher, Hughie 140
Gascoigne, Paul 195, 208
Gateshead Stadium 14
General Strike, 1926 18
George V, King 140
ghosts 14, 96
Gibson, Steve 30
Gillespie, Keith 287
Gladstone, William 15, 18
Glanville, Brian 141